Lighting Fixtures of the Depression Era

BOOK II

Jo Ann Thomas

COLLECTOR BOOKS

A Division of Schroeder Publishing Co., Inc.

The current values in this book should be used only as a guide. They are not intended to set prices, which vary from one section of the country to another. Auction prices as well as dealer prices vary greatly and are affected by condition and demand. Neither the author nor the publisher assumes responsibility for any losses which might be incurred as a result of consulting this guide.

Cover design: Beth Summers
Book design: Holly Long

Searching For A Publisher?

We are always looking for people knowledgeable within their fields. If you feel that there is a real need for a book on your collectible subject and have a large comprehensive collection, contact Collector Books.

Collector Books

P.O. Box 3009

Paducah, KY 42002-3009

www.collectorbooks.com

Copyright © 2001 by Jo Ann Thomas

Contents

Introduction

The decade of 1930s was a somber time after the stock market crash in October, 1929. These were the dust storms years, the Depression Years.

One of the biggest influences during these years was Hollywood motion pictures — the movies. For a few cents people could go to the movies, and, for a while at least, forget their troubles. If it happened to be "bank night" they might even win some dishes. The theaters capitalized on this with extravagant use of electric lighting. From wall sconces, fan shapes in gorgeous, glowing colors appeared on the walls. Miniature sconces at the end of each row of seats turned aisles into colored pathways to fantasyland. Sunsets were visible behind Moorish windows and shimmering moons cast their dreamy light on Spanish balconies. Overhead, in midnight blue skies, stars twinkled brightly as clouds drifted lazily by. I still remember how awestruck I was the first time I went to the Paramount Theatre in my home town of Omaha, Nebraska. I don't recall the movie but, vividly recall the stars and clouds and blue lit aisles and fantastic decorations.

One could still choose from many of the styles of the 1920s, though, in keeping with the times, plainer, less expensive styles, and styles that required no shades became more popular. Sheet brass was formed into shapes and patterns by stamping machines. Many of these stamped brass fixtures and wall sconces had leaves or flowers embossed on them. Quite often the entire fixture or sconce would be painted in ivory or creamy white with the leaves or flowers painted in appropriate colors. Others were painted in blue, green, pink, yellow, or lavender. These made attractive and colorful additions to bedrooms, bathrooms, powder rooms, and sun porches. Bright chrome, aluminum, and brass finishes were used, as well as brushed chrome, aluminum, and brass, which was a satiny finish. Hammered finishes in copper, silver, bronze, aluminum, and iron found much favor during these years, and created a very distinctive style of fixtures and wall sconces. Plastic also began to appear in some fixtures and sconces, as well as being used in making some shades.

Kitchen and bathroom fixtures and wall sconces were made in porcelain, in all the colors of the rainbow as well as black and red. These created lovely accents of color. These were also sometimes decorated with floral designs. The metal fixtures and sconces were often painted and the white shades for these would have matching colored bands on them. Many of the porcelain fixtures and sconces had satin glass shades in contrasting or complimentary colors with sculptured designs on them. Polished chrome was very much in vogue for bathroom fixtures and sconces, many with white cylinder shaped shades.

Eye strain started becoming a big factor with the electric light in the 1920s and many colors were used in shades to soften the light. Many new innovative shapes were used on the fixtures, also to prevent glare and eye strain. The vibrant colored shades of the 1920s gave way, somewhat, to lovely soft pastels in greens, blues, pinks, yellows, and mauves. The various amber-toned shades remained very popular. Shades in creams, beiges, grays, and browns complemented the new finishes being used on the fixtures and wall sconces. Custard glass, so-called because of the color, was widely used for the inverted cup and bowl shaped shades. Many shades were painted on the inside and then fired, giving them a very durable color finish. A completely new finish for many of the shades of this period was the iridescent finish. The shades came in iridescent pearl, ivory, opal, white onyx, and stippled gold. Some of these seemed to have a moire texture to them, very shimmering.

A very popular glass used for some shades was white glass inside with a light champagne colored glass on the outside, called cased glass. This produced a very pleasing, soft light. A new type of glassware that was introduced during this time was Hyperion glass made by Gill Glass and Fixture Co. of Philadelphia. It was designed to be more serviceable by diffusing the harsh, brilliant light of the electric light bulb into a soft, glareless light that is pleasing to the human eye.

A less expensive metal alloy, called French white metal, known better today as spelter, came into use in place of some of the more expensive materials. This alloy had been used in France and Germany for many years for statues and figural lamps. Being a very malleable material, it adapted quite well to the new casting methods now in use in this country. This alloy was used with patinated finishes, in bronze, brass, silver, gold, or dark green or dark brown matte, or, was sometimes painted. When the alloy was used without another finish on it, the piece is said to have a "pewter" finish. When this finish was polished, the piece had a soft, lustrous, satin appearance, very rich and lovely.

A totally new bold and exciting style emerged at this time. The industry called them Luminaires or Luminators. However, some of these fixtures are better known today as "Saturn Discs." The appearance of these fixtures and wall sconces is very "space age," perhaps influenced by the Buck Rogers comic strip of that time. A distinguishing feature is not only the shape of the shades, perfectly round, teardrop, or inverted cone, but also the use of metal rings or louvres to create a "flying saucer" or "Saturn Rings" appearance. These rings or louvres were usually polished chrome or

brushed chrome, sometimes with brass accents. Some of the fixtures and sconces were made entirely of metal, again in polished or brushed chrome. The glass shades were white, ivory, or opal glass. These fixtures and wall sconces were designed for indirect and semi-indirect illumination, primarily for stores, offices, showrooms, and reception areas. They adapt very well to use in homes and have become quite popular with lighting enthusiasts today.

These were truly the "fun years" in electric lighting — for, beginning in the 1940s, most industries began preparing for war production by curtailing new designs and the use of war materials. When the United States entered the war in December of 1941, all production immediately became geared to the war effort. The lighting industry turned the switches off on all of these glorious, magical, and fantastical fixtures and wall sconces for the duration of the war.

Moe-Bridges Artistic Lighting Equipment, 1931

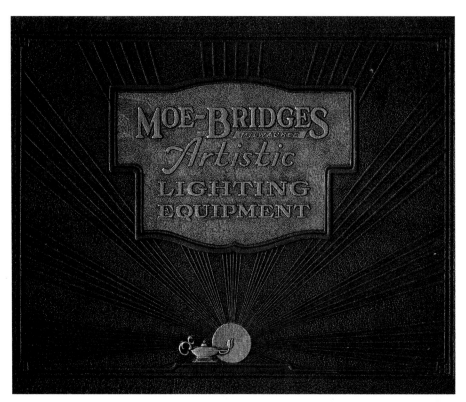

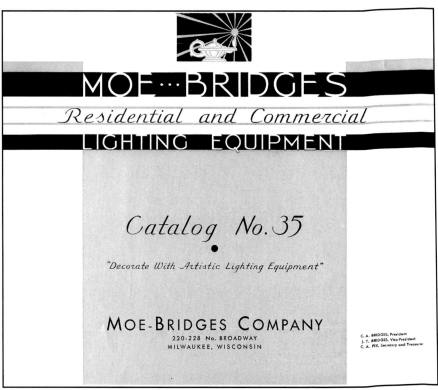

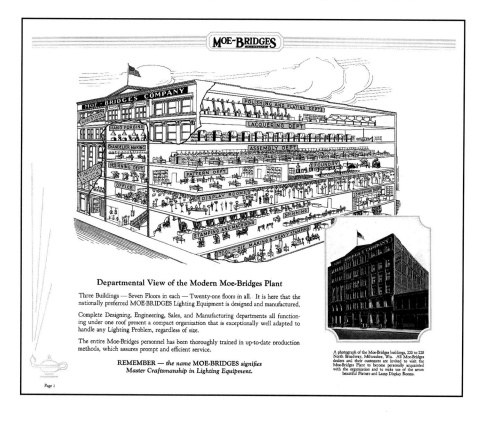

Departmental View of the Modern Moe-Bridges Plant

Three Buildings — Seven Floors in each — Twenty-one floors in all. It is here that the nationally preferred MOE-BRIDGES Lighting Equipment is designed and manufactured.

Complete Designing, Engineering, Sales, and Manufacturing departments all functioning under one roof present a compact organization that is exceptionally well adapted to handle any Lighting Problem, regardless of size.

The entire Moe-Bridges personnel has been thoroughly trained in up-to-date production methods, which assures prompt and efficient service.

REMEMBER — *the name MOE-BRIDGES signifies Master Craftsmanship in Lighting Equipment.*

A photograph of the Moe-Bridges buildings, 220 to 228 North Broadway, Milwaukee, Wis. All Moe-Bridges dealers and their customers are invited to visit the Moe-Bridges Plant to become personally acquainted with the organization and to make use of the seven beautiful Fixture and Lamp Display Rooms.

Page 1

Designs to Please the Most Fastidious
• At Prices to Conform with any Budget

Months of careful research work by Moe-Bridges Designers and Sales Engineers have produced the widest range of popular priced, up-to-date Artistic Lighting Equipment being offered by any single manufacturer today.

Among the scores of styles pictured in this catalog, you will find Shaded Lighting in a variation of period treatments, also Early American, English, Colonial, Georgian, Spanish, and Moderne Period Styles, and a pleasing group of General Types.

You will find, however, in making your selection from the wide variety of Moe-Bridges designs, that charming and beautiful lighting equipment need not be expensive.

The photographs shown on this page illustrate three typical homes—a modest bungalow—a medium priced city residence—a pretentious country home; all equipped with standard Moe-Bridges lighting fixtures.

Thousands of similar Moe-Bridges installations can be found in every section of the United States and Canada, and in many foreign countries.

Page 3

MOE-BRIDGES

How to Buy Lighting Equipment
• For Lasting Satisfaction

It is highly important that lighting equipment be given early consideration in the building of a home. Not many years back, it was the common practice to build a home first, then when it was ready for occupancy, electric fixtures of a nondescript type were installed without giving them any particular thought.

However, during the past few years, there has been a general realization that the thoughtless fixture selections of yesterday have caused more poor eyesight than any other one factor. Educational efforts have also developed an appreciation of the value of correct lighting as an important item in interior decorative plans.

Lasting satisfaction can be assured by developing your home around a central theme—and what could be better than the lighting equipment? Then you can determine in advance, the atmosphere you wish to create in the completed home.

Lighting equipment that properly interprets the setting of each room and enhances the furnishings with glowing beauty—that is the kind you want. Moe-Bridges fixtures do that and more.

In addition to providing perfectly diffused and scientifically correct light, they are in themselves the outstanding decorative feature of the home. Perfect in style and design, rich in their lasting finishes, these fixtures lend exclusive individuality and distinctive charm to every interior.

Page 4

MOE-BRIDGES

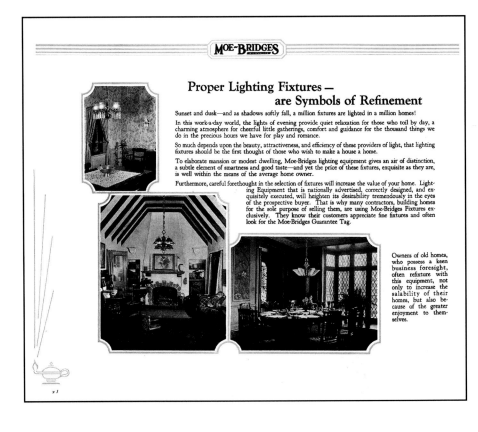

Proper Lighting Fixtures —
are Symbols of Refinement

Sunset and dusk—and as shadows softly fall, a million fixtures are lighted in a million homes!

In this work-a-day world, the lights of evening provide quiet relaxation for those who toil by day, a charming atmosphere for cheerful little gatherings, comfort and guidance for the thousand things we do in the precious hours we have for play and romance.

So much depends upon the beauty, attractiveness, and efficiency of these providers of light, that lighting fixtures should be the first thought of those who wish to make a house a home.

To elaborate mansion or modest dwelling, Moe-Bridges lighting equipment gives an air of distinction, a subtle element of smartness and good taste—and yet the price of these fixtures, exquisite as they are, is well within the means of the average home owner.

Furthermore, careful forethought in the selection of fixtures will increase the value of your home. Lighting Equipment that is nationally advertised, correctly designed, and exquisitely executed, will heighten its desirability tremendously in the eyes of the prospective buyer. That is why many contractors, building homes for the sole purpose of selling them, are using Moe-Bridges Fixtures exclusively. They know their customers appreciate fine fixtures and often look for the Moe-Bridges Guarantee Tag.

Owners of old homes, who possess a keen business foresight, often refixture with this equipment, not only to increase the salability of their homes, but also because of the greater enjoyment to themselves.

S
H
A
D
E
D

L
I
G
H
T
I
N
G

● THE story of man's continued attempts to make light a more friendly friend is both interesting and fascinating. There was no lighting industry in the old candle-light days, but even then, man's urge was to control light. This urge has never ceased, and today we have the pinnacle of perfection in light control—*Shaded Lighting*. Light that is rich in its radiant beauty, yet restful in its soothing softness. Truly, light has never been as friendly to man as it is in shaded lighting.

370-C-2
$300.00+

370-S-1
$185.00+

370-C-5
$475.00+

$485.00+
370-S-5

370-S-3
$395.00+

360-C-3
$385.00+

360-S-1
$150.00+

360-C-5
$450.00+

$500.00+
360-S-5

360-S-3
$400.00+

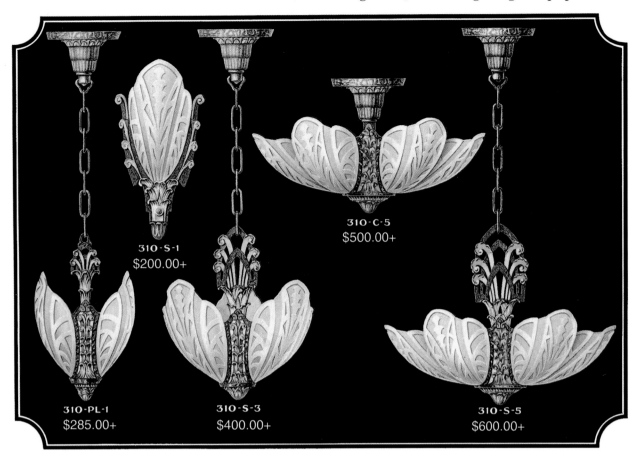

310-S-1
$200.00+

310-C-5
$500.00+

310-PL-1
$285.00+

310-S-3
$400.00+

310-S-5
$600.00+

Above:

Maximum beauty of design, plus quality, at minimum prices.

Biltmore Series

No. 310-PL-1. One light Pendant Lantern Spread 5¼x8½ inches. Length 36 inches. *Price $6.00.*

NOTE: No. 310-PL-1 can be changed to a Ceiling Style, if desired, by eliminating the chain.

No. 310-S-1. One light Wall Bracket. Backplate 6¼x12¼ inches. Covers 4-inch outlet. Extension 4¼ inches. Canopy switch control. *Price $3.90.*

No. 310-S-3. Three light Pendant Fixture. Spread 11½ inches. Length 42 inches. *Price $8.40.*

Finish: Antique Pewter and Gold

NOTE: *No. 310-PL-1 and No. 310-S-1 also furnished in Ivory and Colors for Bedroom and Breakfast Room use. (See Page 48.)*

Glass Shade: No. 24244
Honey Satin Tone.

No. 310-C-3. Three light Ceiling Fixture. (Similar to 310-C-5). Spread 11½ inches. Length 11 inches. *Price $8.40.*

No. 310-C-5. Five light Ceiling Fixture. Spread 17½ inches. Length 11 inches. *Price $13.50.*

No. 310-S-5. Five light Pendant Fixture Spread 17½ inches. Length 42 inches. *Price $13.50.*

Top Left:

A shaded lighting ensemble in Tudor English style.

Croydon Series

No. 370-C-2. Two light Ceiling Fixture. Spread 4⅜x12 inches. Length 17 inches. *Price $10.50.*

No. 370-S-2. Two light Pendant Fixture. (Similar to 370-S-3). Spread 4⅜x12 inches. Length 42 inches. *Price $10.50.*

No. 370-S-5. Five light Pendant Fixture. Spread 17½ inches. Length 42 inches. *Price $19.50.*

No. 370-C-1. Beam Light. Canopy diameter 5¾ inches. *Price $1.50.*

Finish: Croydon Plate
Hand toned with touches of Blue and Red in heraldic shield.

Glass Shade: No. 24229
Hand toned, etched surface, Champagne Colored Glass.

No. 370-S-1. One light Wall Bracket. Backplate 6x10¼ inches. Covers 4-inch outlet. Extension 6¼ inches. Canopy switch control. *Price $5.00.*

No. 370-S-3. Three light Pendant Fixture. Spread 14 inches. Length 42 inches. *Price $13.50.*

No. 370-C-3. Three light Ceiling Fixture. (Similar to 370-C-5). Spread 14 inches. Length 18½ inches. *Price $13.50.*

No. 370-C-5. Five light Ceiling Fixture. Spread 17½ inches. Length 21 inches. *Price $19.50.*

Bottom Left:

Norwich Series

Artistic styling in natural bronze with an unusual adaptable feature.

No. 360-C-3. Three light Ceiling Fixture. Spread 15½ inches. Length 13½ inches. *Price $12.50.*

No. 360-S-5. Five light Pendant Fixture. Spread 18½ inches. Length 42 inches. *Price $17.90.*

No. 360-S-1. One light Wall Bracket. Backplate 5¾x8½ inches. Covers 4-inch outlet. Extension 7½ inches. Canopy switch control. *Price $4.50.*

Finish: Natural Bronze

Glass Shade: No. 24227
Antique Iridescent Frostell Glass. An unusual adaptable feature: Shades can be reversed to reflect the light downward as well as ceilingward.

No. 360-S-3. Three light Pendant Fixture. Spread 15½ inches. Length 42 inches. *Price $12.50.*

No. 360-C-5. Five light Ceiling Fixture. Spread 18½ inches. Length 13½ inches. *Price $17.90.*

No. 450. One light Ceiling Lantern to match 360 Line Norwich Fixtures. Illustrated on Page 48. *Price $6.00.*

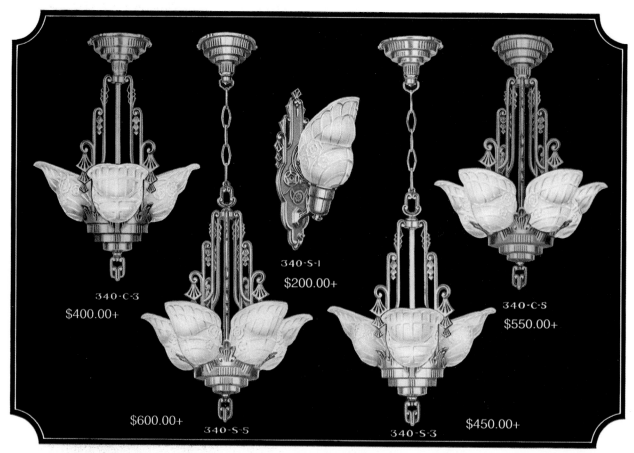

340-C-3
$400.00+

340-S-1
$200.00+

340-C-S
$550.00+

$600.00+

340-S-5

340-S-3 $450.00+

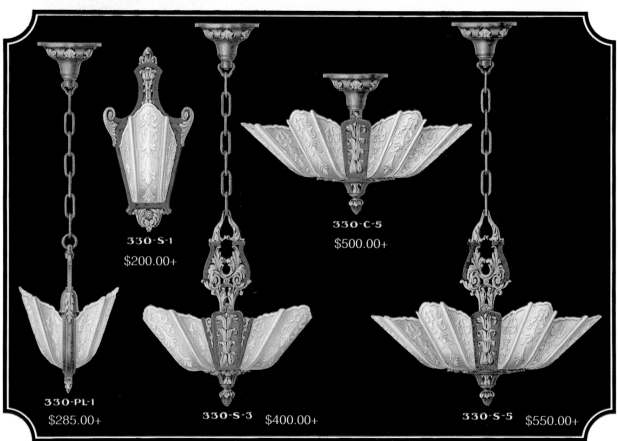

330-S-1
$200.00+

330-C-5
$500.00+

330-PL-1
$285.00+

330-S-3 $400.00+

330-S-5 $550.00+

Please note the beautiful swan in metal work of the frame.

350-S-2
$285.00+

350-S-1
$200.00+

350-S-3
$400.00+

350-L-1
$300.00+

350-S-5
$600.00+

Above:

Commander Series

A shaded lighting group of unusual beauty in the "Moderne" motif.

No. 350-S-3. Three light Pendant Fixture. Spread 11 inches. Length 42 inches. *Price $19.00.*

No. 350-S-2. Two light Wall Bracket. Backplate 4½x11 inches. Covers 4-inch outlet. Spread 9½ inches. Extension 5½ inches. Canopy switch control. *Price $9.00.*

No. 350-L-1. One light Pendant Lantern. Spread 9 inches. Length 36 inches. Glass Cylinder 4x8 inches. *Price $10.50.*

Finish: Ray-O-Gold.

Glassware:

No. 24222
Decorated Aureola Glass Shade for 350-S-1, 2, 3, 5.

No. 24223
Plain Aureola Glass Cylinder for 350-L-1.

No. 350-S-1. One light Wall Bracket. Backplate 4½x11 inches. Covers 4-inch outlet. Extension 6 inches. Canopy switch control. *Price $5.50.*

No. 350-S-5. Five light Pendant Fixture. Spread 18½ inches. Length 42 inches. *Price $29.50.*

Top Left:

Dictator Series

A real "Dictator" that commands the attention of discriminating buyers.

No. 340-C-3. Three light Ceiling Fixture. Spread 16½ inches. Length 20 inches. *Price $16.50.*

No. 340-S-5. Five light Pendant Fixture. Spread 19 inches. Length 42 inches. *Price $22.50.*

No. 340-S-1. One light Wall Bracket. Backplate 5x12 inches. Covers 4-inch outlet. Extension 6 inches. Canopy switch control. *Price $4.50.*

Choice of Finishes: "French Gold" or "French Silver"

Glass Shade: No. 24221
Honey Satin Tone.

No. 340-S-3. Three light Pendant Fixture. Spread 16½ inches. Length 42 inches. *Price $16.50.*

No. 340-C-5. Five light Ceiling Fixture. Spread 19 inches. Length 22½ inches. *Price $22.50.*

Bottom Left:

Quiet dignity—delicate tracery of design artistically embellished in plated Etruscan Gold.

Etruscan Series

No. 330-PL-1. One light Pendant Lantern. Spread 6¾x8½ inches. Length 36 inches. *Price $6.90.*

NOTE: No. 330-PL-1 can be changed to a Ceiling Style, if desired, by eliminating the chain.

No. 330-S-1. One light Wall Bracket. Backplate 6½x12 inches. Covers 4-inch outlet. Extension 5 inches. Canopy switch control. *Price $4.50.*

No. 330-S-3. Three light Pendant Fixture. Spread 16½ inches. Length 42 inches. *Price $10.50.*

Finish: Etruscan Gold
NOTE: No. 330-PL-1 and No. 330-S-1 also furnished in Ivory and Colors for Bedroom and Breakfast Room use. (See Page 48.)

Glass Shade: No. 24243
Champagne Satin Tone.

No. 330-C-3. Three light Ceiling Fixture. (Similar to 330-C-5). Spread 16½ inches. Length 11½ inches. *Price $10.50.*

No. 330-C-5. Five light Ceiling Fixture. Spread 19½ inches. Length 11½ inches. *Price $16.50.*

No. 330-S-5. Five light Pendant Fixture. Spread 19½ inches. Length 42 inches. *Price $16.50.*

EARLY AMERICAN

COLONIAL

ENGLISH

PERIOD STYLES

● A home that reflects the rugged simplicity of early America—the charm and grace of the Colonial days—or, perhaps, the admirable dignity of the Tudor English—that is period styling. And what a selection of motifs the home builder of today has to choose from—for all through the ages, even to the "Moderne" vogue of today, we find characteristics which bear a powerful influence in the building and equipping of the present day home.

Top Right:

A pleasing modernistic ensemble done in ebony and nickel.

Lorraine Series

No. 320-L-1. One light Pendant Lantern. Spread 10 inches. Length 36 inches.
Price Complete with Glass $11.50.

No. 320-K-1. One light Wall Bracket. Backplate 5x10 inches. Covers 4-inch outlet. Extension 5¼ inches. *Price Complete with Shade $8.00.*

Finish: Ebony and Nickel

Shade No. S-1004
3½-inch Parchment for 320-K-1, 320-K-2, 320-K-5. Price $1.80.

Glass No. 24228
4-inch Fitter by 7½ inches Square, Black Striped Ivory Aureola Glass Unit for No. 320-L-1.

No. 320-K-2. Two light Wall Bracket. Backplate 5x10 inches. Covers 4-inch outlet. Extension 5¼ inches. Spread 10¾ inches.
Price Complete with Shades $13.00.

No. 320-K-5. Five light Pendant Fixture. Candle style. Spread 18½ inches. Length 42 inches.
Price Complete with Shades $42.50.

Bottom Right:

No. 380-S-3. Three light Pendant Fixture. Spread 19 inches. Length 42 inches. *Price $22.50.*

No. 380-C-5. Five light Ceiling Fixture. Spread 19 inches. Length 24 inches. *Price $32.50.*

No. 380-S-1. One light bracket. Backplate 4¾x7½ inches. Extension 7½ inches. Covers 4-inch outlet. Canopy switch control. *Price $7.00.*

Finish: Old Iron with Weathered Brass Fonts.
Metal Shades in choice of Hand Toned Green or Red Enamel outside and Ivory inside.

Glass Chimney: No. 24231
Crystal Glass (Lower half outside frosted).

Note: *Will accommodate 25 watt pear shaped or flame type lamps.*

No. 320-K-1
$185.00+

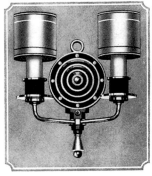

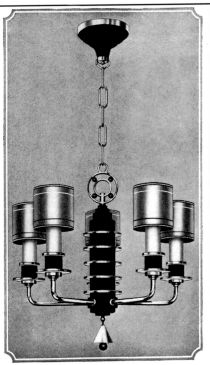

No. 320-L-1
$200.00+

No. 320-K-2
$250.00+

No. 320-K-5
$550.00+

No. 380-S-1
$185.00+

No. 380-C-5
$400.00+

Winthrop Series

No. 380-S-3
$300.00+

No. 380-C-3 $300.00+

$200.00+

No. 380-L-1

NOTE: *Will accommodate 25 watt pear shaped or flame type lamps.*

Winthrop Series

No. 380-C-3. Three light Ceiling Fixture. Spread 19 inches. Length 24 inches.   *Price $22.50.*

No. 380-S-5. Five light Pendant Fixture. Spread 19 inches. Length 42 inches.   *Price $32.50.*

No. 380-L-1. One light Pendant Lantern. Spread 14 inches. Length 42 inches.   *Price $12.50.*

Finish: Old iron with Weathered Brass Fonts. *Metal Shades in choice of Hand Toned Green or Red Enamel outside and Ivory inside.*

Glass Chimney: No. 24231
Crystal Glass (Lower half outside frosted).

skillfully portrayed by Moe-Bridges designers and craftsmen.

No. 380-S-5 $450.00+

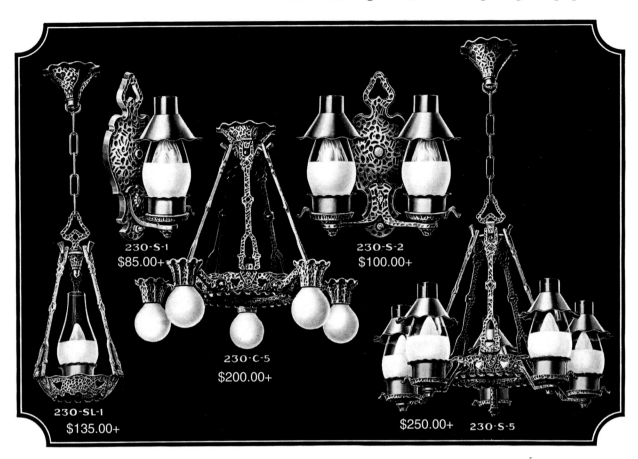

230-S-1
$85.00+

230-S-2
$100.00+

230-C-5
$200.00+

230-SL-1
$135.00+

$250.00+ 230-S-5

— *yet adaptable to English, Italian and Spanish settings.*

No. 230-SL-1. One light Pendant Lantern. Chimney style. Spread 8½ inches. Length 36 inches *Price $7.80.*

No. 230-S-1. One light Wall Bracket. Chimney style. Backplate 4⅜x9⅞ inches. Covers 4-inch outlet. Extension 5¼ inches. Canopy switch control.
Price $3.90.

No. 230-C-5. Five light Ceiling Fixture. Ball style. Spread 20 inches. Length 16½ inches. *Price $14.70.*

No. 230-C-3. Three light Ceiling Fixture. Ball style. Spread 20 inches. Length 16½ inches. *Price $9.90.*

No. 230-S-2. Two light Wall Bracket. Chimney style. Backplate 4⅜x9⅞ inches. Covers 4-inch outlet. Spread 11¼ inches. Extension 4⅝ inches. Canopy switch control. *Price $6.00.*

Finish: Forged Swedish Iron
NOTE: *Fonts and shades on all chimney fixtures finished in Weathered Brass.*
Glass Chimneys:
No. 24231 Large size
No. 24232 Small size (*Used on Brackets only.*)
Crystal Glass (Lower half outside frosted).

Tavern Forge Series

No. 230-S-5. Five light Pendant Fixture. Chimney style. Spread 21¾ inches. Length 42 inches.
Price $21.00.

NOTE: No. 230-S-5 and No. 230-S-3 can be made up in Ceiling Style, similar to No. 230-C-5, if desired. Order as No. 230-SC-5 or No. 230-SC-3.

No. 230-S-3. Three light Pendant Fixture. Chimney style. Spread 21¾ inches. Length 42 inches.
Price $13.80.

MOE-BRIDGES
MILWAUKEE

Finish: Natural Bronze

No. 282-K-2. Two light Wall Bracket — Candle style. Backplate 4x9 inches. Covers 4-inch outlet. Extension 4 inches. Spread 8½ inches. Canopy switch control. *Price $7.50.*

$150.00+

No. 282-K-1. One light Wall Bracket — Candle style. Backplate 4x9 inches. Covers 4-inch outlet. Extension 4 inches. Canopy switch control. *Price $6.00.*

$100.00+

No. 281-L-1. One light Pendant Lantern — Candle style. Spread 6½ inches. Length 36 inches. *Price $13.00.*

$125.00+

No. 282-K-3. Three light Wall Bracket — Candle style. Backplate 4x9 inches. Covers 4-inch outlet. Extension 4 inches. Spread 8½ inches. Canopy switch control. *Price $9.00.*

Stratford Series

$200.00+

No. 280-B-5. Five light Pendant Fixture—Ball style. Spread 22 inches. Length 36 inches. *Price $35.00.*

$300.00+

No. 280-C-5. Five light Ceiling Fixture—Ball style. Spread 22 inches. Length 25 inches. *Price $35.00.*

$300.00+

No. 280-K-5. Five light Pendant Fixture. Candle style. Spread 22 inches. Length 42 inches. *Price $35.00.*

$300.00+

No. 281-K-2. Two light Wall Bracket. Candle style. Backplate 3¾x10¾ inches. Covers three inch outlet. Extension 3¾ inches. Spread 7⅜ inches. Canopy switch control. *Price $5.00*

$150.00+

No. 281-L-3. Three light Pendant Lantern — Candle style. Spread 6½ inches. Length 36 inches. *Price $16.50.*

$200.00+

No. 280-C-1 (*Keyless*). Beam Light. Canopy diameter 5¾ inches. *Price $2.90*

No. 280-C-1P (*Pull Chain*) Same as 280-C-1. *Price $3.50*

$25.00 – 40.00

Finish: Natural Bronze

Stratford Series

No. 281-K-1. One light Wall Bracket. Candle style. Backplate 3¾x10¾ inches. Covers three inch outlet. Extension 3¾ inches. Canopy switch control. *Price $3.50*

$85.00+

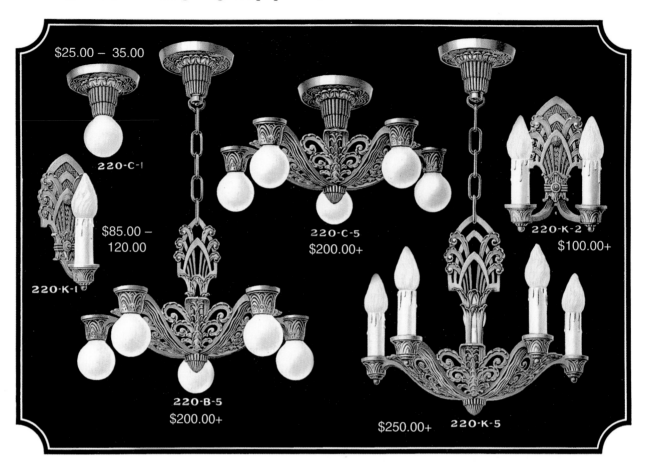

A *pleasing modernistic design at prices that defy comparison.*

Waverly Series

No. 220-K-1. One light Wall Bracket—Candle style. Backplate 4⅝x8 inches. Covers 4-inch outlet. Extension 4⅝ inches. Canopy switch control.
Price $2.40.

No. 220-C-1. Beam Light—Ball style. Canopy diameter 6 inches. *Price $1.20.*

No. 220-B-5. Five light Pendant Fixture—Ball style. Spread 19½ inches. Length 36 inches. *Price $7.50.*

No. 220-B-3. Three light Pendant Fixture (Similar to 220-B-5). Ball style. Spread 16 inches. Length 36 inches. *Price $6.00.*

No. 220-C-5. Five light Ceiling Fixture—Ball style. Spread 19½ inches. Length 8 inches. *Price $7.50.*

No. 220-C-3. Three light Ceiling Fixture. (Similar to 220-C-5.) Ball style. Spread 16 inches. Length 8 inches. *Price $6.00.*

Finish: Antique Pewter and Gold.

No. 220-K-5. Five light Pendant Fixture—Candle style. Spread 19¼ inches. Length 42 inches.
Price $7.50.

No. 220-K-3. Three light Pendant Fixture (Similar to 220-K-5). Candle style. Spread 15¾ inches. Length 42 inches. *Price $6.00.*

No. 220-K-2. Two light Wall Bracket—Candle style. Backplate 4⅝x8 inches. Covers 4-inch outlet. Extension 4¾ inches. Spread 7½ inches. Canopy switch control. *Price $3.30.*

No. 10-S-5

$700.00+

No. 10-S-1

$185.00+

**Choice of Finishes: "Silver and Black"
or "Natural Bronze"** *(Plated)*

Glass Shade No. 24225
*Decorated Cremax for 10-S-1, 10-S-2,
10-S-5.* Price $1.20.

No. 10-S-2

$200.00+

No. 10-S-2. Two light Wall Bracket with Shades.
Backplate 4¼x8 inches. Covers 4-inch outlet. Extension 6¼ inches. Spread 10⅞ inches. Canopy
switch control. *Price $6.50.*

No. 10-S-5. Five light Pendant Fixture with Shades.
Spread 20 inches. Length 42 inches. *Price $18.90.*

No. 10-S-1. One light Wall Bracket with Shade.
Backplate 4¼x8 inches. Covers 4-inch outlet. Extension 6¾ inches. Canopy switch control.
Price $4.30.

GENERAL TYPES

● A man's home is his domain. It reflects his tastes in many ways. His
whims and fancies are mirrored in everything it contains. And if he
should wish to drop away from the conventional in interior styling he
has a myriad of opportunities. To be different is his right, and most of
us permit him a full freedom to that right.

*Note: Cremax glass was also used to make
dinnerware during the Depression era.

MOE-BRIDGES
MILWAUKEE

Finish: Sunset Gold (*Plated*)

$200.00+

No. 120-C-5. Five light Ceiling Fixture—Ball style. Spread 20 inches. Length 19 inches. *Price $18.00.*

No. 120-B-5. Five light Pendant Fixture—Ball style. Spread 20 inches. Length 36 inches. *Price $18.00.*

$200.00+

No. 120-C-1. Beam Light. Canopy diameter 6⅞ inches. *Price $1.80.*

$25.00 – 30.00

No. 120-K-2. Two light Wall Bracket — Candle style. Backplate 4⅜x9 inches. Covers 4-inch outlet. Extension 3¾ inches. Spread 8½ inches. Canopy switch control. *Price $4.50.*

$85.00 – 115.00

$125.00+

No. 120-L-1. One Light Pendant Lantern — Ball style. Spread 8½ inches. Length 36 inches. *Price $7.80.*

No. 120-K-5. Five Light Pendant Fixture—Candle style. Spread 20 inches. Length 42 inches. *Price $18.00.*

$200.00+

$65.00 – 85.00

No. 120-K-1. One light Wall Bracket — Candle style. Backplate 4⅜x9 inches. Covers 4-inch outlet. Extension 3¾ inches. Canopy switch control. *Price $3.00.*

Sungold Series *Its beauty of design and finish is patterned from the glorious brilliancy of the setting sun.*

MOE~BRIDGES
MILWAUKEE

No. 140-C-5. Five light Ceiling Fixture—Ball style. Spread 21½ inches.
Length 19 inches.   *Price $15.90.*

$185.00+

No. 140-B-5. Five light Pendant Fixture—Ball style. Spread 21½ inches.
Length 36 inches.   *Price $15.90.*

$200.00+

**Finish:
Polished Pewter and Gold**

No. 140-K-5. Five light Pendant Fixture—Candle style.   Spread 21½
inches. Length 42 inches.
Price $15.90.

$200.00+

No. 141-C-1. Beam Light.
Canopy   diameter   6½
inches.   *Price $1.30.*

$25.00 – 30.00

No. 141-K-1. One light Wall
Bracket—Candle style. Backplate 4¼x8¾ inches. Covers
4-inch outlet. Extension 4
inches. Canopy switch control.
Price $2.70.

$75.00 – 100.00

$100.00 – 135.00

No. 141-L-1. One light
Pendant Lantern—Ball
style. Spread 7 inches.
Length 36 inches.

No. 141-K-2. Two light
Wall Bracket—Candle
style. Backplate 4¼x
8¾ inches. Covers 4-
inch outlet. Extension
4½ inches. Spread 8½
inches. Canopy switch
control. *Price $3.90.*

$85.00 – 115.00

A conception of modernistic design constructed to meet the requirements of the modest home.

Moderne Series

MOE-BRIDGES
MILWAUKEE

No. 150-C-5. Five light Ceiling Fixture—Ball style. Spread 20 inches. Length 18 inches. *Price $12.90.*

$225.00+

Finish: Sealtone

No. 150-B-5. Five light Pendant Fixture—Ball style. Spread 20 inches. Length 36 inches. *Price $12.90.*

$250.00+

No. 150-K-5. Five light Pendant Fixture—Candle style. Spread 20 inches. Length 42 inches. *Price $12.90*

$250.00+

No. 150-K-2. Two light Wall Bracket — Candle style. Backplate 4½x12 inches. Covers 4-inch outlet. Extension 3¾ inches. Spread 9 inches. Canopy switch control. *Price $3.50.*

$85.00 – 115.00

No. 462 (*Keyless*) — Beam Light. Canopy diameter 6 inches. *Price $1.50 (*6).*

No. 462-P (*Pull Chain*) — Same as No. 462. *Price $2.00 (*6).*

$25.00 – 35.00

No. 150-K-1. One light Wall Bracket — Candle style. Backplate 4½x12 inches. Covers 4-inch outlet. Extension 4½ inches. Canopy switch control. *Price $2.50*

$65.00 – 85.00

No. 150-L-1. One light Pendant Lantern—Ball style. Spread 7½ inches. Length 36 inches. *Price $3.90.*

$125.00 – 140.00

Full sized, sturdily constructed, attractively finished, and economically priced.

Victoria Series

24

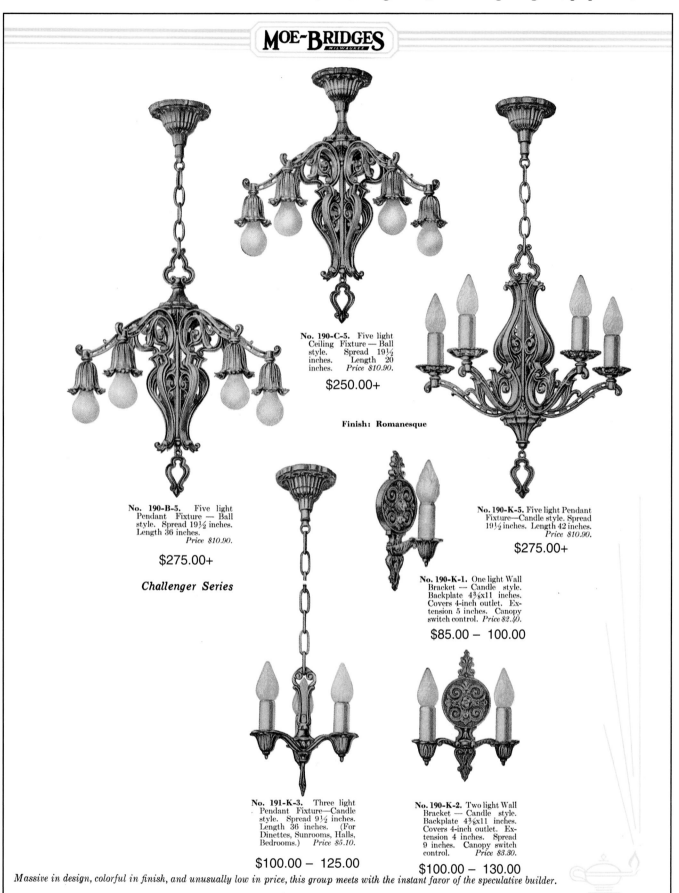

Moe-Bridges
MILWAUKEE

No. 190-C-5. Five light Ceiling Fixture — Ball style. Spread 19½ inches. Length 20 inches. *Price $10.90.*

$250.00+

Finish: Romanesque

No. 190-B-5. Five light Pendant Fixture — Ball style. Spread 19½ inches. Length 36 inches. *Price $10.90.*

$275.00+

Challenger Series

No. 190-K-5. Five light Pendant Fixture—Candle style. Spread 19½ inches. Length 42 inches. *Price $10.90.*

$275.00+

No. 190-K-1. One light Wall Bracket — Candle style. Backplate 4⅜x11 inches. Covers 4-inch outlet. Extension 5 inches. Canopy switch control. *Price $2.40.*

$85.00 — 100.00

No. 191-K-3. Three light Pendant Fixture—Candle style. Spread 9½ inches. Length 36 inches. (For Dinettes, Sunrooms, Halls, Bedrooms.) *Price $5.10.*

$100.00 — 125.00

No. 190-K-2. Two light Wall Bracket — Candle style. Backplate 4⅜x11 inches. Covers 4-inch outlet. Extension 4 inches. Spread 9 inches. Canopy switch control. *Price $3.30.*

$100.00 — 130.00

Massive in design, colorful in finish, and unusually low in price, this group meets with the instant favor of the speculative builder.

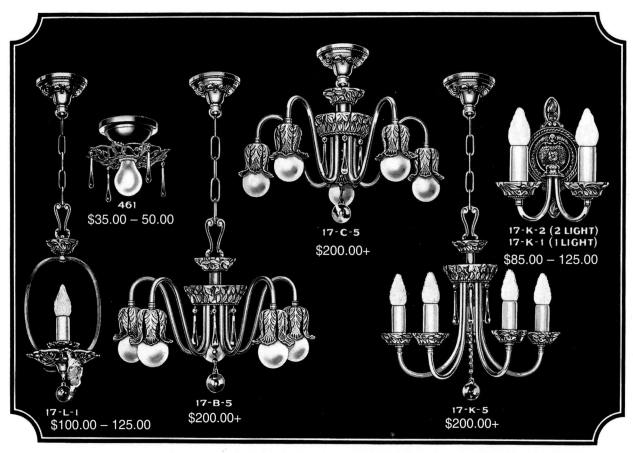

461
$35.00 – 50.00

17-C-5
$200.00+

17-K-2 (2 LIGHT)
17-K-1 (1 LIGHT)
$85.00 – 125.00

17-L-1
$100.00 – 125.00

17-B-5
$200.00+

17-K-5
$200.00+

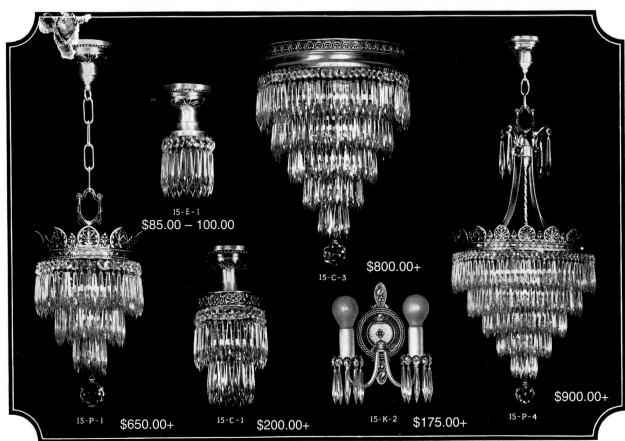

15-E-1
$85.00 – 100.00

$800.00+
15-C-3

$900.00+

15-P-1 $650.00+

15-C-1 $200.00+

15-K-2 $175.00+

15-P-4

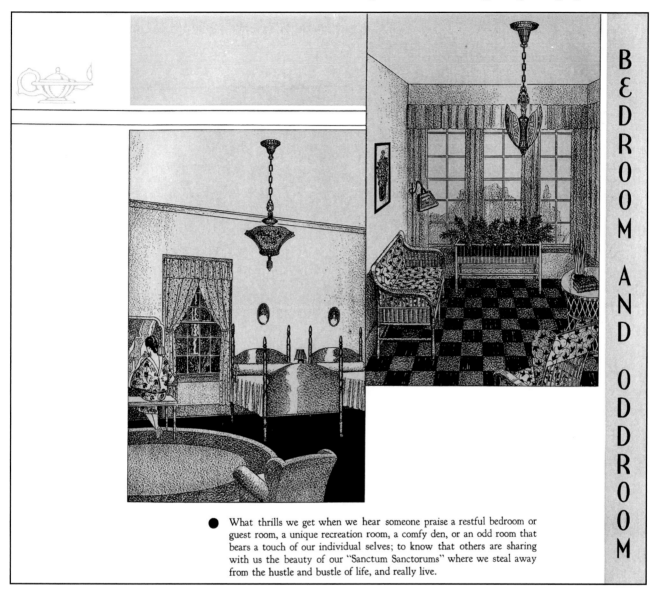

BEDROOM AND ODDROOM

● What thrills we get when we hear someone praise a restful bedroom or guest room, a unique recreation room, a comfy den, or an odd room that bears a touch of our individual selves; to know that others are sharing with us the beauty of our "Sanctum Sanctorums" where we steal away from the hustle and bustle of life, and really live.

Top Left:

Glenwood Series

Symmetrically curved tubing arms and delicately carved castings, artistically trimmed with glass ornaments.

No. 17-L-1. One light Pendant Lantern—Candle style. Spread 7½ inches. Length 36 inches. *Price $7.50.*

No. 461. One light Ceiling Fixture—Ball style. Canopy diameter 5 inches. Ornament diameter 8 inches. *Price $1.90 (*6).*

No. 17-B-5. Five light Pendant Fixture—Ball style. Spread 20 inches. Length 36 inches. *Price $13.90.*

No. 17-B-3. Three light Pendant Fixture—similar to 17-B-5. Spread 20 inches. Length 36 inches. *Price $9.90.*

No. 17-C-5. Five light Ceiling Fixture—Ball style. Spread 20 inches. Length 15 inches. *Price $13.90.*

No. 17-C-3. Three light Ceiling Fixture—similar to 17-C-5. Spread 20 inches. Length 15 inches. *Price $9.90.*

No. 17-K-5. Five light Pendant Fixture—Candle style. Spread 18 inches. Length 42 inches. *Price $13.90.*

Choice of Finishes: "Gold Polychrome" or "Silver & Black"

No. 17-K-3. Three light Pendant Fixture—similar to 17-K-5. Spread 18 inches. Length 42 inches. *Price $9.90.*

No. 17-K-2. Two light Wall Bracket—Candle style. Backplate 5x9 inches. Covers 4-inch outlet. Extension 5 inches. Spread 9¼ inches. Canopy switch control. *Price $4.50.*

No. 17-K-1. One light Wall Bracket—Candle style. Backplate 5x9 inches. Covers 4-inch outlet. Extension 6½ inches. Canopy switch control. *Price $3.30.*

Bottom Left:

Crystal Series

The decorative brilliancy of crystal fixture illumination has a definite place in many modern interior

No. 15-P-1. One light Pendant Fixture. Spread 9 inches. Length 36 inches. *Price $15.00.*

No. 15-E-1. One light Ceiling Fixture. Spread 5 inches. Length 7½ inches. *Price $3.90.*

No. 15-C-1. One light Ceiling Fixture. Spread 7 inches. Length 11 inches. *Price $6.50.*

No. 15-C-3. Three light Ceiling Fixture. Spread 13½ inches. Length 16 inches. *Price $24.00.*

Choice of Finishes: "Silver & Black" or "Burnished Gold"

No. 15-K-2. Two light Wall Bracket—Candle style. Backplate 4½x9 inches. Covers 4-inch outlet. Extension 5 inches. Spread 9 inches. Canopy switch control. *Price $6.50.*

No. 15-K-1. One light Wall Bracket—Candle style. Backplate 4½x9 inches. Covers 4-inch outlet. Extension 6 inches. Canopy switch control. *Price $4.30.*

No. 15-P-4. Four light Pendant Fixture. Spread 15 inches. Length 42 inches. *Price $33.00.*

477-B
$150.00+

478-C
$175.00+

478-A
$175.00+

477-A $150.00+

478-B
$175.00+

477-C
$150.00+

No. 25-C-3 (Three Light)
No. 25-C-2 (Two Light)
$165.00 – 175.00

No. 24-C-3
$165.00 – 175.00

No. 25-S-1
$65.00 – 85.00

No. 25-C-1
$50.00 – 100.00

No. 24-S-1
$50.00 – 75.00

No. 25-B-3 (Three Light)
No. 25-B-2 (Two Light)
$185.00 – 200.00

No. 25-S-3 (Three Light)
No. 25-S-2 (Two Light)
$185.00 – 200.00

* Note: Cremax glass was also used to make dinnerware during the Depression era.

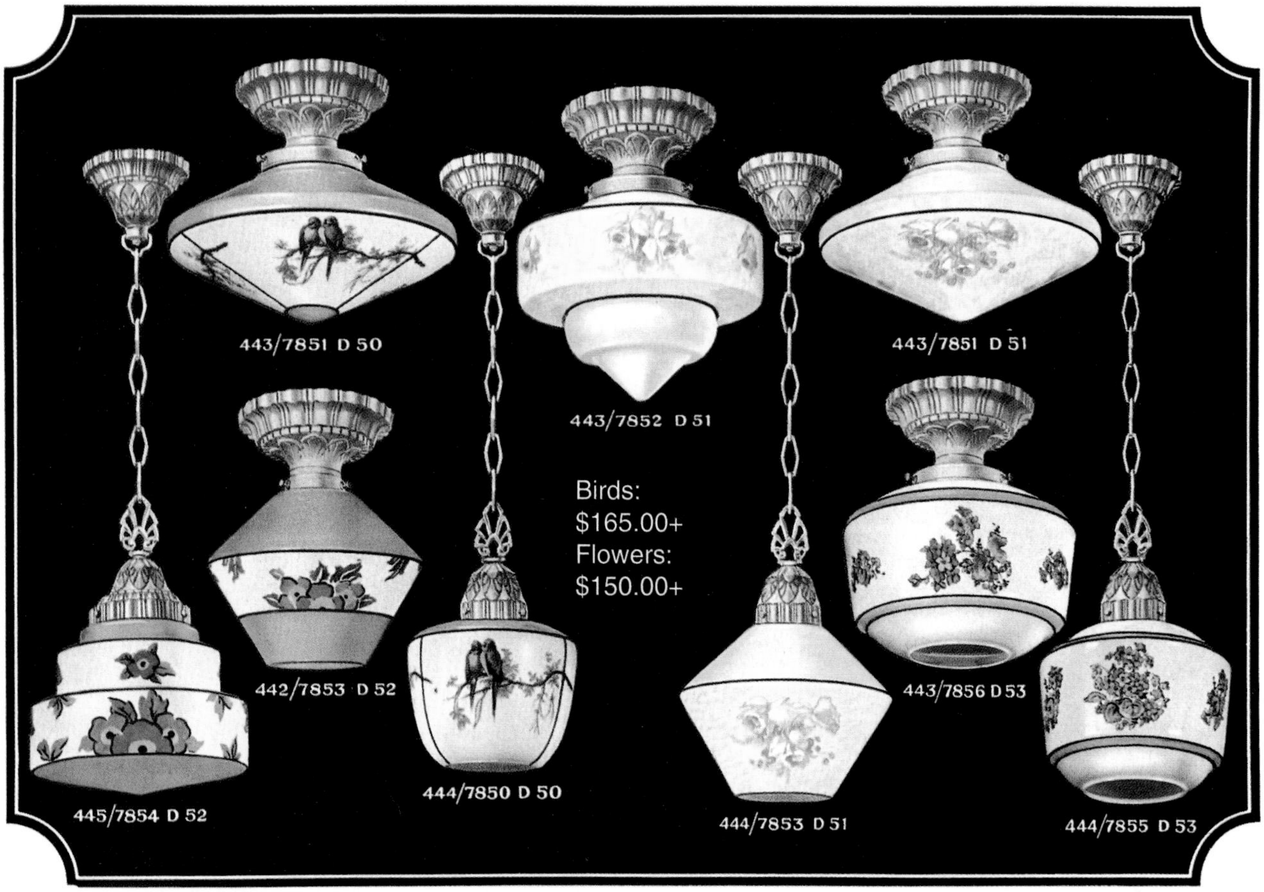
443/7851 D 50
443/7852 D 51
443/7851 D 51
Birds:
$165.00+
Flowers:
$150.00+
442/7853 D 52
443/7856 D 53
445/7854 D 52
444/7850 D 50
444/7853 D 51
444/7855 D 53

Above:

Colorful Glassware in a wide variety of designs and shapes with Metal Holders to match.

COMPLETE AS ILLUSTRATED

CATALOG NO. Holder	Glass	PRICE EACH
No. 445	7854-D52	$9.96 (*4)
No. 443	7851-D50	7.74 (*4)
No. 442	7853-D52	7.64 (*4)
No. 444	7850-D50	7.56 (*12)
No. 443	7852-D51	7.74 (*4)
No. 444	7853-D51	8.50 (*4)
No. 443	7851-D51	7.40 (*4)
No. 443	7856-D53	6.06 (*4)
No. 444	7855-D53	6.34 (*12)

NOTE: *Combinations other than those illustrated above, can be made if desired. Care should be taken, however, to have same size fitter on holder and glass.*

HOLDERS ONLY

CAT. NO.	DESCRIPTION	PRICE EACH
No. 442	2¼" Ceiling Holder	$1.80
No. 443	4" Ceiling Holder (Canopy Diameter, 6¼ inches)	1.90
No. 444	2¼" Pendant Holder	3.00
No. 445	4" Pendant Holder (Canopy Diameter 5 inches) (Length less glass, 30 inches)	3.30

Choice of Finishes on Holders: "Old Ivory and Colors" or "Old Ivory"

NOTE: *Keyless Sockets are standard equipment. Pull Chain Sockets furnished on request at slight additional cost.*

Bedroom, Sunroom, Breakfast Nook Series

GLASSWARE ONLY

CATALOG NO.	DIMENSIONS Fitter	Diam.	Depth	Bottom Opening	Ship. Wt. Per Doz.	PRICE EACH
7850-D50	2¼	8	7	4	33 lbs.	$4.56 (*12)
7851-D50	4	12	6¼	. . .	60	5.84 (*4)
7851-D51	4	12	6¼	. . .	60	5.50 (*4)
7852-D51	4	10	8⅞	. . .	45	5.84 (*4)
7853-D51	2¼	10	8½	4 9/16	42	5.50 (*4)
7853-D52	2¼	10	8½	4 9/16	42	5.84 (*4)
7854-D52	4	10	8¼	. . .	42	6.66 (*4)
7855-D53	2¼	8	7⅛	4	25	3.34 (*12)
7856-D53	4	10	7⅛	4	45	4.16 (*4)

Top Left:

Shaded Lighting for the boudoir in appropriate pastel colors.

No. 478-A—Green Colored Glass.
No. 478-B—Topaz Colored Glass.
No. 478-C—Rose Colored Glass.

One light Ceiling Fixture. Semi-indirect style. Spread 11 inches. Length 12½ inches. Glass accommodates a 60 Watt Lamp. *Price Complete $6.00* (*6).

Finish: Old Ivory

Glassware: No. 24238

Floral Decorated, Satin Finished, Pastel Colored Glass Dish. Diameter 11 inches. Depth 4¾ inches. Drilled Bottom Hole ⅜ inch.

NOTE: **No. 478—Pendant Style.** *Order as Numbers 478P-A, 478P-B, or 478P-C. Pendant Style—Price Complete $7.50* (*6).

Bedroom Series

No. 477-A—Green Silverna Etched Glass.
No. 477-B—Ivory Aureola Lustre Glass.
No. 477-C—Tan Silverna Etched Glass.

Two light Close-up Ceiling Fixture. Spread 10¼ inches. Length 5 inches. Glass accommodates two 60 Watt Lamps. *Price Complete $7.50.*

Finish: French Silver

Glassware: No. 24242

Diameter 10 inches. Depth 4 inches. Drilled Bottom Hole 5/16 inch.

Bottom Left:

Bedroom Series

A wide range of selection is the keynote of this shaded bedroom group.

No. 25-B-3. Three light Pendant Fixture—Drop Shade Style. Spread 13½ inches. Length 36 inches. *Price Complete $9.90.*

No. 25-B-2. Two light Pendant Fixture—Similar to No. 25-B-3. *Price Complete $7.90.*

No. 25-C-3. Three light Ceiling Fixture—Drop Shade Style. Spread 13½ inches. Length 10 inches. *Price Complete $8.50.*

No. 25-C-2. Two light Ceiling Fixture—Similar to No. 25-C-3. *Price Complete $6.50.*

No. 25-S-1. One light Wall Bracket—Torch Shade Style. Backplate 4x7½ inches. Covers 4-inch outlet. Extension 6¼ inches. Canopy switch control. *Price Complete $3.50.*

No. 25-C-1. One light Ceiling Fixture—Drop Shade Style. Canopy diameter 5 inches. Length 8½ inches. *Price Complete $2.20.*

No. 25-S-3. Three light Pendant Fixture—Torch Shade Style. Spread 13½ inches. Length 36 inches. *Price Complete $9.90.*

No. 25-S-2. Two light Pendant Fixture—Similar to No. 25-S-3. *Price Complete $7.90.*

Finish on 25 Line Fixtures: Ivory & Colors.

Glass Shades:
No. 7951D12—Torch Type
No. 7952D12—Drop Type
Cremax Glass with Decalcomania decorations.

No. 24-C-3. Three light Ceiling Fixture—Torch Shade Style. Spread 13 inches. Length 12 inches. *Price Complete $9.90.*

No. 24-S-1. One light Wall Bracket—Torch Shade Style. Backplate diameter 4½ inches. Covers 4-inch outlet. Extension 6¼ inches. Canopy switch control. *Price Complete $3.90.*

Finish on 24 Line Fixtures: Ivory & Gold. (*Hilighted*)

Glass Shade: No. 7951D12—Torch Type.
Cremax Glass with Decalcomania decorations.

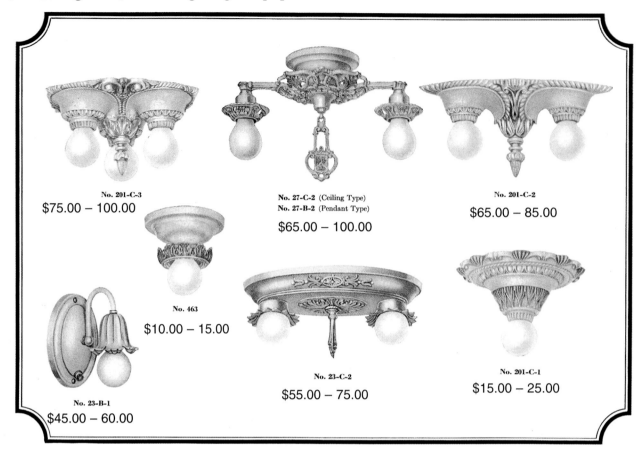

No. 201-C-3
$75.00 – 100.00

No. 27-C-2 (Ceiling Type)
No. 27-B-2 (Pendant Type)
$65.00 – 100.00

No. 201-C-2
$65.00 – 85.00

No. 463
$10.00 – 15.00

No. 23-C-2
$55.00 – 75.00

No. 201-C-1
$15.00 – 25.00

No. 23-B-1
$45.00 – 60.00

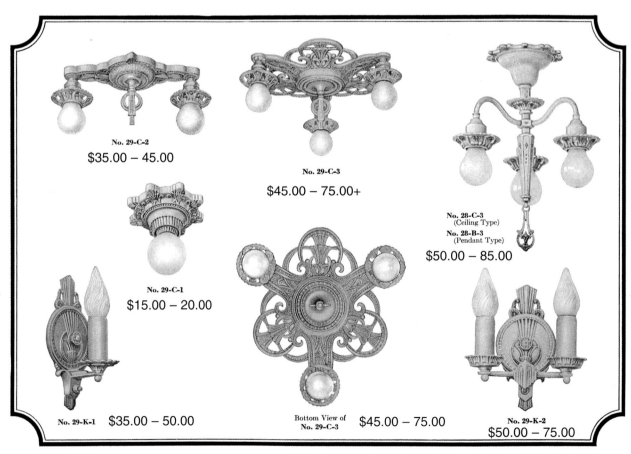

No. 29-C-2
$35.00 – 45.00

No. 29-C-3
$45.00 – 75.00+

No. 28-C-3
(Ceiling Type)
No. 28-B-3
(Pendant Type)
$50.00 – 85.00

No. 29-C-1
$15.00 – 20.00

No. 29-K-1 $35.00 – 50.00

Bottom View of
No. 29-C-3 $45.00 – 75.00

No. 29-K-2
$50.00 – 75.00

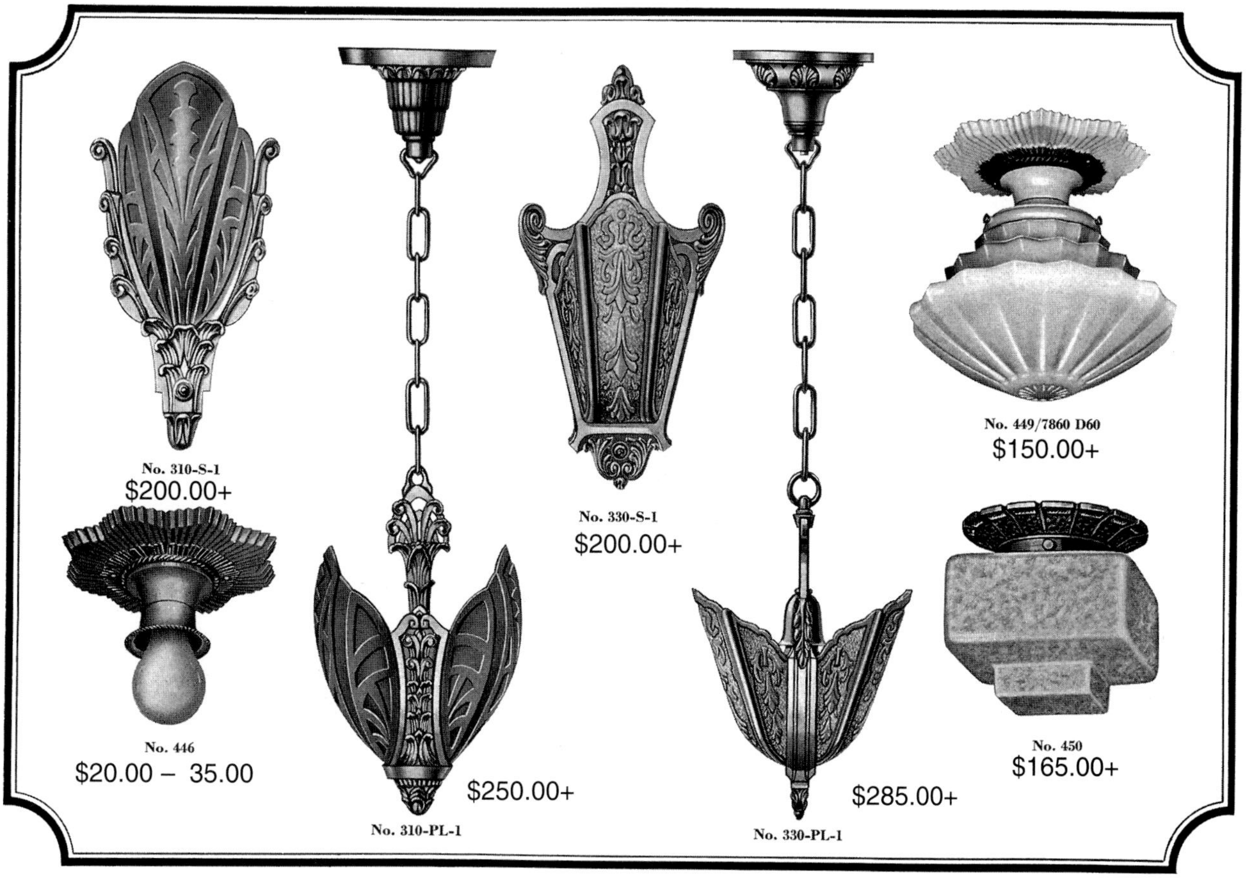
No. 310-S-1
$200.00+
No. 446
$20.00 – 35.00
No. 310-PL-1
$250.00+
No. 330-S-1
$200.00+
No. 330-PL-1
$285.00+
No. 449/7860 D60
$150.00+
No. 450
$165.00+

Above:

Appropriate styles for Bedroom, Sunroom, Hallway, Breakfast Nook, etc., will be found in this group.

Oddroom Series

No. 310-S-1. One light Wall Bracket. Backplate 6¼x12¼ inches. Covers 4-inch outlet. Extension 4¼ inches. Canopy switch control. *Price $3.90.*

No. 310-PL-1. One light Pendant Lantern suitable for Bedroom, Sunroom, and Breakfast Room. Spread 5¼x8½ inches. Length 36 inches. *Price $6.00.*

Choice of Finishes on 310-S-1 and 310-PL-1: "Old Ivory and Colors" or "Antique Pewter and Gold" *(See Page 8)*

Glass Shades: No. 24244 — Honey Satin Tone.

No. 330-S-1. One light Wall Bracket. Backplate 6½x12 inches. Covers 4-inch outlet. Extension 5 inches. Canopy switch control. *Price $4.50.*

No. 330-PL-1. One light Pendant Lantern suitable for Bedroom, Sunroom, and Breakfast Room. Spread 6¾x8½ inches. Length 36 inches. *Price $6.90.*

Choice of Finishes on 330-S-1 and 330-PL-1: "Old Ivory", "Old Ivory and Colors", or "Etruscan Gold". *(See Page 10)*

Glass Shades: No. 24243 — Choice of "Champagne Satin", "Green Lustre", "Orchid Lustre", or "Golden Lustre".

No. 450. One light Ceiling Lantern suitable for use in Sunroom or Hallway. Recommended for use with Norwich Series shown on Page 7. Cast Ceiling Ring diameter 7⅝ inches. Fitter 4 inches. Length Overall with Glass 7 inches. *Price Complete $6.00.*

Finish on No. 450: Natural Bronze *(Plated)*

Glass: No. 24237 — Antique Iridescent Frostell Texture. *(4-inch Fitter x 7½ inches Square).*

No. 446. One light Ceiling Fixture of Modernistic Design suitable for Bedrooms and Hallways. Canopy diameter 8 inches. *Price $1.80* (*6).

No. 449/7860 D60. One light Ceiling Fixture of Modernistic Design suitable for Bedrooms, Sunrooms, Breakfast Nooks, etc. *Price Complete $5.40.*

Holder No. 449—Canopy Diameter 8 inches. Fitter 4 inches. *Price Holder only $2.10* (*6)

Glass No. 7860 D60—Diameter 10 inches. Fitter 4 inches. *Price Glass only $3.30* (*12).

Finishes on No. 446 and No. 449: Choice of "Ivory and Gold", "Green and Gold", or "Orchid and Gold".

(NOTE: *Glassware furnished in "Tan", "Green", or "Orchid" to match finishes on Holder.)*

Top Left:

Bedroom Series

Attractive designs in "Old Ivory and Colors" at extremely modest prices.

No. 23-B-1. One light Wall Bracket. Backplate 4¼x6 inches. Covers 4-inch outlet. Extension 6¼ inches. Canopy switch control. *Price $2.50* (*6).

No. 23-C-2. Two light Ceiling Fixture. Oval Canopy 6⅜x12 inches. Length 5¼ inches. *Price $1.80* (*6).

No. 27-C-2. Two light Ceiling Fixture. Spread 14 inches. Length 8½ inches. *Price $3.90.*

No. 27-B-2. Two light Pendant Fixture. Spread 14 inches. Length 36 inches. *Price $5.40.*

No. 463. Beam Light. Canopy diameter 5 inches. *Price $.98* (*6)

Choice of Finishes: "Old Ivory" or "Old Ivory & Colors"

No. 201-C-1. One light Ceiling Fixture. Canopy diameter 8 inches. *Price $2.00* (*6).

No. 201-C-2. Two light Ceiling Fixture. Spread 12¼ inches. Length 5 inches. *Price $2.50* (*6).

No. 201-C-3. Three light Ceiling Fixture. Spread 9⅜ inches. Length 4½ inches. *Price $3.50* (*6).

Bottom Left:

Pastel colors delicately applied on pleasing designs of modernistic influence gives these fixtures a touch of individuality.

Bedroom Series

No. 29-C-1. Beam Light. Canopy diameter 6½ inches. *Price $1.30*

No. 29-C-2. Two light Ceiling Fixture. Spread 5¾x13¼ inches. Length 5 inches. *Price $3.30.*

No. 29-C-3. Three light Ceiling Fixture. Spread 16 inches. Length 5¾ inches. *Price $5.10.*

No. 29-K-1. One light Wall Bracket. Backplate 4¼x8¾ inches. Covers 4-inch outlet. Extension 4 inches. Canopy switch control. *Price $2.70.*

No. 29-K-2. Two light Wall Bracket. Backplate 4¼x8¾ inches. Covers 4-inch outlet. Extension 4½ inches. Spread 8½ inches. Canopy switch control. *Price $3.90.*

Choice of Finishes on 29 Line:

"Old Ivory" *as shown on 29-C-1.*

"Old Ivory and Colors" *as shown on 29-C-2 and 29-K-2.*

"Pastel Green and Peach" *as shown on 29-K-1.*

"Pastel Orchid and Green" *as shown on 29-C-3.*

No. 28-C-3. Three light Ceiling Fixture. Spread 11½ inches. Length 13 inches. *Price $7.90.*

No. 28-B-3. Three light Pendant Fixture. Spread 11½ inches. Length 36 inches. *Price $9.40.*

Choice of Finishes on 28-C-3 and 28-B-3: "Old Ivory" or "Old Ivory and Colors"

Boudoir Lamps of Unusual Charm

The same inherent qualities that make Moe-Bridges Fixtures most desirable for your home are to be found in the three charming lamps illustrated on this page.

Bedroom, library corner, den, living room, hall, stair landing, are but a few of the places where these lamps are appropriate and will add to the comfort and attractiveness of the home. They can also be used successfully on tables in cafes, hotels, restaurants, and any other similar establishments.

Well designed, sturdily built, and attractively finished, the metal bases blend admirably with the harmonizing parchment paper shades. However our splendid facilities for volume production enable us to sell these lamps at prices far below those usually asked for lamps of like quality.

No. B8/S17. Base diameter, 5 inches. Height overall, 13 inches. Equipped with Turn Knob Candle Socket. 10-inch Cone Shade with applied Godey Fashion Print.
Price Complete $4.50 (*6).

Finish: Antique Pewter

$150.00+

No. B9/S18. Base diameter, 4¾ inches. Height overall, 12½ inches. Equipped with Push Bar Socket. 10-inch Cone Shade with applied Historic Print.
Price Complete $4.50 (*6).

Finish: Sunset Gold

$150.00+

No. B10/S19. Base diameter, 4¾ inches. Height overall, 13¼ inches. Equipped with Push Bar Socket. 8-inch Empire Shade with painted Gold Stripe.
Price Complete $4.50 (*6).

Finish: Ivory and Gold.

$125.00+

Gift Lamps

A solution to the ever perplexing gift problem is presented in these three charming gift lamps.

Appropriate as a gift for Christmas, Graduation, Birthday, Wedding, and other similar occasions when you would like to give something "nice but not too expensive."

Their wide range of adaptability, plus their obvious quality, place the B8, B9, and B10 lamps in a class by themselves.

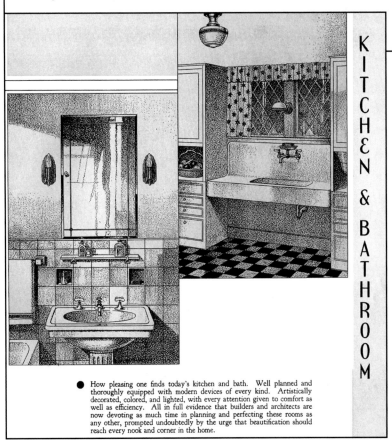

KITCHEN & BATHROOM

● How pleasing one finds today's kitchen and bath. Well planned and thoroughly equipped with modern devices of every kind. Artistically decorated, colored, and lighted, with every attention given to comfort as well as efficiency. All in full evidence that builders and architects are now devoting as much time in planning and perfecting these rooms as any other, prompted undoubtedly by the urge that beautification should reach every nook and corner in the home.

$15.00 — 20.00

P 2635-1

P 2630
$85.00+

P 2637
P 2638

$75.00+

P 2636-1
$150.00+

P 2631-1
P 2632-1

$75.00+

P 2628-1
P 2629-1 $35.00+

P 2633
P 2634 $100.00+

$35.00+   P 2626
P 2627

Porcelain Series

Exclusive Moe-Bridges designs in spotless solid porcelain —

Catalog Number		Wiring Code	Price Each Complete	Catalog Number	Wiring Code	Price Each Comlpete	Catalog Number		Wiring Code		Price Each Complete	Catalog Number		Wiring Code		Price Each Complete
P 2626	White	A	$4.05 (*4)	P 2630-1 or 2	E	$3.45 (*4)	P 2633	White	C		$4.50 (*4)	P 2636	White	E (with glass)		$4.05 (*1)
P 2627	White	B	4.70 (*4)	P 2630-8	E	4.05 (*4)	P 2634	White	D		5.25 (*4)	P 2636-1 or 2		E (with glass)		6.00 (*1)
P 2628	White	C	2.55 (*4)	P 2631 White	C	3.30 (*4)	P 2635	White	E		1.50 (*4)	P 2636-8		E (with glass)		4.95 (*1)
P 2628-1 or 2		C	3.30 (*4)	P 2631-1 or 2	C	4.05 (*4)	P 2635-1 or 2		E		1.95 (*4)	P 2637	White	C (less glass)		2.10 (*4)
P 2629	White	D	3.30 (*4)	P 2632 White	D	4.05 (*4)	P 2636	White	E	(less glass)	1.65 (*1)	P 2637	White	C (with glass)		2.85 (*4)
P 2629-1 or 2		D	4.05 (*4)	P 2632-1 or 2	D	4.80 (*4)	P 2636-1 or 2		E	(less glass)	2.10 (*1)	P 2638	White	D (less glass)		2.40 (*4)
P 2630	White	E	2.70 (*4)				P 2636-8		E	(less glass)	2.55 (*1)	P 2638	White	D (with glass)		3.15 (*4)

NOTE: *Stripes and Colors on this page are designated by suffix numbers:* "White and Black - 1"; "White and Green - 2"; "Ivory - 8". *(For Complete Color Code — see Page 52.)*
WIRING CODE: *Description shown on Page 52.*

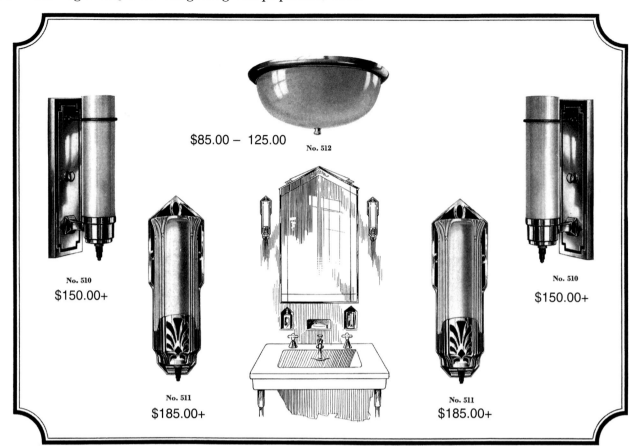

$85.00 – 125.00

No. 512

No. 510
$150.00+

No. 510
$150.00+

No. 511
$185.00+

No. 511
$185.00+

Chromium Bath Series

No. 510. One light Cast Brass Chromium Bathroom Bracket. Backplate 3x8¾ inches. Covers standard switch box outlet (2 inches wide x 3 inches long). Extension 3½ inches. Equipped with insulated turn knob candle socket. *Price Complete $7.50.*

Finish: "Chromium and Black"

Glassware: No. 24233 Cylinder (2x7 inches). Choice of "White" or "Ivory" glass.
Will accommodate 25 watt tubular lamp.

No. 511. One light Cast Durolite Bathroom Bracket. Backplate 3⅝x10⅞ inches. Covers 3-inch outlet. Extension 3 inches. Equipped with insulated turn knob candle socket. *Price Complete $6.00.*

Finish: "Chromium and Black"

Glassware: No. 24239 Moulded "Marbo" Glass Shade (Milky White).
Will accommodate 25 watt tubular lamp.

No. 512. Two light Chromium Ceiling Fixture. Diameter 8½ inches. Depth 3½ inches.
Price Complete $7.50.

Finish: Chromium.

Glassware: No. 24238-A Crystal Frosted for use with No. 511 Bracket.
No. 24238-B Opal White for use with No. 510 Bracket.
(Diameter 7⅜ inches. Depth 3 inches. Drilled Bottom Hole ¼ inch).

OUTDOOR LANTERNS

● A *glowing welcome*—light from charming lanterns is as becoming to dark doorways as smiles to dull faces, transfiguring them into radiant beauty. It is a symbol and a sign that beyond the door will be found light hearts and merry voices; a family whose warm cordiality overflows in the message of the lamps: "*Come in! We want you to come!*"

Bronze Lanterns
of Unusual Distinction

Critics and Art Collectors in all parts of the world admire the ingenious workmanship of the craftsmen of the Middle Ages. Artisans in those days toiled not so much for money as for love of their work. As a result, their skill in creating ornamental metal designs of plants and figures has seldom been equalled.

By careful study and patient effort the outdoor lanterns shown on this page have been created to rival the masterpieces of the Old Guild Craftsmen. Some of them have been developed from treasured pieces among the *objects d'art* in the famous museums of Europe and America. They are presented here as the ultimate in fine exterior lighting equipment.

Choice of Finishes: "Weathered Bronze" or "Black"

Glass: Clear or C. R. I.
(Specify glass desired)

No. 901-B. Wall Plate, 4¾x8⅛ inches. Extension, 9¾ inches. Height Overall, 14½ inches.
Price—$25.00—Weathered Bronze
18.00—Black

$150.00+

No. 903-B. Wall Plate, 4¾x8⅛ inches. Extension, 9¾ inches. Height Overall, 12¾ inches.
Price—
$20.00—Weathered Bronze
13.00—Black

$150.00+

No. 902-B. Wall Plate, 4½x12⅜ inches. Extension 10½ inches. Height Overall, 16 inches.
Price—
$29.50—Weathered Bronze
22.50—Black.

$160.00+

No. 900-B. Wall Plate, 4½x12⅜ inches. Extension 10½ inches. Height Overall, 16½ inches.
Price—
$27.00—Weathered Bronze
20.00—Black

$175.00+

$175.00+

No. 904-B. Wall Plate, 4½x12⅜ inches. Extension, 9⅝ inches. Height Overall, 17 inches.
Price—
$32.00—Weathered Bronze
25.00—Black

NOTE: *Lanterns illustrated on this page also furnished in Pendant Style.*

Pendant Style No.	Weathered Bronze	Black
900-P	$20.00	$15.00
901-P	20.00	15.00
902-P	22.50	17.50
903-P	15.00	10.00
904-P	25.00	20.00

Outdoor Lantern Series

Choice of Finishes on 865, 866 and 867:

"Swedish Iron" with Clear Moss Glass Panels (*As shown on 866*)

"Antique Copper" with Amber Cathedral Glass Panels (*As shown on 867 and 865*).

No. 867. Copper Ceiling Lantern. Cage diameter 6 inches. Depth 10 inches. Length Overall 16 inches. *Price $6.00.*

$150.00+

No. 865. Copper Bracket Lantern— Drop Style. Hexagon Wall Plate 4¼ inch diameter. Cage diameter 6 inches. Depth 10 inches. Extension 8¾ inches. Height Overall 15 inches. *Price $6.00.*

$150.00+

No. 868. Bracket Lantern— Drop Style. Wall Plate 4¼ inches square. Cage 4¼ inches square. Depth 8 inches. Extension 7½ inches. Height Overall 11 inches. *Price $3.75.*

$100.00+

No. 869. Ceiling Lantern. Canopy 4¼ inches square. Cage 4¼ inches square. Depth 8 inches. Length Overall 11 inches. *Price $3.75.*

$100.00+

Finish on 868, 869:
"Black" (*Applied on Galvin Iron*)

Clear Moss Glass Panels

No. 866. Copper Bracket Lantern— Upright Style. Hexagon Wall Plate 4¼ inches diameter. Cage diameter 6 inches. Depth 10 inches. Extension 8¾ inches. Height Overall 15 inches. *Price $6.00.*

$150.00+

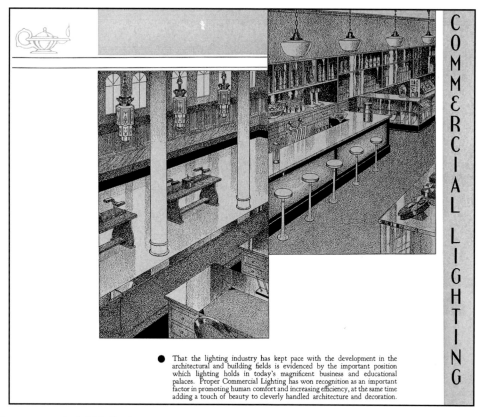

● That the lighting industry has kept pace with the development in the architectural and building fields is evidenced by the important position which lighting holds in today's magnificent business and educational palaces. Proper Commercial Lighting has won recognition as an important factor in promoting human comfort and increasing efficiency, at the same time adding a touch of beauty to cleverly handled architecture and decoration.

COMMERCIAL LIGHTING

Commercial Lighting

UP-TO-DATE business establishments and educational institutions require and demand Proper Lighting. Well-Lighted window displays, store interiors, shops, etc., attract customers and make it easy for them to buy. Proper Illumination in offices and factories protects the eyesight and health of workers in addition to promoting modern production methods. Good Lighting in banks, theatres, and clubs attracts patrons and members. In every community those firms which are keeping ahead of the others, abreast of the times, and able to meet their ever-increasing competition, are benefiting by modern lighting equipment.

Moe-Bridges designers and lighting engineers have been generous contributors to this important phase of the lighting industry—Commercial Lighting. Included in the large variety of plain and ornamental commercial holders illustrated on the succeeding pages will be found the nationally known "Focalite" Holders, "M-B Safety" Holders, "Marvel" Screwless Holders, all patented by Moe-Bridges.

Glassware Description

(See Glassware Illustrations on opposite page — No. 62.)

Catalog No.	Fitter	Diam.	Depth	Shipping Weight Per Std. Pkg.	Price Each
7510-D-30	4	10	6¼	15 lbs.	$ 5.28 (*2)
7512-D-30	6	12	10	10 lbs.	5.85 (*1)
7514-D-30	6	14	12	11 lbs.	6.75 (*1)
7516-D-30	6	16	14	12 lbs.	9.60 (*1)
7521 S.W.	4	6	8¾	35 lbs.	1.05 (*6)
7521-D-31	4	6	8¾	35 lbs.	1.80 (*6)
7522 S.W.	6	10	16¾	10 lbs.	4.95 (*1)
7522-D-31	6	10	16¾	10 lbs.	6.75 (*1)
7523 S.W.	6	12	20	14 lbs.	15.00 (*1)
7523-D-31	6	12	20	14 lbs.	18.00 (*1)
7531-D-32	4	6	9	30 lbs.	2.40 (*12)
7532-D-32	6	10¼	16¼	12 lbs.	6.75 (*1)
7533-D-32	4	9	8	20 lbs.	3.75 (*4)
7534-D-32	6	12½	11¼	11 lbs.	8.25 (*1)

Decoration Description

S.W.—"Snowwhite" Opal Glass.

D-30—This decoration is furnished in 2 finishes as follows: "Silver Gray and Black" — Two tone effect on opal glass. "Mello-tone" — Two tone tan effect on cream background.
NOTE: *Bottom Tassel (crystal glass) is standard equipment on all D-30 Units.*

D-31—Opal Glass, Silver Gray decoration framed by black lines on each of the six plain panels.

D-32—Opal Glass, Black Lines in Ribs; Crystal Glass removable bottom in 7533 and 7534 units.

A Few Representative Moe-Bridges Commercial Lighting Installations

Barnett National Bank Building..Jacksonville, Fla.
Shelton High School..............Shelton, Wash.
Apollo High School................Altoona, Pa.
Hobart Building..............San Francisco, Calif.
Hotel St. Anthony.................Laredo, Texas.
Zuehlke Building.................Appleton, Wis.
Boston Chamber of Commerce......Boston, Mass.
Burton High School..........Grand Rapids, Mich.
Union Building..................San Diego, Calif.
American Trust Building...........Oakland, Calif.
Boys Technical High School.....Milwaukee, Wis.
Convent of Notre Dame..........Elm Grove, Wis.
Foster De Witt Library.........Ft. Atkinson, Wis.
Liberty County Court House.......Liberty, Texas.
Girls Technical High School......Milwaukee, Wis.
Johnson Woods School...........Milwaukee, Wis.
Milwaukee Hospital.............Milwaukee, Wis.
Ishpeming High School..........Ishpeming, Mich.
Sheboygan High School..........Sheboygan, Wis.
Adair County Court House........Stillwell, Okla.
Escanaba Junior High School....Escanaba, Mich.
Jacksonville State Teachers College, Jacksonville, Ala.
San Jose Public School..........San Jose, Calif.
Manteno State Hospital.........Manteno, Ill.
Angell School..................Muskegon, Mich.
Republic Building.............Los Angeles, Calif.
Fox Hospital...............Johnson City, Tenn.
Whittier School................Hampton, Va.
Ypsilanti State Hospital........Ypsilanti, Mich.
Boston Store..................Milwaukee, Wis.
Roosevelt School...............Kenosha, Wis.
Cushing Memorial Hospital...Leavenworth, Kans.
Lord's Department Store..........Waukegan, Ill.
Dodge Motor Plants.............Detroit, Mich.
Dennison Manufacturing Co...Framingham, Mass.
Concordia College.............Milwaukee, Wis.

THE NAME MOE-BRIDGES MILWAUKEE SIGNIFIES MASTER CRAFTSMANSHIP IN LIGHTING EQUIPMENT

$150.00+

$100.00+

$250.00+

$150.00+

MSC 26/7534 D32

MSC 26/7514 D30

MSB 34/7521 D31

MSB 34/7531 D32

MSP 26/7522 D31

MSP 26/7534 D32

MSP 26/7514 D30

MSP 26/7532 D32

MSP 26/7522 SW

$200.00+

$100.00+

$250.00+

$200.00+

$200.00+

No. MSC 26/7541 D33

$200.00+

No. MSC 24/7540 D33

$150.00+

$185.00+

No. MSP 26/7542 (White)

$250.00+

No. MSP 26/7542 D33

Cased Glass Modernistic Units

Cased Glass is made with a thin lining of the highest quality white glass, reinforced with a heavy outer layer of special crystal glass. This texture possesses a deep lustrous beauty that is transformed, when lighted, into a snow-white light of even distribution. Glare is filtered out and the light is perfectly diffused with a minimum of absorption.

* Note: Monax glass also used to make dinnerware during the Depression era.

No. MSC 36/7614 D19
$100.00+

No. MSP 36/7614 D19
$125.00+

No. MSC 36/7114 D18
$65.00+

No. MB 67/7212 D13
$150.00+

Above:

A group of ornamental metal holders with decorated glass units to match.

Commercial Series

No. MSP 36/7614 D19. Six inch Ornamental Pendant Holder No. MSP 36 (Screw Type) Complete with 6x14 inch Tan Decorated Opal Glass Unit No. 7614 D19. *Price Complete $12.24 (*2).* Canopy Diameter, 6 inches. Length 30 inches *(Less glass).*

No. MSC 36/7614 D19. Six inch Ornamental Ceiling Holder No. MSC 36 (Screw Type) Complete with 6x14 inch Tan Decorated Opal Glass Unit No. 7614 D19. *Price Complete $9.99 (*2).* Canopy Diameter, 6 inches. Length 5¼ inches *(Less glass).*

No. MSC 36/7114 D18. Six inch Ornamental Ceiling Holder No. MSC 36 (Screw Type) Complete with 6x14 inch Tan Decorated Opal Glass Unit No. 7114 D18. *Price Complete $9.99 (*2).* Canopy Diameter, 6 inches. Length 5¼ inches *(Less glass).*

Finish on MSP 36 and MSC 36: Statuary Bronze with Natural Bronze Trim. *(Plated)*

No. MB 67/7212 D13. Six inch Ornamental Pendant Holder No. MB 67 (Safety Gravity Grip Type). Complete with 6x12x14 inch Tan Etched Decorated Monax Glass Unit No. 7212 D13. *Price Complete $23.82 (*2).* Canopy Diameter, 6 inches. Length 30 inches *(Less glass).*

Finish on MB 67: Bank Bronze *(Plated).*

NOTE: *Complete price information shown on Page 67.*

Top Left:

"Modernistic" Glass Units in a wide variety of designs and shapes with metal holders to match.

Commercial Series

COMPLETE AS ILLUSTRATED

CATALOG NO. Holder Glass	Price Each	CATALOG NO. Holder Glass	Price Each
No. MSB 34/7521 D31	$ 9.80 (*6)	No. MSP 26/7522 SW	$12.45 (*1)
No. MSB 34/7531 D32	10.40 (*12)	No. MSP 26/7522 D31	14.25 (*1)
No. MSC 26/7514 D30	11.25 (*1)	No. MSP 26/7532 D32	14.25 (*1)
No. MSC 26/7534 D32	12.75 (*1)	No. MSP 26/7534 D32	15.75 (*1)
No. MSC 26/7514 D30	14.25 (*1)		

NOTE: *Combinations, other than those illustrated above, can be made if desired. Care should be taken, however, to have same size fitter on holder and glass. (See opposite page for descriptions and prices on glass units.)*

HOLDERS ONLY

No. MSB-34. 4-inch Wall Bracket. Back Plate diameter 5 inches. Extension 9¼ inches. Canopy switch control.
Price $8.00. (*12).

No. MSC-26. 6-inch Ceiling Holder. Canopy diameter 6 inches. *Price $4.50. (*12).* Wired Mogul *Price 4.80. (*12).*

NOTE: *Also made in 4 inch size—No. MSC-24.*

No. MSP-26. 6-inch Pendant Holder with "Focalite" Feature (See Page 65). Canopy diameter 8¾ inches. Length less glass 30 inches. *Price $7.50. (*12).* Wired Mogul *Price 7.80. (*12).*

NOTE: *Also made in 4 inch size—No. MSP-24. (All canopies have knockout for Levolier Switch)*

Choice of Finishes: "Stained Nickel" or "Stained Bronze"

Bottom Left:

Commercial Series

Commercial Lighting in the "Modernistic" Vogue furnishes excellent illumination, plus added beauty and style.

CATALOG NUMBER Holder Glass	Type	GLASSWARE DESCRIPTION Diam.	Depth	Fitter	Suggested Wattage	EACH PRICES Glass Only	Holder Only	Complete Only
MSC 24/7540 White	4" Ceiling	9	7⅞	4	100	$1.35 (*8)	$4.50 (*12)	$5.85 (*8)
MSC 24/7540 D-33	4" Ceiling	9	7⅞	4	100	2.70 (*1)	4.50 (*12)	7.20 (*1)
MSC 26/7541 White	6" Ceiling	12½	10	6	150-200	4.20 (*1)	4.50 (*12)	8.70 (*1)
MSC 26/7541 D-33	6" Ceiling	12½	10	6	150-200	5.85 (*1)	4.50 (*12)	10.35 (*1)
MSP 24/7540 White	4" Pendant	9	7⅞	4	100	1.35 (*8)	7.50 (*12)	8.85 (*8)
MSP 24/7540 D-33	4" Pendant	9	7⅞	4	100	2.70 (*1)	7.50 (*12)	10.20 (*1)
MSP 26/7542 White	6" Pendant	10	16	6	200-300	5.50 (*1)	7.50 (*12)	13.00 (*1)
MSP 26/7542 D-33	6" Pendant	10	16	6	200-300	7.50 (*1)	7.50 (*12)	15.00 (*1)

HOLDER DESCRIPTIONS

Finishes: Choice of "Stained Nickel" or "Stained Bronze"

Extra Lengths: Extra Chain complete with wire $.60 per Foot.

Canopies: All canopies have knockout for levolier switch. (Switch installed $1.80.)

For additional descriptions and prices on holders only, refer to page 62.

GLASSWARE DESCRIPTIONS

White: Undecorated White Cased Glass.

D-33: Conventional Decorated "Modernistic" Design in Black on White Cased Glass.

SPECIAL CREATIONS

● Individuality is the word which best describes that "certain something" toward which every Architect is striving. Modern Public Buildings, Churches, Hotels, Clubs, Theatres, and Large Residences, though usually bearing the earmarks of Early European Architecture, are characterized by the individual art of today's architects. This Individuality is obtained thru various sources, one of the most important being the proper expression of Modern Illumination, and Moe-Bridges is prepared to be of assistance with Special Lighting Fixture Creations to meet with specific conditions.

Note: It is not possible to put prices on items shown on the following pages.

Special Creations

Theatres, Hotels, Churches, Clubs, Educational Buildings, Large Residences, Court Houses, Banks, and many types of Public Buildings which are being built today, have been or are being equipped with Moe-Bridges lighting equipment. In addition to the items selected from the Moe-Bridges standard line, "Special Creations," such as those illustrated on the following three pages, were designed and manufactured by Moe-Bridges to harmonize with the Architectural Plan of the buildings in which they were installed.

Use the Moe-Bridges Engineering Service—a complete department combining exceptional Designing, Manufacturing and Sales facilities that is placed at the disposal of Architects, Builders, Contractors and Electrical Dealers where the problems of proper selection and placing of Lighting Equipment demand the assistance of Specialists.

MOE-BRIDGES
MILWAUKEE

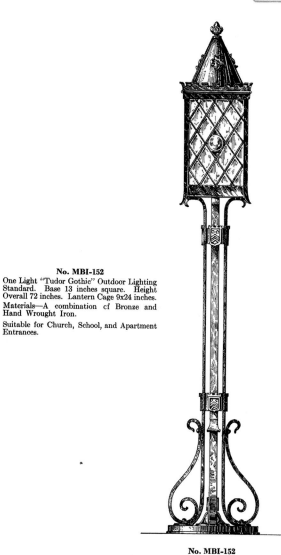

No. MBI-152

One Light "Tudor Gothic" Outdoor Lighting Standard. Base 13 inches square. Height Overall 72 inches. Lantern Cage 9x24 inches.

Materials—A combination of Bronze and Hand Wrought Iron.

Suitable for Church, School, and Apartment Entrances.

No. MBI-152

No. MBI-192

One Light Outdoor Lighting Standard of "Classical" Design, used in the new Milwaukee County Courthouse.

Base 36 inches square. Height overall 126 inches. Materials—Cast Bronze with 20-inch Opal Glass Ball.

No. MBI-192

NOTE: On Pages 74, 75 and 76 are illustrations of but a few of the "Special Creations" which have been designed and manufactured by the Moe-Bridges Company for installations in all sections of the United States and Canada. (*Prices furnished upon application.*)

No. MBI-193

Indirect Lighting Standard of "Classical" Design mounted on pedestal in center of large rotunda in the new Milwaukee County Courthouse.

Diameter 44 inches. Height overall 30½ inches. Materials—Cast Bronze.

MOE-BRIDGES
MILWAUKEE

No. MBE-351

One Light "Spanish" Lantern. Lantern Cage 10x24 inches. Length Overall 48 inches. Materials—A combination of Bronze and Iron metals with Amber Glass Panels.

Suitable for vestibules and halls in Clubs, Theatres, and Large Residences.

No. MBD-351

Twelve Light "Italian Renaissance" Candle Chandelier. Spread overall 33 inches. Length Overall 56 inches.

Materials—Spinnings and castings of brass.

Suitable for Dining Room or Lounge in Hotels, Clubs, and Large Residences.

No. MBE-316

One Light "Gothic" Pendant Lantern. Lantern Cage 10x28 inches. Length Overall 48 inches. Materials—Copper with Antique Acid Etched Crystal Glass Panels.

Suitable for vestibule and halls in Churches, Schools, and any Public Building of Gothic Architecture.

NOTE: Moe-Bridges Sales Representatives are located in all sections of the United States. They are trained and equipped to assist you on "Special Jobs" requiring "Made-to-Order" Lighting Equipment. We will be pleased to place our Designing, Engineering, and Sales facilities at your disposal when you are estimating your next "Special Job."

MOE-BRIDGES
MILWAUKEE

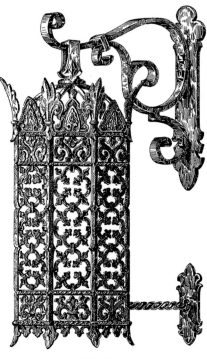

No. MBE-271

Six Light Candle Lantern. Diameter overall 20 inches. Length of Lantern Cage 48 inches. Overall Length (*Optional*). Materials—Cast Bronze with Clear Glass Panels.

Suitable for Stair Wells, Large Hallways, Hotel and Theatre Lobbies, etc., of the "French" and "Georgian" influence.

No. MBE-204

One Light "Louis XVI" Lantern. Diameter 12 inches. Length Overall 40 inches. Materials—Cast Brass with Beveled Clear Glass Panels.

Suitable for Residential and Hotel Reception Halls.

No. MBB-328

One Light "Spanish" Outdoor Bracket Lantern. Lantern Cage 14x30 inches. Extension Overall 24 inches. Length Overall 36 inches. Materials—Cast Bronze with Amber Glass Panels.

Suitable for Exterior Lighting of Apartments, Office Buildings, Banks, etc.

NOTE: Consult the Moe-Bridges Engineering Department for Layouts, Sketches, and Quotations on Specially Designed Custom-Built Lighting Equipment for Public Buildings, Apartments, Theatres, Churches, etc.

Hi-Glo Lighting Fixtures
by Sears, 1934

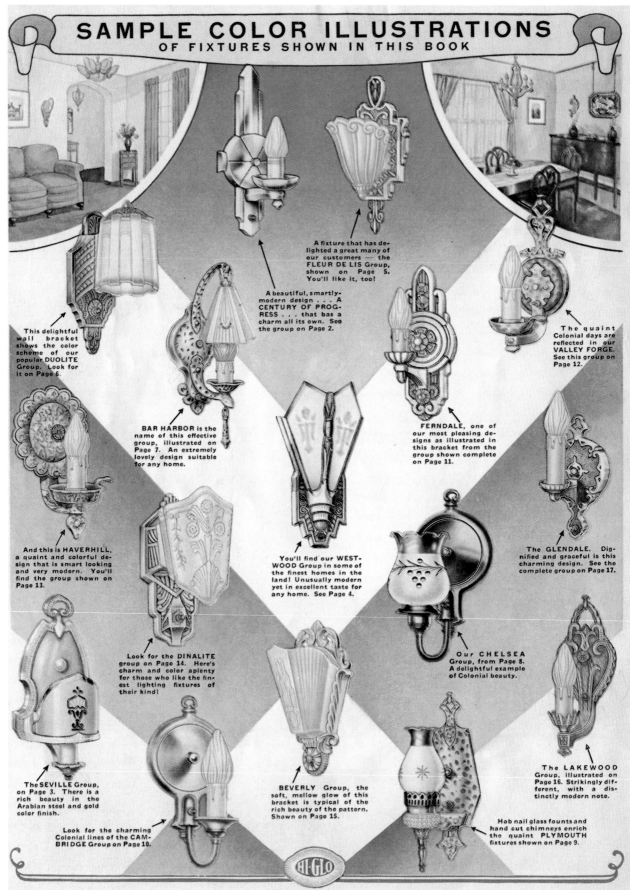

SAMPLE COLOR ILLUSTRATIONS
OF FIXTURES SHOWN IN THIS BOOK

A fixture that has delighted a great many of our customers — the FLEUR DE LIS Group, shown on Page 5. You'll like it, too!

A beautiful, smartly-modern design . . . A CENTURY OF PROGRESS . . . that has a charm all its own. See the group on Page 2.

The quaint Colonial days are reflected in our VALLEY FORGE. See this group on Page 12.

This delightful wall bracket shows the color scheme of our popular DUOLITE Group. Look for it on Page 6.

BAR HARBOR is the name of this effective group, illustrated on Page 7. An extremely lovely design suitable for any home.

FERNDALE, one of our most pleasing designs as illustrated in this bracket from the group shown complete on Page 11.

And this is HAVERHILL, a quaint and colorful design that is smart looking and very modern. You'll find the group shown on Page 13.

You'll find our WESTWOOD Group in some of the finest homes in the land! Unusually modern yet in excellent taste for any home. See Page 4.

The GLENDALE. Dignified and graceful is this charming design. See the complete group on Page 17.

Look for the DINALITE group on Page 14. Here's charm and color aplenty for those who like the finest lighting fixtures of their kind!

Our CHELSEA Group, from Page 8. A delightful example of Colonial beauty.

The SEVILLE Group, on Page 3. There is a rich beauty in the Arabian steel and gold color finish.

Look for the charming Colonial lines of the CAMBRIDGE Group on Page 10.

BEVERLY Group, the soft, mellow glow of this bracket is typical of the rich beauty of the pattern. Shown on Page 15.

Hob nail glass founts and hand cut chimneys enrich the quaint PLYMOUTH fixtures shown on Page 9.

The LAKEWOOD Group, illustrated on Page 16. Strikingly different, with a distinctly modern note.

643F.1.8-9-34

SAMPLE COLOR ILLUSTRATIONS
OF FIXTURES SHOWN IN THIS BOOK

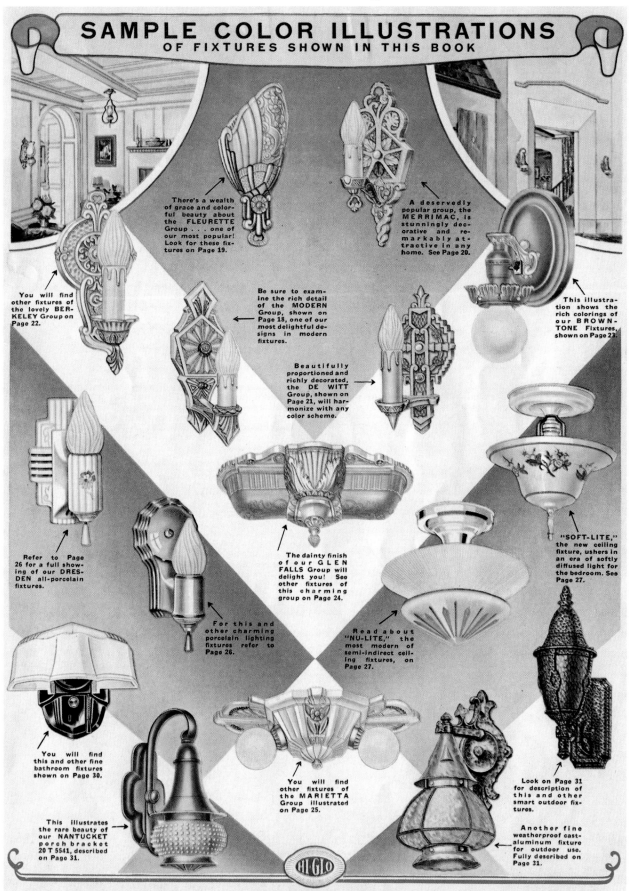

There's a wealth of grace and colorful beauty about the FLEURETTE Group . . . one of our most popular! Look for these fixtures on Page 19.

A deservedly popular group, the MERRIMAC, is stunningly decorative and remarkably attractive in any home. See Page 20.

You will find other fixtures of the lovely BERKELEY Group on Page 22.

Be sure to examine the rich detail of the MODERN Group, shown on Page 18, one of our most delightful designs in modern fixtures.

This illustration shows the rich colorings of our BROWN-TONE Fixtures, shown on Page 23.

Beautifully proportioned and richly decorated, the DE WITT Group, shown on Page 21, will harmonize with any color scheme.

Refer to Page 26 for a full showing of our DRESDEN all-porcelain fixtures.

The dainty finish of our GLEN FALLS Group will delight you! See other fixtures of this charming group on Page 24.

"SOFT-LITE," the new ceiling fixture, ushers in an era of softly diffused light for the bedroom. See Page 27.

For this and other charming porcelain lighting fixtures refer to Page 26.

Read about "NU-LITE," the most modern of semi-indirect ceiling fixtures, on Page 27.

You will find this and other fine bathroom fixtures shown on Page 30.

You will find other fixtures of the MARIETTA Group illustrated on Page 25.

Look on Page 31 for description of this and other smart outdoor fixtures.

This illustrates the rare beauty of our NANTUCKET porch bracket 20 T 5541, described on Page 31.

Another fine weatherproof cast-aluminum fixture for outdoor use. Fully described on Page 31.

HI-GLO

WHY

SEARS SAVE YOU MOST
AND OFFER FINER QUALITY
IN LIGHTING FIXTURES

Sears, Roebuck and Co., the largest retail distributors of electric lighting fixtures in the world, buy in immense quantities, for cash, obtaining the benefits of all discounts and securing the lowest freight charges, due to carload shipments. Consequently, Sears buy lighting fixtures *for less* . . . Because we sell direct to the user, we save the extra profits associated with less economical methods of distribution.

We Save You Fully 50%!

By eliminating these extra profits and expenses that add nothing to the value of the fixtures, Sears save you fully 50% on lighting fixtures. Comparisons will prove that a quality usually retailing for $15.00 sells at Sears for $7.50 to $8.00, while one usually priced to retail at $10.00 costs but $5.00 at Sears. You will find prices in this book as low or lower than most wholesale prices on fixtures of equal quality.

Sears Electric Lighting Fixtures are QUALITY products, each the very finest value for the money that our buyers can find. Whether you buy our lowest priced fixtures, or our most expensive, you always get the very best materials for that type of fixture. Not one detail of Hi-Glo Fixtures is skimped to meet a price.

Most of Sears Hi-Glo Fixtures are made from fine aluminum castings. Aluminum is more expensive than cast iron or various cheap alloys often used for lighting fixtures. But Sears have found that aluminum castings are better in every way . . . have clean-cut, sharp detail, finish smoothly and are much lighter in

weight than any other material we could possibly use. Aluminum is practically indestructible, because of its resistance to corrosion or oxidation. And you save money on delivery charges, due to its lighter weight.

We need say but little about the superiority of Hi-Glo designs, for those shown in this catalog speak for themselves!

Anyone Can Install Hi-Glo Fixtures

Hi-Glo Fixtures are completely wired and very easy to install. No special tools are necessary. A screwdriver is the only tool you need. We supply special connectors with each fixture, which require no solder or tape. Anyone can do a safe, workmanlike job without previous experience. The connectors are listed as standard by the Underwriters' Laboratories. When you order Sears Hi-Glo Fixtures *you have nothing else to buy!*

All wiring, switches, sockets and fittings in Hi-Glo Fixtures are approved types. They are absolutely safe. All fixtures hung from a chain can be adjusted for any desired height of fixture.

Now is the time to re-fixture your home! Prices were never lower. Qualities are unsurpassed. Re-fixture when you re-decorate. You will be amazed at the improvement new fixtures bring to your home. And you will be delighted with the extremely low cost of a complete new installation of Hi-Glo Fixtures.

Refer to the inside cover pages of this catalog for exact color finishes of Hi-Glo Lighting Fixtures, and use the small illustrations below to identify the various types of fixtures you plan to order.

For Prices Refer to Complete Price List Enclosed

WALL BRACKET

HALL

CEILING

SEMI CEILING

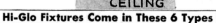
Hi-Glo Fixtures Come in These 6 Types

DROP

CANDLE

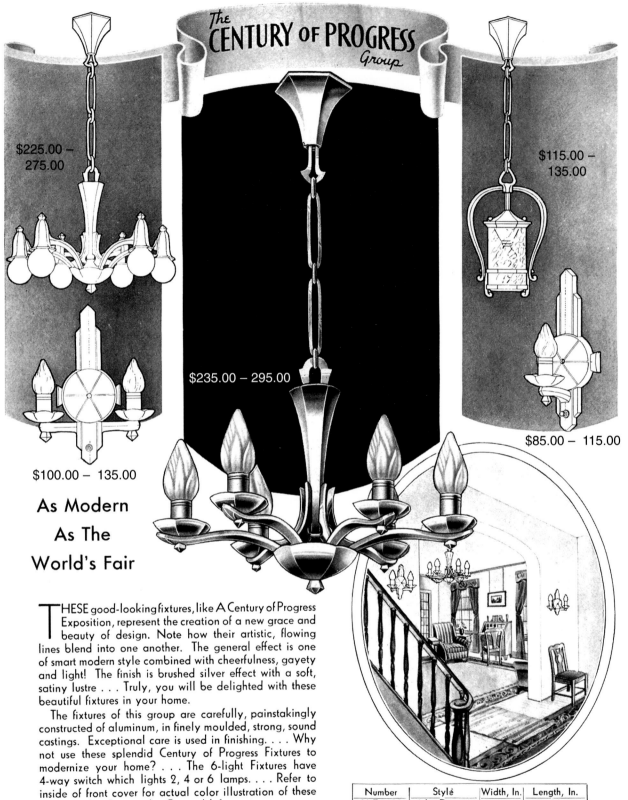

The CENTURY OF PROGRESS Group

$225.00 – 275.00

$115.00 – 135.00

$235.00 – 295.00

$100.00 – 135.00

$85.00 – 115.00

As Modern As The World's Fair

THESE good-looking fixtures, like A Century of Progress Exposition, represent the creation of a new grace and beauty of design. Note how their artistic, flowing lines blend into one another. The general effect is one of smart modern style combined with cheerfulness, gayety and light! The finish is brushed silver effect with a soft, satiny lustre . . . Truly, you will be delighted with these beautiful fixtures in your home.

The fixtures of this group are carefully, painstakingly constructed of aluminum, in finely moulded, strong, sound castings. Exceptional care is used in finishing. . . . Why not use these splendid Century of Progress Fixtures to modernize your home? . . . The 6-light Fixtures have 4-way switch which lights 2, 4 or 6 lamps. . . . Refer to inside of front cover for actual color illustration of these fixtures. See Page 1 for General Information.

For Prices Refer to Complete Price List Enclosed

Number	Style	Width, In.	Length, In.
20 T 5630	6-Lt. Drop	21	36
20 T 5631	6-Lt. Candle	21	36
20 T 5634	2-Lt. Bracket	11	13
20 T 5632	1-Lt. Hall	10	36
20 T 5633	1-Lt. Bracket	5	13

643F

SEARS, ROEBUCK AND CO.

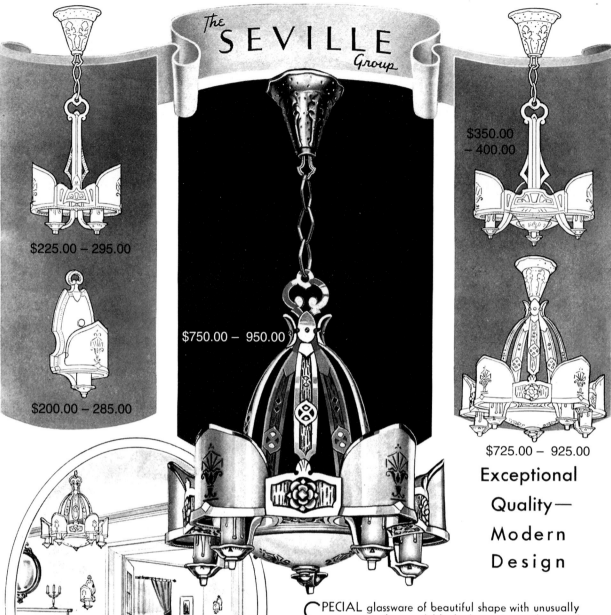

The SEVILLE Group

$350.00 – 400.00

$225.00 – 295.00

$200.00 – 285.00

$750.00 – 950.00

$725.00 – 925.00

Exceptional Quality— Modern Design

SPECIAL glassware of beautiful shape with unusually attractive silver and black decoration, softens and subdues the light from the fixtures of the Seville Group. Due to the novel arrangement of the shades the fixture gives exceptionally good illumination directly below, while light reaches the rest of the room through the glassware or by reflection from the ceiling . . . These semi-shaded fixtures are deservedly popular. They are made from the finest aluminum castings, carefully finished and strongly assembled. Superb Arabian Steel finish relieved with touches of gold color makes them distinctive. Every item of material in these fixtures is the very finest quality, insuring a lifetime of service . . . Seven light candle type has 4-way switch giving 7, 5 or 2 lights. Refer to Inside Front Cover for actual color scheme of these fixtures. See Page 1 for General Information.

For Prices Refer to Complete Price List Enclosed

Number	Style	Width In.	Length In.
20T5260	7-Lt. Candle	17	36
20T5261	7-Lt. Ceiling	17	20
20T5262	3-Lt. Candle	9	36
20T5263	2-Lt. Candle	10	36
20T5264	1-Lt. Bracket	6	12

SEARS, ROEBUCK AND CO.

643F

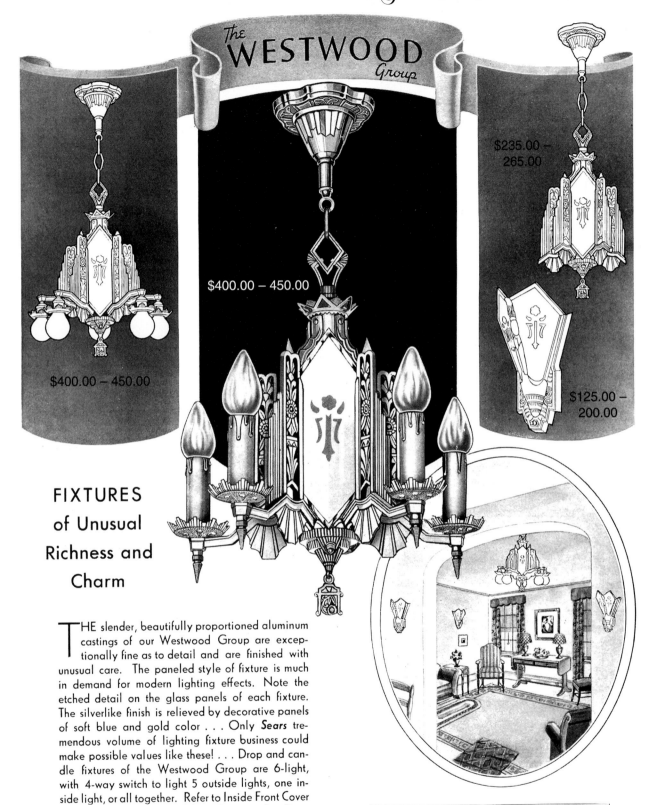

The WESTWOOD Group

$400.00 – 450.00

$400.00 – 450.00

$235.00 – 265.00

$125.00 – 200.00

FIXTURES of Unusual Richness and Charm

THE slender, beautifully proportioned aluminum castings of our Westwood Group are exceptionally fine as to detail and are finished with unusual care. The paneled style of fixture is much in demand for modern lighting effects. Note the etched detail on the glass panels of each fixture. The silverlike finish is relieved by decorative panels of soft blue and gold color . . . Only *Sears* tremendous volume of lighting fixture business could make possible values like these! . . . Drop and candle fixtures of the Westwood Group are 6-light, with 4-way switch to light 5 outside lights, one inside light, or all together. Refer to Inside Front Cover for actual color scheme of these fixtures. See Page 1 for General Information.

For Prices Refer to Price List Enclosed

Number	Style	Width, In.	Length, In.
20 T 5391	6-Lt. Candle	18	36
20 T 5390	6-Lt. Drop	18	36
20 T 5392	1-Lt. Bracket	7	12
20 T 5389	1-Lt. Hall	11	36

The DUOLITE Group

$245.00 – 285.00

$450.00 – 675.00

$225.00 – 285.00

They Provide
Two Forms
of
Lighting

HERE is the delightful Duolite Group—lighting fixtures with a new beauty and a new utility! Charmingly designed of cast aluminum of the finest quality . . . . finished in a rich polychrome gold color. The soft, light cream color shades, tinted with brown, are **reversible**. Use these fixtures to throw the light downwards, for the dining room, or, by reversing the shades, use them for semi-indirect lighting for the living room or other parts of the house. The two-light drop illustrated at the left above has one shade reversed to show how Duolite Fixtures may be used to throw light up or down. Drop fixtures have "on and off" switch. Refer to Inside Front Cover for reproduction of actual colors of these fixtures. See Page 1 for General Information.

For Prices Refer to Complete Price List Enclosed

Number	Style	Width, In.	Length, In.
20 T 5460	5-Lt. Drop	19	36
20 T 5642	2-Lt. Drop	13	36
20 T 5641	1-Lt. Bracket	4½	10

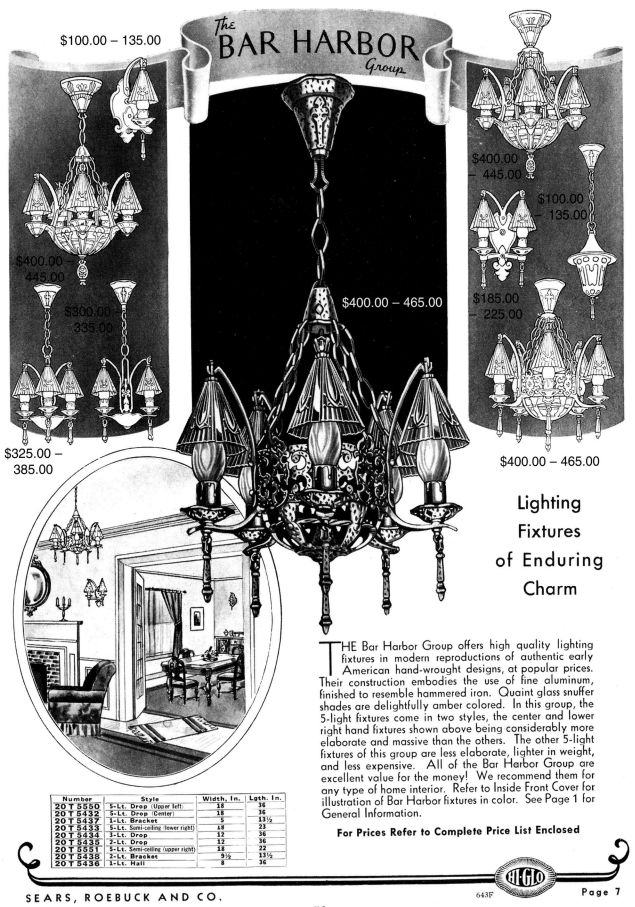

The **BAR HARBOR** *Group*

$100.00 – 135.00

$400.00 – 445.00

$300.00 – 335.00

$400.00 – 465.00

$325.00 – 385.00

$400.00 – 445.00

$100.00 – 135.00

$185.00 – 225.00

$400.00 – 465.00

Lighting Fixtures of Enduring Charm

THE Bar Harbor Group offers high quality lighting fixtures in modern reproductions of authentic early American hand-wrought designs, at popular prices. Their construction embodies the use of fine aluminum, finished to resemble hammered iron. Quaint glass snuffer shades are delightfully amber colored. In this group, the 5-light fixtures come in two styles, the center and lower right hand fixtures shown above being considerably more elaborate and massive than the others. The other 5-light fixtures of this group are less elaborate, lighter in weight, and less expensive. All of the Bar Harbor Group are excellent value for the money! We recommend them for any type of home interior. Refer to Inside Front Cover for illustration of Bar Harbor fixtures in color. See Page 1 for General Information.

For Prices Refer to Complete Price List Enclosed

Number	Style	Width, In.	Lgth. In.
20 T 5550	5-Lt. Drop (Upper left)	18	36
20 T 5432	5-Lt. Drop (Center)	18	36
20 T 5437	1-Lt. Bracket	5	13½
20 T 5433	5-Lt. Semi-ceiling (lower right)	18	23
20 T 5434	3-Lt. Drop	12	36
20 T 5435	2-Lt. Drop	12	36
20 T 5551	5-Lt. Semi-ceiling (upper right)	18	22
20 T 5438	2-Lt. Bracket	9½	13½
20 T 5436	1-Lt. Hall	8	36

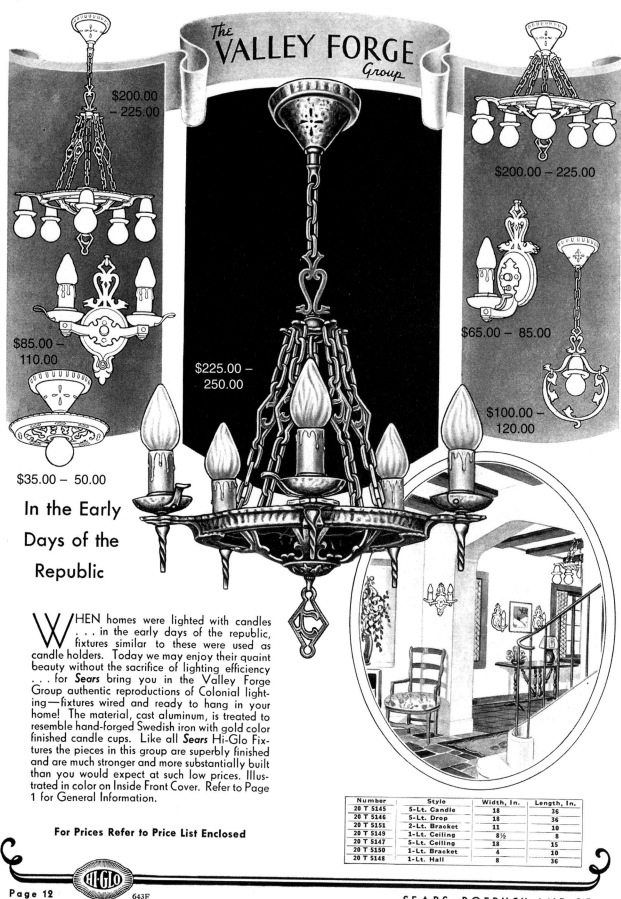

The VALLEY FORGE Group

$200.00 – 225.00

$200.00 – 225.00

$85.00 – 110.00

$65.00 – 85.00

$225.00 – 250.00

$100.00 – 120.00

$35.00 – 50.00

In the Early Days of the Republic

WHEN homes were lighted with candles . . . in the early days of the republic, fixtures similar to these were used as candle holders. Today we may enjoy their quaint beauty without the sacrifice of lighting efficiency . . . for *Sears* bring you in the Valley Forge Group authentic reproductions of Colonial lighting—fixtures wired and ready to hang in your home! The material, cast aluminum, is treated to resemble hand-forged Swedish iron with gold color finished candle cups. Like all *Sears* Hi-Glo Fixtures the pieces in this group are superbly finished and are much stronger and more substantially built than you would expect at such low prices. Illustrated in color on Inside Front Cover. Refer to Page 1 for General Information.

For Prices Refer to Price List Enclosed

Number	Style	Width, In.	Length, In.
20 T 5145	5-Lt. Candle	18	36
20 T 5146	5-Lt. Drop	18	36
20 T 5151	2-Lt. Bracket	11	10
20 T 5149	1-Lt. Ceiling	8½	8
20 T 5147	5-Lt. Ceiling	18	15
20 T 5150	1-Lt. Bracket	4	10
20 T 5148	1-Lt. Hall	8	36

The HAVERHILL Group

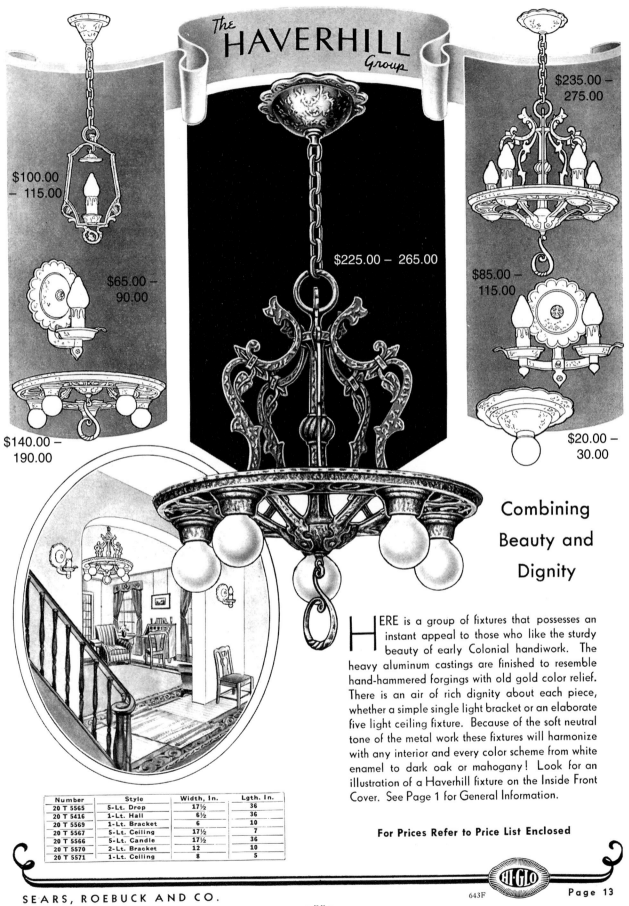

$100.00 – 115.00

$65.00 – 90.00

$140.00 – 190.00

$225.00 – 265.00

$235.00 – 275.00

$85.00 – 115.00

$20.00 – 30.00

Combining Beauty and Dignity

HERE is a group of fixtures that possesses an instant appeal to those who like the sturdy beauty of early Colonial handiwork. The heavy aluminum castings are finished to resemble hand-hammered forgings with old gold color relief. There is an air of rich dignity about each piece, whether a simple single light bracket or an elaborate five light ceiling fixture. Because of the soft neutral tone of the metal work these fixtures will harmonize with any interior and every color scheme from white enamel to dark oak or mahogany! Look for an illustration of a Haverhill fixture on the Inside Front Cover. See Page 1 for General Information.

For Prices Refer to Price List Enclosed

Number	Style	Width, In.	Lgth. In.
20 T 5565	5-Lt. Drop	17½	36
20 T 5416	1-Lt. Hall	6½	36
20 T 5569	1-Lt. Bracket	6	10
20 T 5567	5-Lt. Ceiling	17½	7
20 T 5566	5-Lt. Candle	17½	36
20 T 5570	2-Lt. Bracket	12	10
20 T 5571	1-Lt. Ceiling	8	5

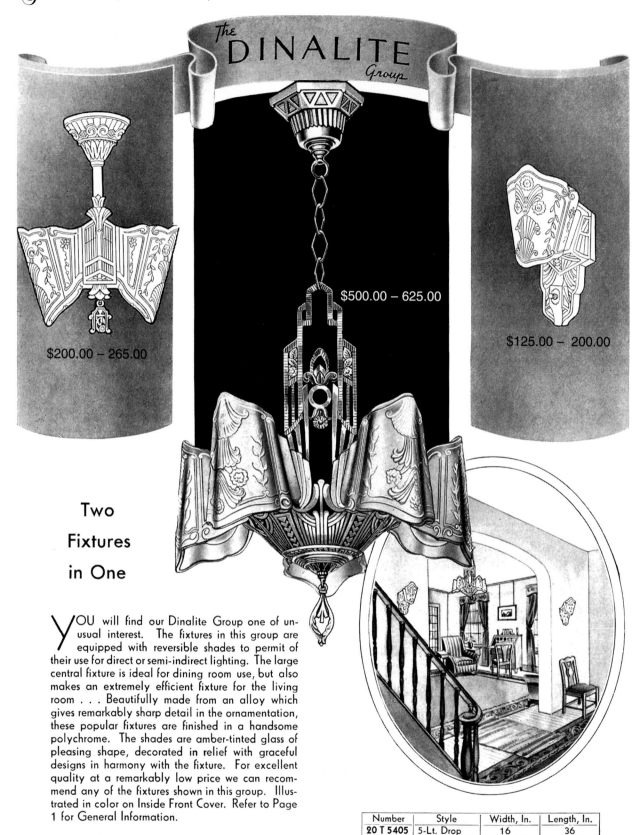

The DINALITE Group

$200.00 – 265.00

$500.00 – 625.00

$125.00 – 200.00

Two Fixtures in One

YOU will find our Dinalite Group one of unusual interest. The fixtures in this group are equipped with reversible shades to permit of their use for direct or semi-indirect lighting. The large central fixture is ideal for dining room use, but also makes an extremely efficient fixture for the living room . . . Beautifully made from an alloy which gives remarkably sharp detail in the ornamentation, these popular fixtures are finished in a handsome polychrome. The shades are amber-tinted glass of pleasing shape, decorated in relief with graceful designs in harmony with the fixture. For excellent quality at a remarkably low price we can recommend any of the fixtures shown in this group. Illustrated in color on Inside Front Cover. Refer to Page 1 for General Information.

For Prices Refer to Price List Enclosed

Number	Style	Width, In.	Length, In.
20 T 5405	5-Lt. Drop	16	36
20 T 5420	2-Lt. Ceiling	13½	15
20 T 5421	1-Lt. Bracket	4½	9

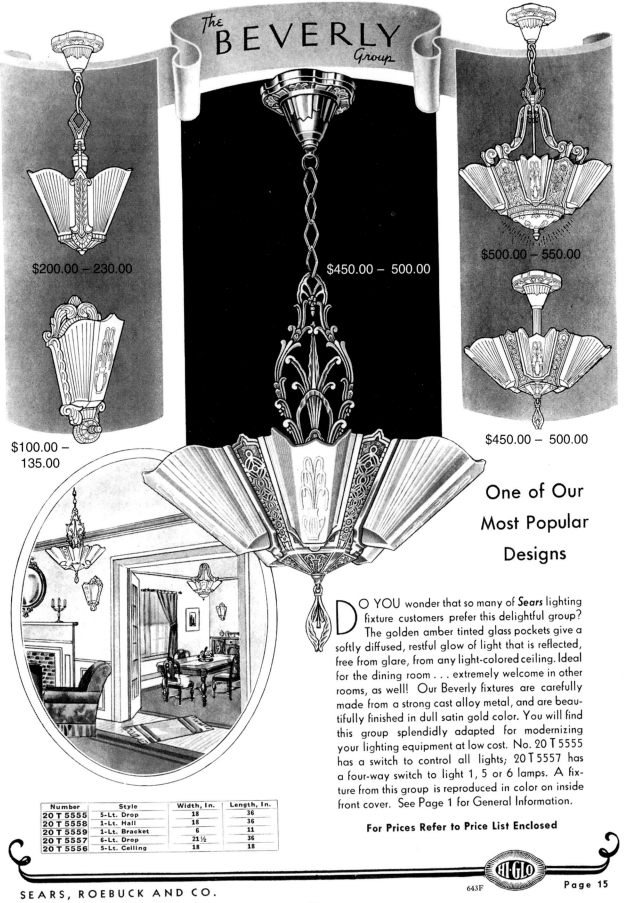

The BEVERLY Group

$200.00 – 230.00

$100.00 – 135.00

$450.00 – 500.00

$500.00 – 550.00

$450.00 – 500.00

One of Our Most Popular Designs

DO YOU wonder that so many of *Sears* lighting fixture customers prefer this delightful group? The golden amber tinted glass pockets give a softly diffused, restful glow of light that is reflected, free from glare, from any light-colored ceiling. Ideal for the dining room . . . extremely welcome in other rooms, as well! Our Beverly fixtures are carefully made from a strong cast alloy metal, and are beautifully finished in dull satin gold color. You will find this group splendidly adapted for modernizing your lighting equipment at low cost. No. 20 T 5555 has a switch to control all lights; 20 T 5557 has a four-way switch to light 1, 5 or 6 lamps. A fixture from this group is reproduced in color on inside front cover. See Page 1 for General Information.

For Prices Refer to Price List Enclosed

Number	Style	Width, In.	Length, In.
20 T 5555	5-Lt. Drop	18	36
20 T 5558	1-Lt. Hall	18	36
20 T 5559	1-Lt. Bracket	6	11
20 T 5557	6-Lt. Drop	21½	36
20 T 5556	5-Lt. Ceiling	18	18

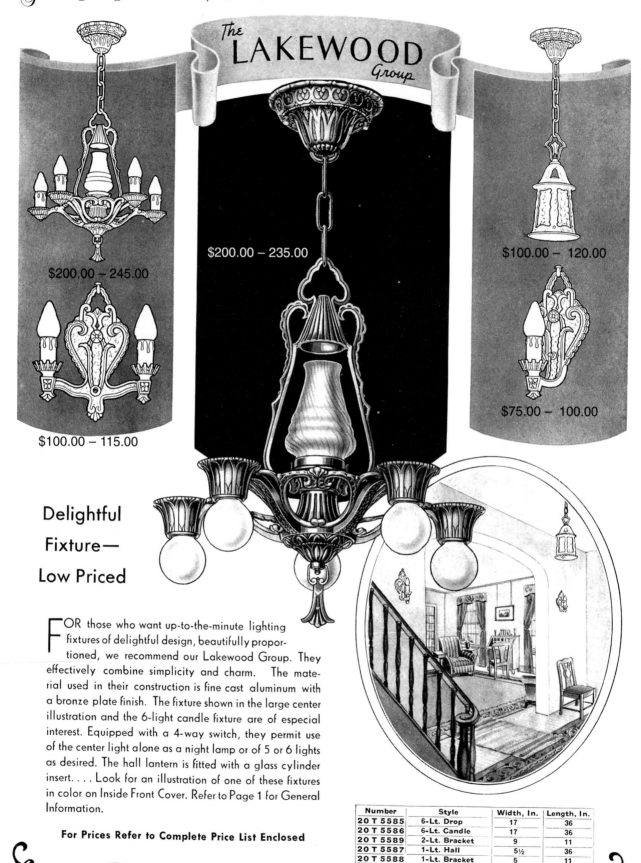

The LAKEWOOD Group

$200.00 – 245.00

$100.00 – 115.00

$200.00 – 235.00

$100.00 – 120.00

$75.00 – 100.00

Delightful Fixture— Low Priced

FOR those who want up-to-the-minute lighting fixtures of delightful design, beautifully proportioned, we recommend our Lakewood Group. They effectively combine simplicity and charm. The material used in their construction is fine cast aluminum with a bronze plate finish. The fixture shown in the large center illustration and the 6-light candle fixture are of especial interest. Equipped with a 4-way switch, they permit use of the center light alone as a night lamp or of 5 or 6 lights as desired. The hall lantern is fitted with a glass cylinder insert. . . . Look for an illustration of one of these fixtures in color on Inside Front Cover. Refer to Page 1 for General Information.

For Prices Refer to Complete Price List Enclosed

Number	Style	Width, In.	Length, In.
20 T 5585	6-Lt. Drop	17	36
20 T 5586	6-Lt. Candle	17	36
20 T 5589	2-Lt. Bracket	9	11
20 T 5587	1-Lt. Hall	5½	36
20 T 5588	1-Lt. Bracket	5	11

The GLENDALE Group

$85.00 – 115.00

$65.00 – 100.00

$185.00 – 200.00

$185.00 – 200.00

$150.00 – 175.00

Good Looking— Yet Inexpensive

NOTE especially the well balanced design of these fixtures and the carefully worked-out designs which ornament them . . . While ideal for so-called Spanish type interiors, they may be used with equally happy results in any home. The material is cast aluminum, beautifully finished. You will be surprised to find how little it costs to liven up your home with these lighting fixtures. Why not decide today that you will modernize your home with Hi-Glo fixtures? Available in Arabian steel finish as shown on Inside Front Cover page, or in bronze color with polychrome tinting. Be sure to state color wanted. Refer to Page 1 for General Information.

For Prices Refer to Complete Price List Enclosed

Number	Style	Width, In.	Length, In.
20 T 5220	5-Lt. Drop	19	36
20 T 5222	1-Lt. Bracket	4½	10½
20 T 5223	2-Lt. Bracket	8	12
20 T 5219	5-Lt. Semi-Ceiling	19	17
20 T 5221	5-Lt. Candle	19	36

The MODERN *Group*

$165.00 – 185.00

$85.00 – 100.00

$150.00 – 175.00

$100.00 – 120.00

$150.00 – 175.00

$20.00 – 30.00

$65.00 – 85.00

A New Design of Rare Beauty

HERE is a group that is thoroughly modern in every line . . . yet, like most of our best designs in lighting fixtures, is derived from a very old motif. Its smart style makes it ideal for those newer homes furnished in the modern manner. On the other hand, it fits well into any surroundings. Try fixtures from the Modern Group in your home. You will find them all we claim for them in beauty, value and satisfaction. The material is cast metal; the finish, silver gray with polychrome decorations. These fixtures may be obtained in a variety of styles and shapes, either in the drop type for "ball" lamps, or in the candle type, preferred by so many. Illustrated in color on Inside Back Cover. Refer to Page 1 for General Information.

For Prices Refer to Price List Enclosed

Number	Style	Width, In.	Length, In.
20 T 5135	5-Lt. Drop	18	36
20 T 5136	5-Lt. Candle	18	36
20 T 5139	2-Lt. Bracket	9	10½
20 T 5191	2-Lt. Ceiling	14	11
20 T 5137	5-Lt. Ceiling	18	12
20 T 5138	1-Lt. Bracket	4½	10½
20 T 5192	1-Lt. Ceiling	5½	6½

The
FLEURETTE
Group

$200.00 –
250.00

$125.00 –
150.00

$500.00+

$550.00

$250.00 –
285.00

Its Satin Textured Glass Glows With Light

PICTURE these lovely fixtures in your home . . . the satin textured glass shades aglow with golden amber light! What wonderfully soft tones and colors they cast upon ceilings and walls, transforming any interior into a place of radiant beauty! The six light drop is designed especially for dining rooms, the additional light in the central glass illuminating the table. The glassware in the fixtures of the Fleurette Group is easily removed for cleaning. No. 20 T 5440 has a tassel switch control for all lights. No. 20 T 5445, the dining room fixture referred to, has a four way switch for controlling 1, 5 or 6 lights. The material used in these fixtures is fine aluminum, carefully cast. The finish is a harmony of silvery aluminum and gold color that blends nicely with the amber textured glass pockets. Shown in color on Inside Back Cover. Refer to Page 1 for General Information.

For Prices Refer to Price List Enclosed

Number	Style	Width, In.	Length, In.
20 T 5440	5-Lt. Drop	17	36
20 T 5443	1-Lt. Hall	7	36
20 T 5441	1-Lt. Bracket	6	11½
20 T 5445	6-Lt. Drop	17	36
20 T 5442	2-Lt. Ceiling	15	10

$165.00 – 190.00

$100.00 – 120.00

$150.00 – 185.00

$100.00 – 125.00

$75.00 – 85.00

Gold Color Finished, In Rich Relief

IN OUR Merrimac Group we have produced an un-usually artistic fixture along modern lines, at a remark-ably low price. The material used, a cast metal, lends itself to fine, sharp, clear detail. The finish is gold color, in relief, with delicate polychrome decorations, giving a most pleasing effect. All of the fixtures in this group are equally pleasing, whether intended to hang from ceiling or wall. You will make no mistake in choosing the Merrimac Group for refixturing your home. It is a design that will adapt itself to any surroundings or fur-nishings and will please you for many years . . . a most important consideration in selecting fixtures. Drop fix-tures are equipped with switch to control lights. Refer to Inside Back Cover for illustration in color. For General Information refer to Page 1.

For Prices Refer to Complete Price List Enclosed

Number	Style	Width, In.	Length, In.
20T5595	5-Lt. Drop	18	36
20T5596	5-Lt. Candle	17	36
20T5599	2-Lt. Bracket	8	11
20T5597	1-Lt. Hall	8	36
20T5598	1-Lt. Bracket	5	11

The DE WITT Group

$165.00 – 200.00

$75.00 – 100.00

$175.00 – 200.00

$185.00 – 210.00

$100.00 – 115.00

A New Pattern That Has Unusual Beauty

THIS group comprises lighting fixtures of unusual beauty. They are designed along modern lines, yet will harmonize nicely with any furnishings. The material is a sturdy aluminum, cast clean and sharp with excellent detail in the decorations. Superbly finished in gold with highlights touched with red . . . These and other Hi-Glo Lighting Fixtures should not be confused with cheap, inferior fixtures usually built to sell at a price. Surprising, isn't it, that you pay no more at *Sears* for really fine fixtures than you would expect to pay for less stylish and durable ones. That's because *Sears* sell more lighting fixtures than any other store in the world, and always bring you greatest value for your money. Refer to Inside Back Cover for illustration in color. See Page 1 for General Information.

For Prices Refer to Complete Price List Enclosed

Number	Style	Width, In.	Lgth., In.
20 T 5330	5-Lt. Drop	17	36
20 T 5338	5-Lt. Ceiling	17	14
20 T 5341	1-Lt. Bracket	4½	9
20 T 5337	5-Lt. Candle	17	36
20 T 5340	2-Lt. Bracket	8	9

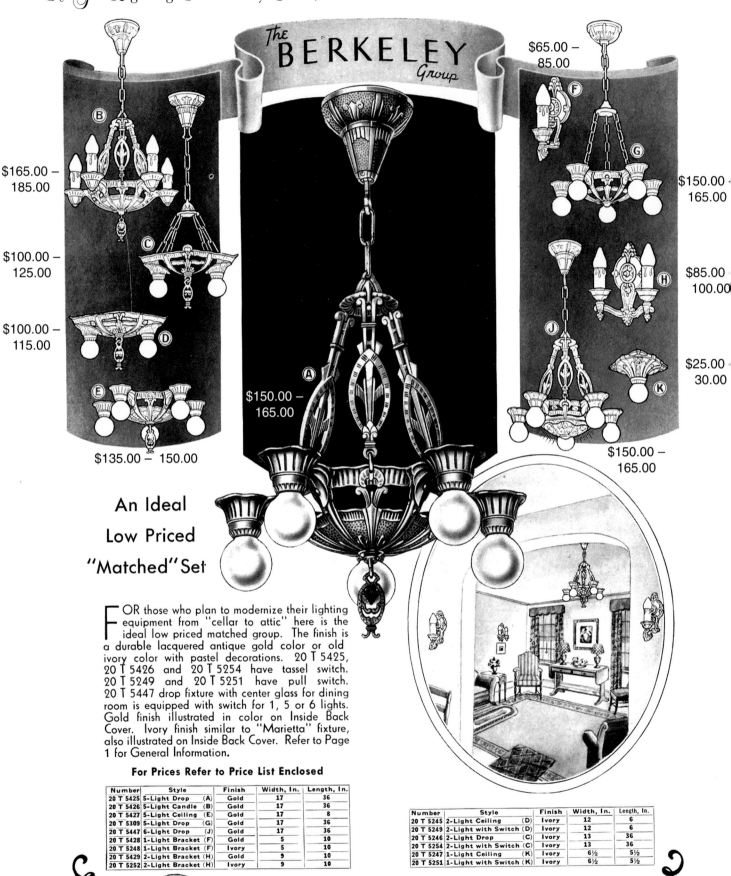

The Berkeley Group

$65.00 – 85.00

$165.00 – 185.00

$100.00 – 125.00

$100.00 – 115.00

$135.00 – 150.00

$150.00 – 165.00

$85.00 – 100.00

$25.00 – 30.00

$150.00 – 165.00

$150.00 – 165.00

An Ideal Low Priced "Matched" Set

FOR those who plan to modernize their lighting equipment from "cellar to attic" here is the ideal low priced matched group. The finish is a durable lacquered antique gold color or old ivory color with pastel decorations. 20 T 5425, 20 T 5426 and 20 T 5254 have tassel switch. 20 T 5249 and 20 T 5251 have pull switch. 20 T 5447 drop fixture with center glass for dining room is equipped with switch for 1, 5 or 6 lights. Gold finish illustrated in color on Inside Back Cover. Ivory finish similar to "Marietta" fixture, also illustrated on Inside Back Cover. Refer to Page 1 for General Information.

For Prices Refer to Price List Enclosed

Number	Style		Finish	Width, In.	Length, In.
20 T 5425	5-Light Drop	(A)	Gold	17	36
20 T 5426	5-Light Candle	(B)	Gold	17	36
20 T 5427	5-Light Ceiling	(E)	Gold	17	8
20 T 5309	5-Light Drop	(G)	Gold	17	36
20 T 5447	6-Light Drop	(J)	Gold	17	36
20 T 5428	1-Light Bracket	(F)	Gold	5	10
20 T 5248	1-Light Bracket	(F)	Ivory	5	10
20 T 5429	2-Light Bracket	(H)	Gold	9	10
20 T 5252	2-Light Bracket	(H)	Ivory	9	10

Number	Style		Finish	Width, In.	Length, In.
20 T 5245	2-Light Ceiling	(D)	Ivory	12	6
20 T 5249	2-Light with Switch	(D)	Ivory	12	6
20 T 5246	2-Light Drop	(C)	Ivory	13	36
20 T 5254	2-Light with Switch	(C)	Ivory	13	36
20 T 5247	1-Light Ceiling	(K)	Ivory	6½	5½
20 T 5251	1-Light with Switch	(K)	Ivory	6½	5½

The BROWNTONE *Group*

$100.00 – 120.00

$50.00 – 65.00

$125.00 – 150.00

$120.00 – 140.00

A Group That Offers Much but Costs Little

FIXTURES of the Browntone Group, long favorites with our customers, still enjoy a deserved popularity. They are beautifully finished with the artistically designed bodies "Browntoned"—the arms polished and gilded and then the entire fixture lacquered to preserve its glowing color for years. All fixtures have individual key sockets, giving complete control of the lights. The construction of these fixtures is of extremely high quality—a quality that we maintain by rigid inspection. We believe you will find it extremely difficult, if not altogether impossible, to match the high quality of these fixtures at anywhere near *Sears* low prices. Refer to Inside Back Cover for illustration of one of these charming Browntone fixtures in natural color. See Page 1 for General Information.

For Prices Refer to Price List Enclosed

Number	Style	Width, In.	Length, In.
20 T 5777	4-Lt. Drop	20	36
20 T 5183	1-Lt. Bracket	4	8½
20 T 5253	2-Lt. Drop	16	36
20 T 5298	3-Lt. Drop	16	36

The GLEN FALLS Group

$200.00 – 240.00

$125.00 – 150.00

$200.00 – 250.00

Charming Fixtures For the Bedroom

You know how much attractive lighting fixtures contribute to the appearance of the bedroom. This charming shaded light group of cast metal comes in a choice of two popular finishes: (1) Gold color finish tinted with colors and "golden glow" glass shades, and (2) Toned Ivory color finish with blended colors and delicately "satin rose" glass shades. Please specify finish when ordering. . . . You will find the gold color finish in actual colors on the Inside Back Cover of this catalog. Refer to Page 1 for General Information concerning all *Sears* Hi-Glo Lighting Fixtures.

Number	Style	Size, In.
20 T 5255	2-Lt. Ceiling (Keyless)	6x16
20 T 5256	3-Lt. Ceiling (Keyless)	6x14
20 T 5258	2-Lt. Ceiling (Chain Pull)	6x16
20 T 5259	3-Lt. Ceiling (Chain Pull)	6x14
20 T 5257	1-Lt. Bracket	5½x10

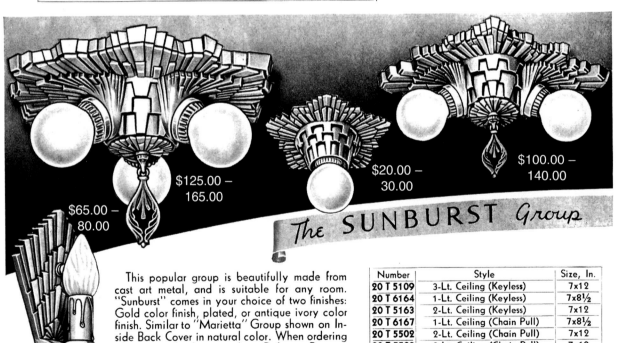

$125.00 – 165.00

$20.00 – 30.00

$100.00 – 140.00

$65.00 – 80.00

The SUNBURST Group

This popular group is beautifully made from cast art metal, and is suitable for any room. "Sunburst" comes in your choice of two finishes: Gold color finish, plated, or antique ivory color finish. Similar to "Marietta" Group shown on Inside Back Cover in natural color. When ordering please state finish you prefer. Refer to Page 1 for General Information regarding all *Sears* Hi-Glo Lighting Fixtures.

Number	Style	Size, In.
20 T 5109	3-Lt. Ceiling (Keyless)	7x12
20 T 6164	1-Lt. Ceiling (Keyless)	7x8½
20 T 5163	2-Lt. Ceiling (Keyless)	7x12
20 T 6167	1-Lt. Ceiling (Chain Pull)	7x8½
20 T 5502	2-Lt. Ceiling (Chain Pull)	7x12
20 T 5503	3-Lt. Ceiling (Chain Pull)	7x12
20 T 6165	1-Lt. Bracket	9½x5½

For Prices Refer to Price List Enclosed

The MARIETTA Group

$20.00 – 30.00

$120.00 – 130.00

$65.00 – 80.00

$125.00 – 150.00

Daintily Finished in Eggshell Ivory

You will find these charming fixtures among the very nicest of all for bedrooms! The finish is a dainty eggshell ivory color, delicately tinted with light pastel colors. The material used in their construction is cast aluminum alloy, which insures clear sharp detail in the decorations. Equipped with multiple pull chain arrangement permitting individual lighting of lamps. No. 20 T 5339 is provided with an extra outlet—as well as the usual switch. Refer to inside back cover page for an illustration of the actual color scheme of this group. See Page 1 for General Information concerning all *Sears* Hi-Glo Lighting Fixtures.

Number	Style	Width, In.	Length, In.	Number	Style	Width, In.	Length, In.
20 T 5334	2-Lt. Ceiling (Keyless)	13	5	20 T 5331	1-Lt. Ceiling (Chain Pull)	5	10
20 T 5333	2-Lt. Ceiling (Chain Pull)	13	5	20 T 5339	1-Lt. Bracket	5	4½
				20 T 5336	3-Lt. Ceiling (Keyless)	11	4½
20 T 5332	1-Lt. Ceiling (Keyless)	5	6	20 T 5335	3-Lt. Ceiling (Chain Pull)	11	5

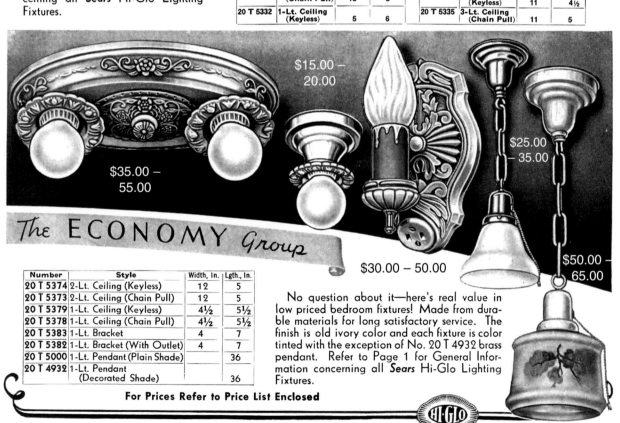

$15.00 – 20.00

$35.00 – 55.00

$25.00 – 35.00

$30.00 – 50.00

$50.00 – 65.00

The ECONOMY Group

Number	Style	Width, In.	Lgth., In.
20 T 5374	2-Lt. Ceiling (Keyless)	12	5
20 T 5373	2-Lt. Ceiling (Chain Pull)	12	5
20 T 5379	1-Lt. Ceiling (Keyless)	4½	5½
20 T 5378	1-Lt. Ceiling (Chain Pull)	4½	5½
20 T 5383	1-Lt. Bracket	4	7
20 T 5382	1-Lt. Bracket (With Outlet)	4	7
20 T 5000	1-Lt. Pendant (Plain Shade)		36
20 T 4932	1-Lt. Pendant (Decorated Shade)		36

No question about it—here's real value in low priced bedroom fixtures! Made from durable materials for long satisfactory service. The finish is old ivory color and each fixture is color tinted with the exception of No. 20 T 4932 brass pendant. Refer to Page 1 for General Information concerning all *Sears* Hi-Glo Lighting Fixtures.

For Prices Refer to Price List Enclosed

NOVELTIES *for* **SUN PORCHES** *or* **BEDROOMS**

$200.00+

$200.00 – 235.00

NU-LITE Brings a New Glow of Beauty to the Home

Something absolutely new—something altogether delightful in a ceiling fixture for the bedroom, breakfast nook or sunroom—NU-LITE provides a new thrill in lighting! When lighted, its soft glow of color is reflected upward from the bowl to the etched corona of uncolored glass. Has spread of 11 inches. Choice of rose decorated glass bowl or green decorated glass bowl, with plain coronas. The holder is ivory color enamel finish. State choice of color wanted.

20 T 5224—Nu-Lite Fixture, Complete.

SOFT-LITE Is a Dainty Bedroom Fixture

One of the most charming of all the new bedroom fixtures is SOFT-LITE. It furnishes a softly subdued indirect light from the ceiling and permits a certain amount of light to come direct from the lamp through the amber-tinted, daintily decorated shade. The overall diameter of shade is 9 inches; of base, 6 inches. Base is finished in ivory colored enamel. Depth, 10 inches. You will find SOFT-LITE a most pleasing addition to your bedroom or boudoir.

20 T 5225—SOFT-LITE Fixture, Complete.

For Prices Refer to Complete Price List Enclosed

· GLASS - WARE ·

HI-GLO glassware is of the very highest quality, the product of the nation's leading glass factories, and guaranteed to equal or excel in workmanship, design and finish any glassware on the market, regardless of price. On this and the following pages you will find selections of glassware suitable for various types of HI-GLO Lighting Fixtures.

$25.00 – 35.00

LARGE IVORY COLOR FLORAL DESIGN

This rich-looking shade is made of delicately ivory-tinted glass with embellishments of full color floral designs and horizontal stripings. It is 6 inches in diameter at its widest point, and 5 inches high.

20 T 9058
$50.00 – 60.00

ATTRACTIVE STRIPED BELL SHADE

White opal glass. Choice of green or black stripe. State choice.

20 T 9057
$25.00 – 30.00

MOST POPULAR OF ALL

Frosted, with choice of white, green, rose or amber tint. State color.

20 T 9050
$25.00 – 35.00

DECORATED IVORY COLOR SHADE

Matches in color and decoration our No. 20T9058 at left. Rich-appearing.

20 T 9059
$25.00 – 35.00

POPULAR FLARED RIBBED TYPE

This large white ribbed design shade is extremely popular. Diameter, 8 in. White only. Suitable for Bathroom, Hall, Stores, in fact anywhere a single drop light is used.

20 T 9056

WEATHERPROOF OUTDOOR FIXTURES

The "FOREST HILL"

Lifetime cast aluminum. Hand wrought effect with two-tone copper and forged iron finish. The amber glass shade has green lines between sections. Bracket is 13 in. high and extends 8 in. Lantern is 14 in. in length. See Inside Back Cover for actual color illustration.

20 T 7021—Ceiling Lantern.
20 T 7022—Wall Bracket.

Both: $60.00 – 85.00

The "KENILWORTH"

Cast aluminum, finished in the hand wrought style resembling forged iron. These lanterns are especially designed for larger homes or apartment buildings. 20 T 5562 and 20 T 5563 are 17 in. high and extend 8½ in. 20 T 5564 is 16½ in. in length.

20 T 5562—Upright Bracket. (Shown on inside back cover.)
20 T 5563—Downward Bracket.
20 T 5564—Ceiling Fixture.

Both: $75.00 – 90.00

Rustproof Aluminum Bracket

Made of cast aluminum. Design has sharp details and is finely finished. Black only, with white ball shade. Shade, 3¼ opening, 6-in. diameter.

20 T 7031—Wall Bracket.
20 T 7032—Ceiling Light.
20 T 9225—Ball shade only.

$40.00 – 50.00

Weatherproof Outdoor Bracket

Strongly made of heavily galvanized steel pipe with 10-in. metal reflector. Arm extends 22 inches from wall. Will give long service.
20 T 7062

$20.00 – 30.00

Outdoor Floodlight

Powerful reflecting surface, highly polished. Gives a brilliant flood of light. 9-inch lens. Use 150 or 200-watt lamp.

20 T 7077—Outdoor Floodlight.
20 T 7078—Indoor Floodlight. Complete with 6 color sheets instead of glass lens.

$35.00 – 50.00

The "GLEN ELLYN"

Finished in rich forged iron, these attractive lanterns of lifetime cast aluminum have that sought-after hand-wrought effect. Amber crackled glass cylinder. These fixtures are stunning by day—fascinating at night when lighted! 20 T 7026 is 10 in. high and extends 7 in. 20 T 7027 is 12 in. long. Ideal for the front or side porch.

20 T 7026—Wall Bracket.
20 T 7027—Ceiling Lantern.

Both: $60.00 – 90.00

The "NANTUCKET"

A delightful new Colonial design. Beautified by the shade of "hobnail" glass. Cast aluminum. Finished in weathered bronze color. One of our most distinctive outdoor fixtures. 20 T 5541 is 12 in. high and extends 8 in. 20 T 5540 is 13½ in. in length. See Inside Back Cover for actual color illustration of this charming Colonial design.

20 T 5540—Ceiling Lantern.
20 T 5541—Wall Bracket.

Both: $50.00 – 75.00

Attractive Octagon Shade Fixtures

Weatherproof black finish that harmonizes with any style of architecture or decoration. The octagon crackled glass shade is amber tinted, has 3¼ in. opening, and is 6 in. in diameter.

20 T 7034—Ceiling light.
20 T 7033—Wall Bracket.
20 T 9226—Shade only.

Both: $45.00 – 65.00

Outdoor Ceiling Fixture

Attractive cast aluminum ceiling fixture in natural finish. Has amber tint glass panels on six sides and one in bottom. Extends 4½ in. from ceiling.

20 T 7008—Ceiling Fixture.

$30.00 – 40.00

Metal Reflector

High quality, made from heavy gauge steel. Will give years of service, even if exposed to weather because heavily porcelain enameled. Rust and corrosion proof.

20 T 9033—12-in. Porcelain enameled. Green outside, white inside. Fits 2¼ in. holder.

$25.00 – 35.00

Cast Aluminum Outdoor Bracket

Rustproof, built for lifetime service. Black finish, with polished 10-in. reflector. Extends 16 in.

20 T 7039—Complete, less lamp.

$30.00 – 50.00

Low-Priced Metal Reflector

Made from steel, plain enamel finish. Green outside, white inside. Diameter, 10 in. A serviceable low-priced reflector.

20 T 9034—Metal Reflector.

$20.00 – 30.00

For Prices Refer to Complete Price List Enclosed

LIGHTING *for* STORES
SCHOOLS, PUBLIC HALLS

BRONZE FINISH FIXTURES

Sturdily made, of copper-face steel, finished in a rich bronze, these 36-inch drop fixtures will give splendid service for store, school or hall lighting. Drop fixture 36 in. long.

20 T 7500—6-in. drop holder.
20 T 7502—4-in. drop holder.
20 T 7520—6-in. ceiling holder.
20 T 7522—4 in. ceiling holder.

MODERNISTIC TYPE FIXTURES

A striking new design with thoroughly modern lines now so much in vogue. The finish is a non-tarnishing chromium plate. Ideal for up-to-date store lighting use. Drop fixtures 36 in. long.

20 T 7508—6-in. drop holder.
20 T 7510—4-in. drop holder.
20 T 7528—6-in. ceiling holder.
20 T 7530—4 in. ceiling holder.

KITCHEN GLASS SHOWN ON PAGES 28 and 29 FIT 4-INCH HOLDERS LISTED ABOVE.

$30.00 – 45.00

$25.00 – 40.00

HIGHEST QUALITY GLASSWARE

The very newest of the new in modernistic style glassware for the lighting of stores, schools, halls, churches, etc. Beautiful fluted design of plain white glass that permits a wealth of light to pass but eliminates glare. Supplied in two sizes, as follows:

20 T 9108—Modernistic shade in white glass, for 4-in. holder, 9 inches across.
20 T 9107—Modernistic shade in white glass, for 6-in. holder, 12 inches across.

$30.00 – 40.00

A POPULAR PATTERN IN TWO PREFERRED SIZES

We can supply this popular pattern shade in two sizes usually chosen for store and other public lighting purposes. Made of highest quality opal glass in soft, pearly white color. Priced to save you money, and guaranteed to equal or surpass in quality any similar glassware on the market. Use with 6-inch holder.

20 T 9117—White glass shade, 12-inch diameter.
20 T 9119—White glass shade, 14-inch diameter.

$20.00 – 30.00

GLOLITE · *For Indirect Lighting*

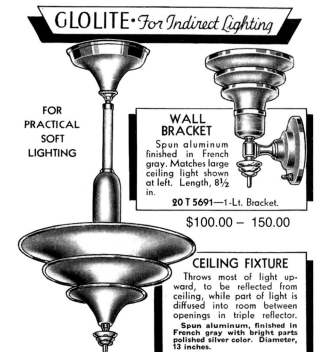

FOR PRACTICAL SOFT LIGHTING

WALL BRACKET

Spun aluminum finished in French gray. Matches large ceiling light shown at left. Length, 8½ in.

20 T 5691—1-Lt. Bracket.

$100.00 – 150.00

CEILING FIXTURE

Throws most of light upward, to be reflected from ceiling, while part of light is diffused into room between openings in triple reflector.

Spun aluminum, finished in French gray with bright parts polished silver color. Diameter, 13 inches.

20 T 5690—Ceiling Fixture.

$175.00 – 250.00

For Prices Refer to Complete Price List Enclosed

HI·GLO

Fleurette

Seville

Plymouth

Berkeley

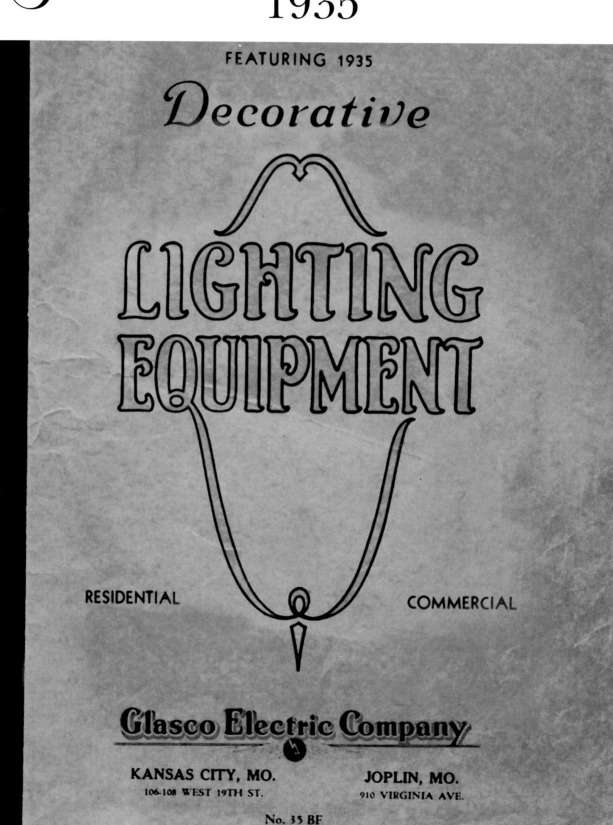

FEATURING 1935

Decorative

LIGHTING EQUIPMENT

RESIDENTIAL

COMMERCIAL

Glasco Electric Company

KANSAS CITY, MO.
106-108 WEST 19TH ST.

JOPLIN, MO.
910 VIRGINIA AVE.

No. 35 BF

New...1935
Decorative Lighting Equipment
for BETTER LIGHT — BETTER SIGHT

THIS book presents a complete style range of Lighting Fixtures...the product of the nation's best designers and most skilled craftsmen.

In accord with the high standards of the BETTER LIGHT ...BETTER SIGHT movement, many lines shown here incorporate the newest developments in indirect and semi-indirect illumination, and combine rare beauty, charm, and refinement with the highest degree of lighting efficiency. Other new lines embody the justly popular "shaded light" principle, and produce a softened, mellow glow of illumination ideal for the present-day trend toward decorative light. Every line shown is a revelation in beauty, smartness, and craftsmanship.

From this elaborate showing you may select Fixtures for every room in your home...and to harmonize perfectly with every type of modern decoration.

In addition to the extensive presentation of residential Lighting Fixtures we display a most comprehensive selection of Commercial Lighting Equipment newly styled for the finest commercial establishments, offices, taverns, stores, etc.

The surprisingly low prices shown in this book are eloquently expressive of the super values created by today's efficient manufacturing methods. You can now own and enjoy fine quality, distinctive lighting equipment at extremely low cost.

OUR LIGHTING FIXTURES
ARE AVAILABLE ONLY THROUGH AUTHORIZED DEALERS

The Dealer who presents this book for your fixture selection is our authorized representative in your community. Place your order with him. His experience and equipment assure you of a safe installation and complete satisfaction. We urge you to look to him for all your electrical requirements.

"DELPHI" SERIES

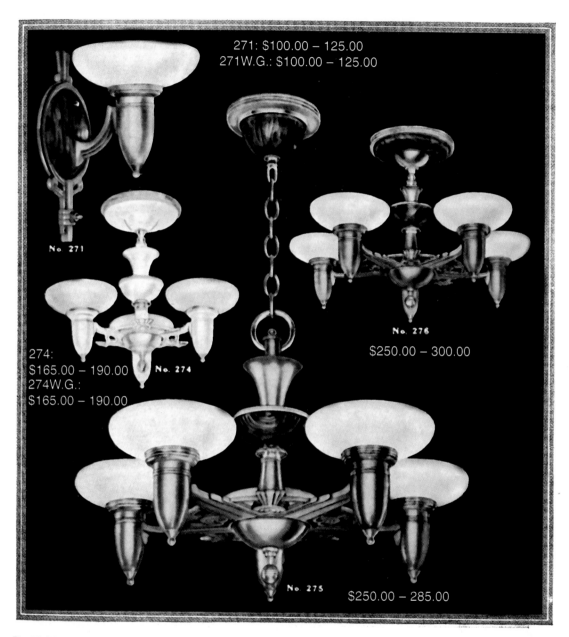

271: $100.00 – 125.00
271W.G.: $100.00 – 125.00

No. 271

274:
$165.00 – 190.00
274W.G.:
$165.00 – 190.00

No. 274

No. 276

$250.00 – 300.00

No. 275

$250.00 – 285.00

The "Delphi" line represents a new and original treatment for home lighting. Combining modern art with period styling, these unusual fixtures blend harmoniously with most any decorative scheme. The white inside cased, light champagne colored glass shades produce a delightfully pleasing illumination and add a touch of warmth and beauty. No. 275 has convenient switch in bottom for controlling 2, 3 or 5 lights as desired.

No.		Finish	Spread	Length	Extends
271	—1 Light Bracket	Bronze and Chromium with Walnut trim	5 in.	9 in.	7 in.
271-W.G.	—1 Light Bracket	Empire White and Gold	5 in.	9 in.	7 in.
274	—3 Light Celing	Bronze and Chromium with Walnut trim	17 in.	14 in.	
274-W.G.	—3 Light Ceiling	Empire White and Gold	17 in.	14 in.	
275	—5 Light Drop	Bronze and Chromium with Walnut trim	21 in.	40 in.	
276	—5 Light Ceiling	Bronze and Chromium with Walnut trim	21 in.	16 in.	

(Companion pieces on reverse side of this page.)

"DELPHI" SERIES

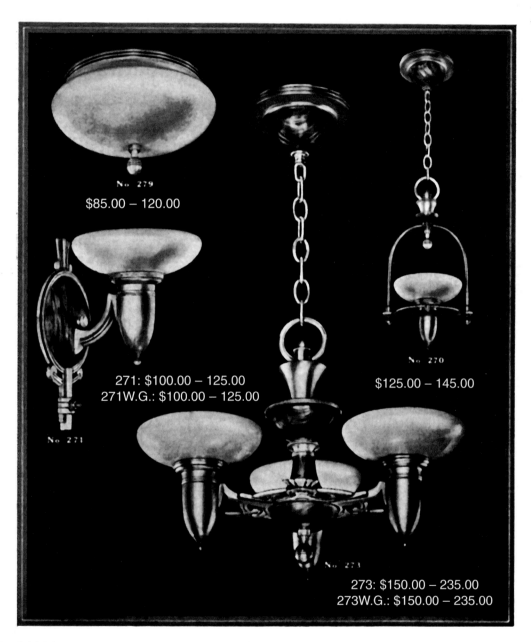

No. 279

$85.00 – 120.00

271: $100.00 – 125.00
271W.G.: $100.00 – 125.00

No. 271

No. 270

$125.00 – 145.00

273: $150.00 – 235.00
273W.G.: $150.00 – 235.00

The "Delphi" Line represents a new and original treatment for home lighting. Combining modern art with period styling, these unusual fixtures blend harmoniously with most any decorative scheme. The white inside cased, light champagne colored glass shades produce a delightfully pleasing illumination and add a touch of warmth and beauty.

No.		Finish	Spread	Length	Extends
279	—2 Light Ceiling	Bronze and Chromium with Walnut trim	9 in.	6 in.	
271	—1 Light Bracket	Bronze and Chromium with Walnut trim	5 in.	9 in.	7 in.
271-W.G.	—1 Light Bracket	Empire White and Gold	5 in.	9 in.	7 in.
273	—3 Light Drop	Bronze and Chromium with Walnut trim	17 in.	40 in.	
273-W.G.	—3 Light Drop	Empire White and Gold	17 in.	40 in.	
270	—1 Light Drop	Bronze and Chromium with Walnut trim	8 in.	32 in.	

(Companion pieces on reverse side of this page.)

"SAVOY" SERIES

361: $100.00 – 135.00
361W.G.: $100.00 – 135.00

No. 361

No. 366

$200.00 – 275.00

No. 365

$200.00 – 300.00

The "Savoy" Line offers a unique combination of the very latest modern styling with a distinctive simplicity that adds charm and beauty to the home. The white inside cased, light champagne colored glass shades produce an unusually efficient soft light that is free from eyestrain. No. 365 has convenient switch in bottom for controlling 2, 3, or 5 lights as desired.

No.		Finish	Spread	Length	Extends
361	—1 Light Bracket	Walnut and Chromium	5 in.	5 in.	6½ in.
361-W.G.	—1 Light Bracket	Empire White and Gold	5 in.	5 in.	6½ in.
365	—5 Light Drop	Walnut and Chromium	21 in.	40 in.	
366	—5 Light Ceiling	Walnut and Chromium	21 in.	17 in.	

(Companion pieces on reverse side of this page.)

"SAVOY" SERIES

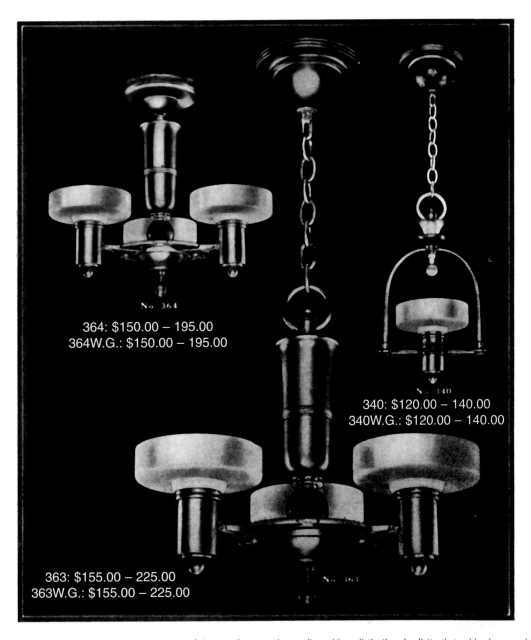

364: $150.00 – 195.00
364W.G.: $150.00 – 195.00

340: $120.00 – 140.00
340W.G.: $120.00 – 140.00

363: $155.00 – 225.00
363W.G.: $155.00 – 225.00

The "Savoy" Line offers a unique combination of the very latest modern styling with a distinctive simplicity that adds charm and beauty to the home. The white inside cased, light champagne colored glass shades produce an unusually efficient, soft light that is free from eye strain.

No.		Finish	Spread	Length
364	—3 Light Ceiling	Walnut and Chromium	15½ in.	15 in.
364-W.G.	—3 Light Celing	Empire White and Gold	15½ in.	15 in.
363	—3 Light Drop	Walnut and Chromium	15½ in.	40 in.
363-W.G.	—3 Light Drop	Empire White and Gold	15½ in.	40 in.
340	—1 Light Drop	Walnut and Chromium	8½ in.	36 in.
340-W.G.	—1 Light Drop	Empire White and Gold	8½ in.	36 in.

(Companion pieces on reverse side of this page.)

The "HAMPTON" Line

Combines the Designs of Old England with Shaded Light

9601-A
$150.00 – 185.00

9625-A
$375.00 – 400.00

9675-A
$385.00 – 425.00

This set is made of Cast Ferro Metal and finished in a beautiful Antique Gold. The Glassware, decorated in Suntan with **Brown** shading is so designed that the light is diffused from all sides of the ring and produces a continuous circle of soft cheerful illumination.

NO.	LIGHTS	FINISH	DIMENSIONS
9601-A	1 Lt. Bracket	Antique Gold	11″ x 7½″
9625-A	5 Lt. Semi-Ceiling	Antique Gold	19″ Diameter
9675-A	5 Lt. Drop	Antique Gold	19″ Diameter

(Lamps not included with above fixtures)

The "WARWICK" Line

Shaded Light of Unusual Beauty

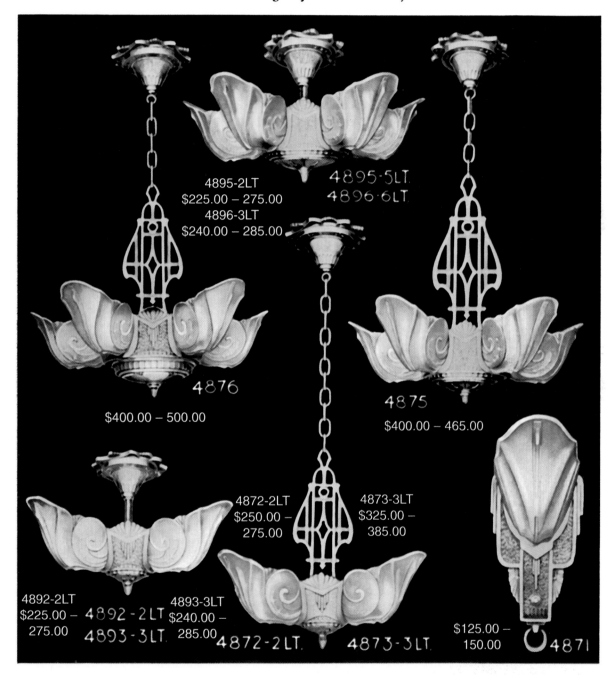

4895-2LT
$225.00 – 275.00
4896-3LT
$240.00 – 285.00

4895-5LT.
4896-6LT.

4876
$400.00 – 500.00

4875
$400.00 – 465.00

4872-2LT
$250.00 –
275.00

4873-3LT
$325.00 –
385.00

4892-2LT
$225.00 –
275.00

4893-3LT
$240.00 –
285.00

$125.00 –
150.00   4871

The "Warwick" line is a new moderately priced shaded light series of unusual beauty. Metal work in Cast Ferro Metal beautifully finished in Antique Gold and equipped with Suntan Glassware.

NO.	DESCRIPTION	FINISH	DIMENSIONS	NO.	DESCRIPTION	FINISH	DIMENSIONS
4871	1 Lt. Bracket	Antique Gold	9½" x 4½"	4892	2 Lt. Semi-Ceiling	Antique Gold	12½" Diameter
4872	2 Lt. Drop	Antique Gold	12½" Diameter	4893	3 Lt. Semi-Ceiling	Antique Gold	15½" Diameter
4873	3 Lt. Drop	Antique Gold	15½" Diameter	4895	5 Lt. Semi-Ceiling	Antique Gold	18½" Diameter
4875	5 Lt. Drop	Antique Gold	18½" Diameter	4896	6 Lt. Semi-Ceiling	Antique Gold	19" Diameter
4876	6 Lt. Drop	ntique Gold	19" Diameter				

(Lamps not included with above fixtures)

The "GLORIA" Line
Emphasizing the Modern Beauty of Shaded Light

2922 2 Light
2923 3 Light

2922:
$225.00 – 275.00
2923:
$240.00 – 285.00

2912 2 Light
2913 3 Light

2912:
$200.00 – 250.00
2913:
$235.00 – 265.00

$130.00 – 150.00

2941

2915

$385.00 – 425.00

The "Gloria" line comprises a wide selection in types and sizes for every room in the home or apartment. All are **attractively** designed in the popular modern shaded light vogue. Finished in rich Old Gold with Tan Iridescent shades.

No.	Description	Size		No.	Description	Size
2912	2 Lt. Drop	16″ Diameter		2922	2 Lt. Ceiling	16″ Diameter
2913	3 Lt. Drop	16″ Diameter		2923	3 Lt. Ceiling	16″ Diameter
2915	5 Lt. Drop	17½″ Diameter		2941	1 Lt. Drop	6″ Diameter

(Lamps not included with above fixtures)
(Companion designs to match this line are shown on reverse side of this page) Printed in U. S. A.

The "GLORIA" Line
Emphasizing the Modern Beauty of Shaded Light

2925

$375.00 – 400.00

2901

$125.00 – 150.00

2982

$150.00 – 175.00

2936

$400.00 – 450.00

The Modern Art Vogue is beautifully presented in these graceful new fixtures. They are well made of cast metal skillfully designed and attractively finished in rich Old Gold with Tan Iridescent shades to match. No. 2936 has a unique shade built into the hanger which affords beauty and is very practical for a night light as it can be lighted individually.

No.	Description	Size	No.	Description	Size
2901	1 Lt. Bracket	10½" x 5½"	2936	6 Lt. Drop	17½" Diameter
2925	5 Lt. Ceiling	17½" Diameter	2982	2 Lt. Bowl	13½" Diameter

(Lamps not included with above fixtures)

(Companion designs to match this line are shown on reverse side of this page)

Printed in U. S. A.

The "MODERNDALE" Line
An Outstanding Design Development in Colorful Shaded Light

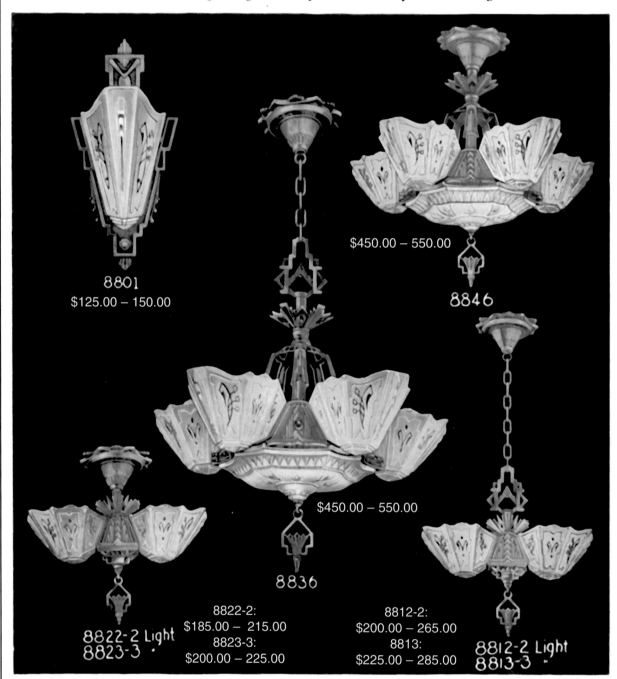

8801
$125.00 – 150.00

$450.00 – 550.00
8846

$450.00 – 550.00
8836

8822-2 Light
8823-3

8822-2:
$185.00 – 215.00
8823-3:
$200.00 – 225.00

8812-2:
$200.00 – 265.00
8813:
$225.00 – 285.00

8812-2 Light
8813-3

Beauty, refinement and lighting efficiency are incorporated in these new fixtures. Glassware produced in lustrous satin effect attractively embossed in harmony with the metalwork of the fixture. The glass bottom of No. 8836-8846 provides increased lighting efficiency. No. 8836 has a small switch on side of fixture for controlling outside lights, permitting central light to be used independently. Metal parts produced in polished plated bronze, a finish of super quality and durability.

No.	Description	Size	No.	Description	Size
8801-A	1 Lt. Bracket	12" x 5½"	8823-A	3 Lt. Ceiling	17" Diameter
8812-A	2 Lt. Drop	15" Diameter	8836-A	7 Lt. Drop	20" Diameter
8813-A	3 Lt. Drop	17" Diameter	8846-A	7 Lt. Ceiling	20" Diameter
8822-A	2 Lt. Ceiling	15" Diameter	All drop fixtures are 36" long overall.		

The "VILLA-ROSE" Line

Charming Styles for Bed Rooms, Sun Rooms, Halls, Breakfast Nooks, etc.

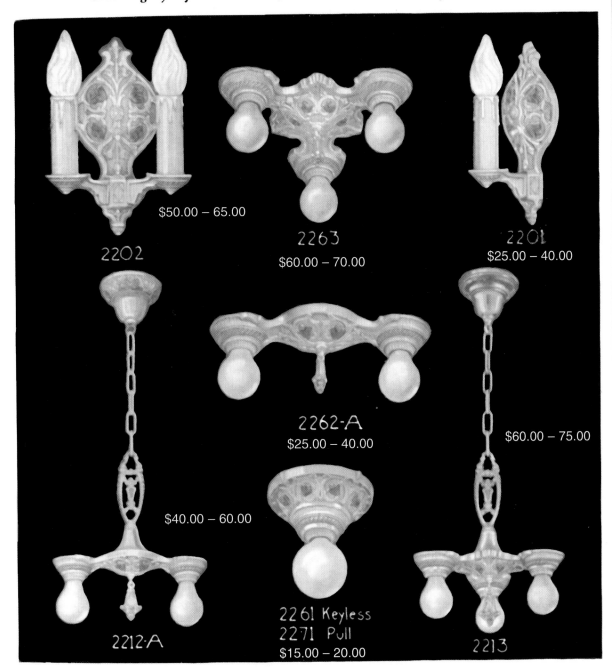

$50.00 – 65.00

2263
$60.00 – 70.00

2201
$25.00 – 40.00

2202

2262-A
$25.00 – 40.00

$60.00 – 75.00

$40.00 – 60.00

2212-A

2261 Keyless
2271 Pull
$15.00 – 20.00

2213

These striking new styles in Sun Room and Bed Room fixtures are well made of cast metal attractively embossed in graceful design. All types are finished in Rich Old Ivory with softly blended color tints effectively applied.

No.	Description	Size	No.	Description	Size
2201	1 Lt. Bracket	4½" x 9½"	2262-A	2 Lt. Ceiling	12½" Diameter
2202	2 Lt. Bracket	4½" x 9½"	2263	3 Lt. Ceiling	13" Diameter
2212-A	2 Lt. Drop	12½" Diameter	2261	1 Lt. Ceiling	6" Diameter
2213	3 Lt. Drop	13" Diameter	2271	1 Lt. Ceiling	6" Diameter

All drop fixtures are 36" long.

(Lamps not included with above fixtures)

Printed in U. S. A.

The "FONTAINE" Line

Inspired by the Beauty of the Directoire Period

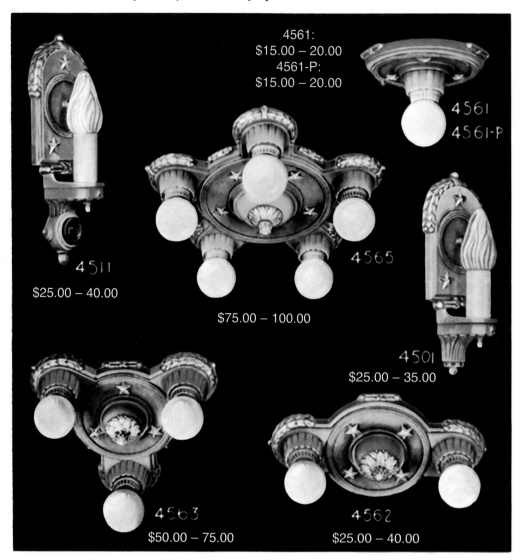

4561:
$15.00 – 20.00
4561-P:
$15.00 – 20.00

4561
4561-P

4511

$25.00 – 40.00

4565

$75.00 – 100.00

4501

$25.00 – 35.00

4563

$50.00 – 75.00

4562

$25.00 – 40.00

Inspired by the beauty of the Directoire Period this series has been designed to co-ordinate with the newest in furniture and decorations. Note the faithful attention to detail in metal and finish. Made of Cast Ferro Metal, finished in Herald Brown and Silver.

NO.	DESCRIPTION	DIMENSIONS	NO.	DESCRIPTION	DIMENSIONS
4501	1 Lt. Bracket	10" x 4¼"	4562	2 Lt. Ceiling	12" x 7"
*4511	1 Lt. Bracket	11" x 4¼"	4563	3 Lt. Ceiling	13" Diameter
4561	1 Lt. Ceiling	7" Diameter	4565	5 Lt. Ceiling	16" Diameter
4561P	Same as 4561 except wired Pull Chain		*4511 With Convenience Outlet.		

(Lamps not included with above fixtures)

The "MIRRO-CHROME" Line

A Most Unusual Development in New Ivory and Chrome Fixtures

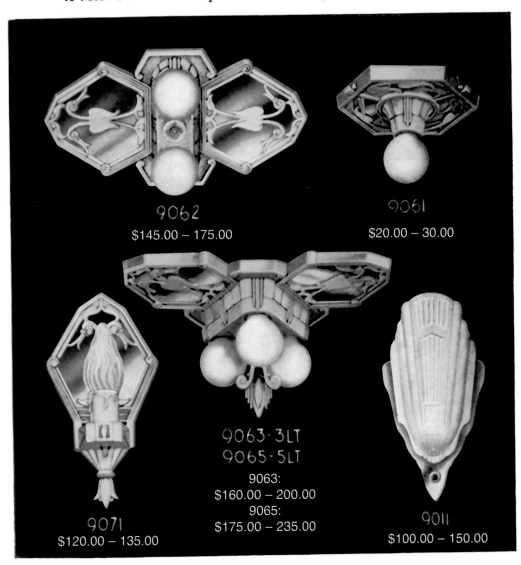

9062
$145.00 – 175.00

9061
$20.00 – 30.00

9063·3LT
9065·5LT
9063:
$160.00 – 200.00
9065:
$175.00 – 235.00

9071
$120.00 – 135.00

9011
$100.00 – 150.00

The Mirro-Chrome offers a unique style which will win the instant admiration of those seeking different and exclusive creations for Bed Rooms, Sun Rooms, Smart Shops, etc.   Finished as pictured in rich Old Ivory and color inset with chrome plate mirror effect. Wall bracket No. 9011 finished in chrome and equipped with modernistic embossed shade.

NO.	DESCRIPTION	FINISH	DIMENSIONS
9011	1 Lt. Bracket	All Chrome	9½" x 5¼"
9061	1 Lt. Ceiling	Ivory and Chrome	7½" Diameter
9062	2 Lt. Ceiling	Ivory and Chrome	13" x 6¾"
9063	3 Lt. Ceiling	Ivory and Chrome	15" Diameter
9065	5 Lt. Ceiling	Ivory and Chrome	18" Diameter
9071	1 Lt. Bracket	Ivory and Chrome	10" x 5¼"

(Lamps not included with above fixtures)

Printed in U. S. A.

SANITARY CHROMIUM PLATED FIXTURES

These modern, easy to clean fixtures embody the highest qualities of lighting efficiency and simple, pleasing designs which fit into most any decorative schemes. They are ideal for kitchens, breakfast rooms, bath rooms, bedrooms, halls, small stores, refreshment booths, wash rooms, hospitals, schools and numerous other places where small, efficient, attractive lighting fixtures are desired.

All metal parts are brass, beautifully finished in durable chromium plate.

No. 792 Ceiling Fixture
Length overall 7½ in.
Opal glass 7 in. in diameter
$40.00 – 60.00

No. 793 Beam Light
Diam. of base 5½ in. Length 5½ in.
$10.00 – 20.00

No. 795 Ceiling Fixture
Opal glass 9 in. in diameter
Length overall 9 in.
$35.00 – 45.00

No. 791 Bracket—with pull socket
Back 3¼ x 6 in. Extends 5½ in.
Opal glass shade
No. 791—No convenience outlet
No. 791C—With convenience outlet
$100.00 – 135.00

No. B147—G3 Bracket
Plain white glass 4½ x 3½ in.
Back 6 x 6 in.
Equipped with turn switch
$100.00 – 115.00

No. 788 Bracket—with pull socket
Back 3½ x 6 in. Extends 4½ in.
No. 788—No convenience outlet
No. 788C—With convenience outlet
$20.00 – 30.00

No. B145—G2 Bracket
White Modernistic glass, 6 x 2½ in. with black raised stripes. Back 9 x 3 in. Equipped with turn switch
$150.00 – 200.00

No. B146—G1E Bracket
Crystal etched striped glass 6 x 2½ in. Back 6¼ x 3¾ in. Equipped with turn switch
$150.00 – 200.00

No. B146—G3 Bracket
Plain white glass 4½ x 3½ in. Back 6¼ x 3¾ in. Equipped with turn switch
$135.00 – 165.00

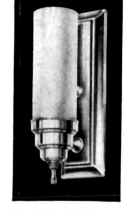

No. B145—G1 Bracket
Plain white glass, 6 x 2½ in. Back 9 x 3 in. Equipped with turn switch
$140.00 – 175.00

INDIRECT The EDWIN F. Guth COMPANY ILLUMINATORS

THE BEST LIGHT FOR THE EYES AND FOR MERCHANDISE DISPLAY — MAKING THEM IDEAL FOR COMMERCIAL OR INSTITUTIONAL INSTALLATIONS

Guth Super Illuminators not only produce the maximum amount of light for wattage used—but they also properly distribute the light over a wide area through the use of wide angle reflectors. They produce efficient, uniform lighting intensities, eliminating glare, shadows and undesirable reflection.

Equipped with metal reflectors, with patented lower bowls of satin finished glass that illuminate the outside of the reflectors without glare and add a touch of warmth and beauty.

They are extremely easy to clean or relamp, simply unhook one of the supports for instant access to the lamp or the reflecting surface.

No. R-4910 SUPER ILLUMINATOR

Decorative type chain suspension. Built of brass and aluminum. Finished in Pewter and Old Gold with decalcomania decoration on outside of reflector. Inside of reflector finished in white oxide. Satin finish glass lower bowl.

No.	Diam. Refl.	Socket	Lamp Size Watts
R-4910	12 in	Medium	100
R-4912	14 in.	Medium	150-200

Overall length: No. R-4910, 26 in.; No. R-4912, 30 in.

$200.00 – 250.00

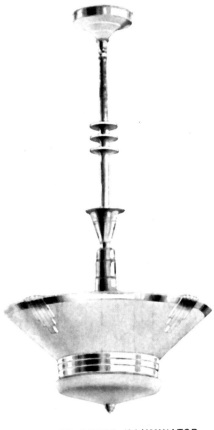

No. R-4671 SUPER ILLUMINATOR

Decorative semi-rigid suspension type, equipped with swivel joint. Brass and aluminum construction. Finished in combination of Chromium and Satin and Polished Aluminum. Satin glass lower bowl. Inside of reflector, white oxide.

No.	Diam. Refl.	Length	Socket	Lamp Size Watts
R-4671	14 in.	30 in.	Medium	150-200
R-4672	18 in.	36 in.	Mogul	300-500
R-4673	22 in.	42 in.	Mogul	750-1500

$300.00 – 400.00

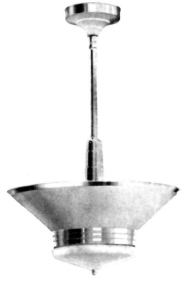

No. R-4355 SUPER ILLUMINATOR

Semi-rigid suspension type, equipped with swivel joint. Constructed of brass and aluminum. Combination of Chromium and Satin and Polished Aluminum finish. Inside of reflector finished in white oxide. Satin finish glass lower bowl.

No.	Diam. Refl.	Socket	Lamp Size Watts
R-4355	14 in.	Medium	150-200
R-4357	18 in.	Mogul	300-500
R-4359	22 in.	Mogul	750-1500

Overall lengths: No. R-4355, 30 in.; No. R-4357, 36 in.; No. 4359, 42 in.

$285.00 – 350.00

INDIRECT  ILLUMINATORS

THE BEST LIGHT FOR THE EYES OR FOR MERCHANDISE DISPLAY
MAKING THEM IDEAL FOR COMMERCIAL OR INSTITUTIONAL INSTALLATIONS

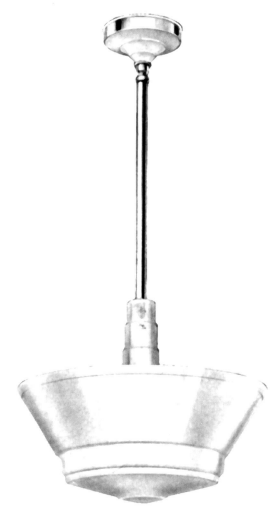

GUTH LUMO-VITRO INDIRECT-LITE

The inside of the one piece metal reflectors is finished with the new exclusive Guth Lumo-Vitro white Enamel, with the outside in Lumo-Vitro Ivory. The chain and canopy of the chain type are finished in Ivory; the suspension of the semi-rigid type in polished Chrome. These finishes will retain their original lustre indefinitely.

They are extremely easy to clean and relamp. Unhook one support for instant access to the reflector surface, from which all dust is quickly and easily removed by a damp cloth.

Adjustable socket permits raising or lowering the lamp to obtain the proper focus.

NEW GUTH SUPER INDIRECT

Numerous tests prove the New Guth Super Indirect to be one of the most efficient indirect lighting units ever devised.

Durably built of porcelain enameled steel — handsomely finished in Ivory and White, with Chromium stem.

The exclusive Guth Luma-Vitro reflecting surface plus the correct design of the reflecting bowl account for its remarkable illuminating efficiency.

Made in one size only, for lamps ranging from 300 to 1500 watts. A simple, easily attached adapter is supplied with each fixture to raise the socket cover when 300 or 500 watt lamp is used.

Semi-rigid Stem	Chain Stem	Diam.	Length	Socket	Lamp Size Watts
R-5355	R-3751	14 in.	30 in.	Medium	200
R-5357	R-3753	18 in.	36 in.	Mogul	300-500
R-5358	R-3754	18 in.	36 in.	Mogul	750-1000
R-5359	R-3755	22 in.	42 in.	Mogul	750-1500

all: $150.00 – 300.00

No.	Diam.	Length	Socket	Lamp Size Watts
R-5230	18 in.	42 in.	Mogul	300 to 1500

$150.00 – 200.00

INDIRECT AND SEMI-INDIRECT FIXTURES

On this and the reverse side of this page, beauty and light at its best are presented in newly styled fixtures of outstanding designs, that blend with any decorative scheme. Incorporating the modern trend of lighting efficiency, they are especially suited for those stores, shops, offices, etc. where efficient illumination by means of something other than the ordinary styled lighting equipment is in demand. The metal reflectors give an indirect light of unsurpassed quality.

No. R-6761
One Light Bracket

An exclusively designed candle-type bracket with a 3 in. x 8 in. glass half cylinder. Wall plate is 5½ in. wide. Length over all, 10½ in. Canopy switch control. **Finished in Silverna and Gold.**

$125.00 – 160.00

No. R-6442S—2-Light Louvre Type Pendant

The pyramid arrangement of the metal louvres illuminates the upper ring with a soft light and develops an indirect ceiling illumination of daylight proportion. Spread 18 in.

Finished in Silverna and Black.

$250.00 – 350.00

No. R-8042—2-Light Louvre Type Pendant

The arrangement of the metal louvres allows the light to illuminate the outside of these units, adding life and beauty.

Spread 18 in., glass bottom bowl 8 in. in diameter, length 36 in. Finished in Silverna and Black.

$250.00 – 385.00

No. R-6461S
One Light Bracket

An exquisite one light wall bracket that harmonizes perfectly with these unusually fine fixtures. Wallplate 7½ in. wide, overall length, 11 in.

Finished in Silverna and Black.

$150.00 – 185.00

SEMI-INDIRECT LIGHT COMMERCIAL FIXTURES

Incorporating the two essential features of fine lighting equipment . . . . beauty and efficiency, these modern fixtures are outstanding in quality, style and value.

The glass bottom plates, which produce the semi-indirect feature, give an added touch of warmth and charm to these unusually fine fixtures.

No. R-6861
One Light Bracket

This unique bracket of modern, yet pleasingly simple design has a double sand blast glass disc 5½ in. in diameter. Overall length 8½ in. Canopy switch control. Finished in Silverna.

$150.00 – 200.00

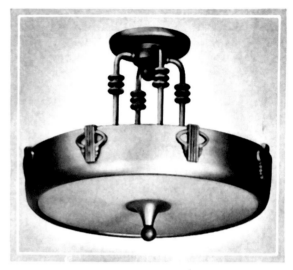

No. R-6824—4-Light Semi-Ceiling Fixture

Bottom plate of double sand blast glass. Diameter, 18 in. Length, 14 in. Metal in beautiful Silverna.

$185.00 – 225.00

No. R-6844—4-Light Pendant

Diameter, 18 in. Double sand blast glass bottom. Metal parts beautifully finished in Silverna.

$200.00 – 235.00

No. R-6744—4-Light Pendant

Eighteen inch metal reflecting bowl. Iridescent opal glass at bottom adds beauty and charm to this fixture.
Finished in Silverna and Gold.
(For bracket to match this pendant see No. R-6761 on reverse side of page).

$225.00 – 245.00

"EXCELITE" SEMI-INDIRECT LIGHTING UNITS

Commercial Lighting Units of unusual beauty, combined with a maximum of lighting efficiency

Especially recommended for use in stores, offices, showrooms, schools, hospitals, public buildings and other places where good, adequate illumination, without eye-strain, is essential.

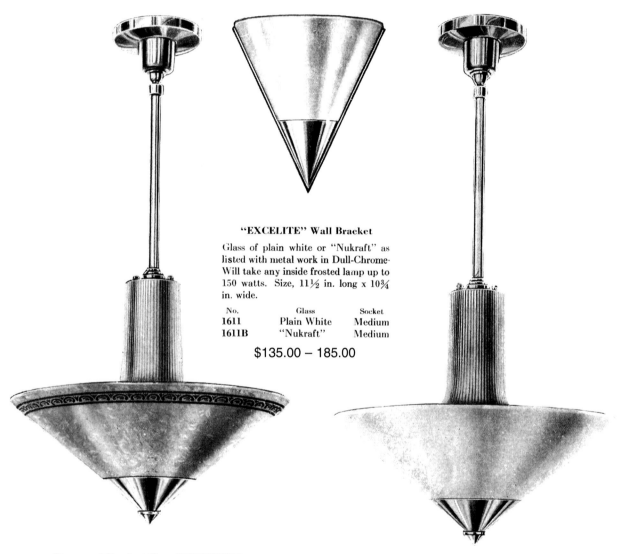

"EXCELITE" Wall Bracket

Glass of plain white or "Nukraft" as listed with metal work in Dull-Chrome. Will take any inside frosted lamp up to 150 watts. Size, 11½ in. long x 10¾ in. wide.

No.	Glass	Socket
1611	Plain White	Medium
1611B	"Nukraft"	Medium

$135.00 – 185.00

Decorated Pendant Type "EXCELITE"

Glass bowls of Ivory "Nukraft", a new permanent finish producing the effect of an uneven, beautiful embossed stipple design on the glass. Luminous glass socket covers. Metal parts finished in Dull-Chrome.

No.	Diam. Glass	Socket	Lamp Size, Watts
1616B	16 in.	Medium	200
1620B	20 in.	Mogul	300-500

$225.00+

Plain Pendant Type "EXCELITE"

Plain white glass bowls and white luminous glass socket covers. Metal parts finished in Dull-Chrome.

No.	Diam. Glass	Socket	Lamp Size, Watts
1616	16 in.	Medium	200
1620	20 in.	Mogul	300-500

$200.00+

SEMI-INDIRECT LIGHTING FIXTURES

Commercial Lighting Units of unusual beauty, combined with a maximum of lighting efficiency

Especially recommended for use in stores, offices, showrooms, schools, hospitals, public buildings and other places where good, adequate illumination, without eye-strain, is essential.

The "NEW YORKER"

An especially attractive semi-indirect lighting fixture, with diffusing bowl of special density glass especially developed for high reflection and low light absorption. Metal work finished in polished chrome.

No.	Diam. Glass	Socket	Lamp Size, Watts
4516	15¼ in.	Medium	150-200
4518	18½ in.	Medium	150-200

$150.00 – 185.00

The "Superlux"

Plain, yet dignified in appearance. Lightly polished glass diffusing bowl perfected for high reflection and low light absorption, resulting in high percentage of light output being converted into useful light. Metal parts finished in "Metalustre" - an applied finish very similar in appearance to Brushed Aluminum

"Superlux" with Plain Glass

No.	Diam. Glass	Socket	Lamp Size, Watts
416	16 in.	Medium	200-300
420	20 in.	Mogul	300-500

"Superlux" with Decorated Glass
(As Illustrated)

No.		Socket	
416E	16 in.	Medium	200-300
420E	20 in.	Mogul	300-500

$250.00+

The "ULTRALITE"

Made of aluminum, except the small bottom diffusing dish which is made of Daylite glass. Inner surface of large reflector is finished in white porcelain type enamel. Entire fixture is finished in gray enamel with highly polished aluminum highlights.

No.	Diam. Reflector	Socket	Lamp Size, Watts
016R	16 in.	Medium	200-300
020R	20 in.	Mogul	300-500

$250.00+

"SYMPHONY" MODERN LOUVRE LUMINAIRES

For Commercial and Institutional Illumination

With pure white hyperion glass, polished chrome finished louvres and remaining metal parts in soft brushed aluminum, these Moderne Louvre Luminaires have an especially strong "eye appeal" in addition to their unusually high illuminating qualities.

The "SYMPHONY" Bracket Type

No.	Diam. Glass	Lamp Size, Watts
701-L1708	8 in.	75-100

$165.00 – 200.00

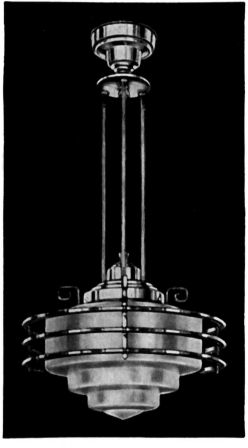

The "SYMPHONY" Pendant Type

No.	Diam. Glass	Lamp Size, Watts
716-L1712	12 in.	100-150
716-L1714	14 in.	150-200
716-L1716	16 in.	300-500

$260.00+

▼

The "SYMPHONY" Ceiling Type

No.	Diam. Glass	Lamp Size, Watts
726-L1712	12 in.	100-150
726-L1714	14 in.	150-200
726-L1716	16 in.	300-500

$250.00+

"CHIEFTON" MODERN LOUVRE LUMINAIRES

For Commercial and Institutional Illumination

With pure white hyperion glass, polished chrome finished louvres and remaining metal parts in soft brushed aluminum, these Moderne Louvre Luminaires have an especially strong "eye appeal" in addition to their unusually high illuminating qualities.

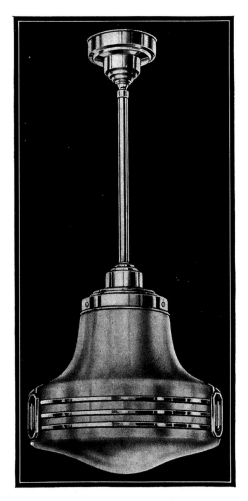

The "CHIEFTON" Ceiling Type

No.	Diam. Glass	Sockets	Lamp Size Watts
708-L3510	10 in.	2	75-100
710-L3512	12 in.	2	100-150
712-L3514	14 in.	3	150-200

$125.00 – 150.00

The "CHIEFTON" Pendant Type

No.	Diam. Glass	Lamp Size, Watts
716-L3312	12 in.	100-150
716-L3314	14 in.	150-200
716-L3316	16 in.	300-500

Length Overall, 39 inches

$200.00+

The superior illuminating efficiency of hyperion glass has been proven by many tests.

The "CHIEFTON" Ceiling Type

No.	Diam. Glass	Lamp Size, Watts
726-L3312	12 in.	100-150
726-L3314	14 in.	150-200
726-L3316	16 in.	300-500

$150.00 – 200.00

MODERN ART STYLED DECORATED FIXTURES

These unusually attractive fixtures are an excellent combination of modern art styling and high illuminating efficiency. They add a tone of distinction to stores, shops and other establishments.

The holders and hangers are smoothly surfaced and attractively finished in durable plated statuary bronze.

The glass unit of the "PREMIER" has panels beautifully patterned in black.

The glass of the "KINGSTON" is attractively decorated with a contrasting blackline effect.

The "PREMIER" Ceiling Type

No.	Glass Size	
	Diam.	Long
686-2260E	12¾ in.	x 10½ in.
686-2258E	10 in.	x 17 in.

$140.00 – 200.00

The "PREMIER" Hanging Type

No.	Glass Size	
	Diam.	Long
683-2258E	10 in.	x 17 in.
683-2260E	12¾ in.	x 10½ in.

$175.00 – 250.00

●

BRONZE PLATED HOLDERS AND HANGERS

The "KINGSTON" Ceiling Type

No.	Glass Size	
	Diam.	Long
1607-1460D	12½ in.	x 10¾ in.

$125.00 – 150.00

New "KINGSTON" Hanging Type

No.	Glass Size	
	Diam.	Long
1602-1458D	10¼ in.	x 16¼ in.
1602M-1461D	12½ in.	x 20 in.

Note: No. 1602M-1461D has Mogul socket.

$135.00 – 175.00

●

GENUINE HYPERION HIGH EFFICIENCY GLASS

"PROGRESS" and "CENTURION" FIXTURES

The simplicity of the hangers, smoothly finished in durable plated statuary bronze, contrasts pleasingly with the modernly designed pure white hyperion glass units and gives these fixtures a combination of attractiveness and illuminating efficiency that can hardly be surpassed at anywhere near their prices.

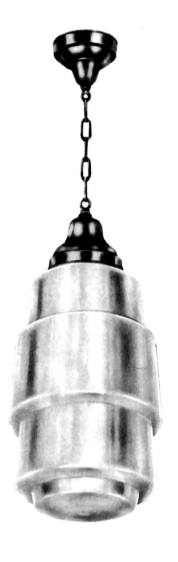

GENUINE HYPERION
HIGH EFFICIENCY GLASS
BRONZE PLATED HANGERS

The "PROGRESS" Hanging Type

No.	Glass Size Diam.	Long	Lamp Size, Watts
1001-2816	10¾ in. x	16 in.	200-300
1001M-2818	10¾ in. x	18 in.	300-500

Note: 1001M-2818 has Mogul socket.

$150.00 – 175.00

The "CENTURION" Hanging Type

No.	Glass Size Diam.	Long	Lamp Size Watts
1001-2258	10 in. x	17 in.	200-300

$125.00 – 150.00

The "CENTURION" Hanging Type

No.	Glass Size Diam.	Long	Lamp Size, Watts
1001-2260	12½ in. x	10¾ in.	150-200

$100.00 – 125.00

PRISMATIC REFLECTOR COMMERCIAL FIXTURES

Especially well suited for use in stores, shops, assembly rooms, entrances, lobbies and halls of public buildings or wherever else brilliant general illumination by means of attractive lighting fixtures is such a desirable feature.

The pure white, modernly styled hyperion glass units have polished crystal prismatic glass reflecting bottoms which magnify and distribute the light rays over a large area.

The hangers and ceiling holders are made of brass and are smoothly finished in durable plated statuary bronze.

The "SENATOR" Ceiling Type

No.	Glass Size Diam. Long	Lamp Size, Watts
1084-2300	9 in. x 12 in.	150-200

$75.00 – 100.00

The "CARTHAGE" Hanging Type
Length Overall, 42 inches

No.	Glass Size Diam. Long	Lamp Size, Watts
1001-165	13 in. x 12½ in.	300

$85.00 – 120.00

The "CARTHAGE" Ceiling Type

No.	Glass Size Diam. Long	Lamp Size, Watts
1084-165	13 in. x 12½ in.	300

$85.00 – 120.00

The "SENATOR" Hanging Type
Length Overall, 42 inches

No.	Glass Size Diam. Long	Lamp Size, Watts
1001-2300	9 in. x 12 in.	150-200

$75.00 – 100.00

Lightmaster Lighting Fixtures by Sears, 1936

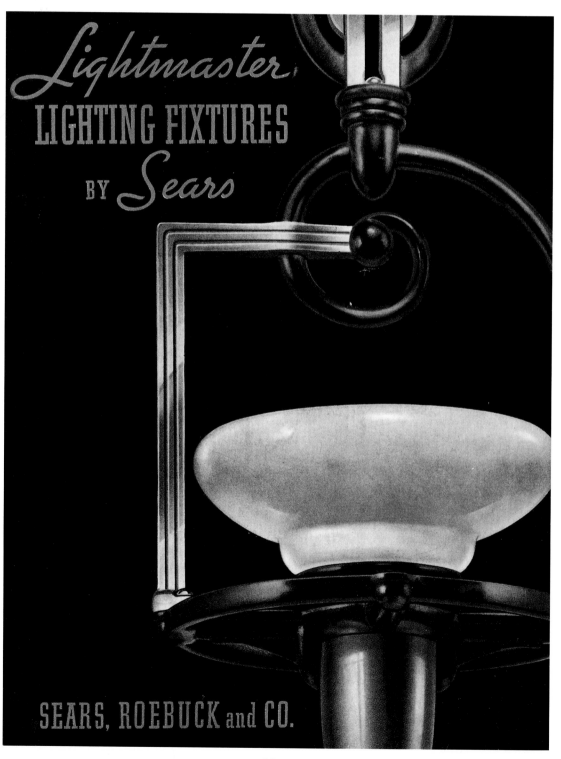

Lightmaster

SEARS CONTRIBUTION TO BETTER LIGHT ·· BETTER SIGHT

WHEN day is done our activities go on—often far into the night. We read, work or play by artificial light that is usually inadequate for healthy eyesight.

On a clear summer day under the shade of a tree, where reading conditions are ideal, nature provides one thousand units of light. Yet after dark many of us read indoors under 5 units of light or only one-half of one percent of what nature provides. To protect your eyes you must have not only enough light, but it must be balanced light.

Balanced Light

It is quite a simple matter to get *enough* light, but if you were to read under a 100 watt bulb with no other light in the room, your eyes would be subjected to an intense strain from glare. The contrast between light on the printed page and the comparatively dark room would be too great.

Balanced light eliminates this sharp contrast by furnishing enough general illumination in the room. By using LIGHTMASTER fixtures in conjunction with auxiliary portable lamps, you get balanced light that approaches the light provided by nature.

Why Sears Save You Money on Lighting Fixtures

Sears, Roebuck and Co., the largest retailer of electric lighting fixtures in the world, buy for cash in carload quantities and sell direct to you. By eliminating costly methods of distribution, we are able to pass on to you substantial savings up to 50%. You not only save money but you are assured of highest quality.

All LIGHTMASTER fixtures in this book are listed as standard by Underwriters' Laboratories which is your assurance of highest quality and safe construction. This includes all switches, sockets, fittings and wiring.

LIGHTMASTER Fixtures Are Easy to Install

LIGHTMASTER fixtures are completely wired and the only tools needed for installing them are a screwdriver and a pair of pliers. They are supplied with one of the two types of connectors illustrated at the right, both of which also are listed as standard by Underwriters' Laboratories. Connections are made quickly and easily without solder or tape.

When you modernize or redecorate, give thought to your lighting fixtures. Make them a definite part of your room settings. Look at the many new groups in this book and select the one best suited to your home. Your investment will be returned many times in beauty as well as better light—better sight.

LIGHTMASTER *Fixtures are Listed as Standard by Underwriters' Laboratories*

SEARS, ROEBUCK AND CO.

Lightmaster
Electric
Lighting Fixtures Are Easy to Install

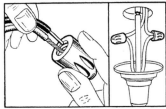

● Remove about ½ inch of insulation from wires in outlet box and about ¾ inch from wires in fixture. Be sure to scrape both clean. Hold wire from fixture and wire from outlet box together so that insulation is even. Insert into porcelain thimble-like connector held in right hand. By pushing and turning to right a safe permanent connection is made. No tape—no solder. Listed by Underwriters' Laboratories.

● Remove insulation from wires as described above and twist securely together. Then insert in bakelite connector as shown above and tighten screw securely. This clamps both wires tightly in a safe, trouble-proof connection. No tape—no solder. Listed by Underwriters' Laboratories.

GOLDEN JUBILEE—for Modern Indirect Lighting

EYESIGHT cannot be replaced, but you *can* replace lighting fixtures with those that save your eyes. The GOLDEN JUBILEE group shown above was designed especially for Sears to conform with I.E.S. Engineers' requirements. They are made of spun steel finished in antique ivory with gold color stars and trimming. The light is thrown against the ceiling to be reflected down without glare and practically no shadows. A louvre opening near the top emits just enough light to give the fixture a rich effect when lighted. A favored type for new modern homes.

20 N 5762	20 N 5761	20 N 5763	20 N 5760
Ceiling type.—*Lower left.* Length, 11½ in. Diam. 10¾ in. Especially good for bedroom or halls. We recommend using a bulb of at least 100-watt size. For wall switch.	Ceiling type.—*Upper left.* Length, 13½ in. Diam. 16½ in. Ideal for living rooms or dining rooms. We recommend using two bulbs of at least 100-watt size. For wall switch.	Bracket type.—*In the center.* Height, 7¼ inches. Width, 5 inches. Useful as auxiliary lights on the wall of any room. We recommend using a 60-watt bulb. With turn switch.	Drop style.—*Above at right.* Length, 33 in. Diameter 16½ in. Well suited to dining rooms. We recommend using two bulbs of at least 100-watt size. For wall switch.
$125.00 – 140.00	$140.00 – 175.00	$100.00 – 125.00	$150.00 – 200.00

Refer to Enclosed Price List for Prices

"AMBASSADOR"
See Page 16

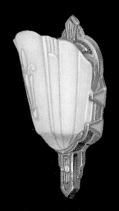
"WINDSOR"
See Page 17

"FLEURETTE"
See Page 18

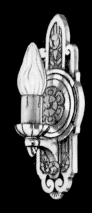
"FERNDALE"
See Page 19

"BROADWAY"
See Page 20

SAMPLE COLOR ILLUSTRATIONS
of Fixtures Shown in this Book

"HARTFORD"
See Page 21

"BERKELEY"
See Page 22

"EMPIRE"
See Page 23

"MARIETTA"
See Page 24

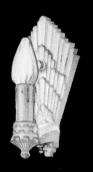
"SUNBURST"
See Page 24

"JAMESTOWN"
See Page 24

"ECONOMY"
See Page 25

"CANTON"
See Page 25

"DRESDEN"
See Page 25

"NEO-CLASSIC"
See Page 2

"PROGRESS"
See Page 3

"ZEPHYR"
See Page 4

"LOUVRE"
See Page 5

SAMPLE COLOR ILLUSTRATIONS
of Fixtures Shown in this Book

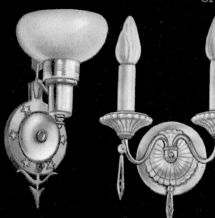

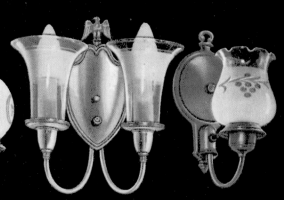

"FEDERAL"
See Page 6

"ARISTOCRAT"
See Page 7

"STUYVESANT"
See Page 8

"ARGYLE"
See Page 9

"CHELSEA"
See Page 10

"CAMBRIDGE"
See Page 11

"PLYMOUTH"
See Page 12

"VALLEY FORGE"
See Page 13

"ROYAL"
See Page 14

"FLEUR-DE-LIS"
See Page 15

·PROGRESS·
New as Tomorrow··yet not Extreme

$200.00 – 275.00

$145.00 – 175.00

$225.00 – 300.00

$120.00 – 145.00

$100.00 – 125.00

An Example of Chromium Finish Tastefully Used

THE smart new lines—the contrast of polished chrome and rich maroon are instantly appealing in the PROGRESS group. Modern it is, but it's just as livable as your favorite chair. Constructed with a framework of durable castings finished in deep maroon. Canopies, shade holders and the shapely risers just below the chains, are polished chromium plate. The saucer shades of glossy ivory color glass, diffuse the light evenly, while a portion of it is reflected indirectly from the ceiling. The 5-light fixture Ⓐ has a 4-way switch permitting 2, 3 or 5 lights to be turned on. The PROGRESS group is a wise choice for those who are modernizing as well as for those who are building. It is a design that will be pleasing today, tomorrow and years from now. These fixtures will also add a fresh note to your room interiors. *Refer to enclosed price list for prices.*

Ⓐ 20 N 5700	Ⓑ 20 N 5701	Ⓒ 20 N 5703	Ⓓ 20 N 5704	Ⓔ 20 N 5702
Five-Light Drop with 4-Way Switch	Five-Light Semi-Ceiling	Three-Light Semi-Ceiling	One-Light Hall	One-Light Bracket with Turn Switch
Width, 20¼ inches	Width, 20 inches	Width, 14¾ inches	Width, 7½ inches	Width, 6¼ inches
Length, 38 inches	Length, 15 inches	Length, 9 inches	Length, 36¼ inches	Length, 5½ inches

Removable chain links permit adjusting length to height of ceiling.

SEARS, ROEBUCK AND CO. 〖 3

· NEO-CLASSIC ·
Combination Modern and Classic

B $225.00 – 250.00

C $145.00 – 185.00

E $25.00 – 35.00

D $100.00 – 125.00

A $250.00 – 300.00

F $115.00 – 125.00

Outstanding Design . . . Two Beautiful Color Combinations

"SOMETHING old, something new"—and the result is this beautiful group of fixtures shown above. A motif from the ancient Greeks adapted to modern trends makes one of the most striking designs we have ever seen—an exclusive Sears product. Made of spun brass with straight hand decorated opal glass shades. A chaste wreath design is carried out on both the fixture and the shades. You have your choice of two smart color combinations: Antiqued Chinese Red with decorations in Gold color or Corn Yellow with decorations in Black and Gold color. The 5-light fixture Ⓐ has a 4-way switch making it possible to turn on 2, 3 or 5 lights. Specify color combination when ordering. The NEO-CLASSIC group has wide application because it will harmonize with almost any type of furnishings—in homes new or old. *Refer to enclosed price list for prices.*

Ⓐ 20 N 5750	Ⓑ 20 N 5755	Ⓒ 20 N 5751	Ⓓ 20 N 5752	Ⓔ 20 N 5754	Ⓕ 20 N 5753
Five-Light Drop Type; 4-way Switch	Five-Light Semi-Ceiling	Three-Light Semi-Ceiling	One-Light Ceiling Hall Light	One-Light Ceiling	One-Light Bracket with Turn Switch
Width, 16½ in.	Width, 16½ in.	Width, 11 inches	Width, 6¼ in.	Width, 6 inches	Width, 3½ inches
Length, 36 in.	Length, 11¾ in.	Length, 12 inches	Length, 10½ in.	Length, 2 inches	Length, 7½ inches

Removable chain links in drop fixtures permit adjusting length to height of ceiling.

22 SEARS, ROEBUCK AND CO.

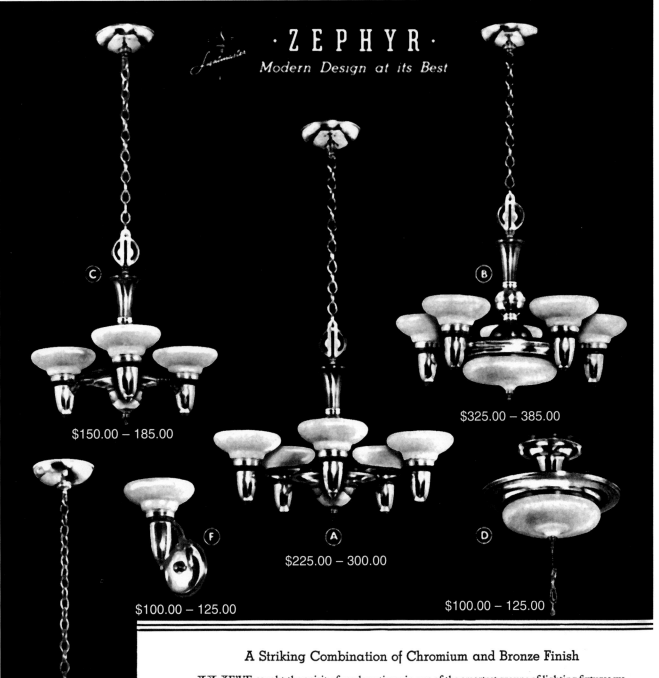

· Z E P H Y R ·
Modern Design at its Best

$150.00 – 185.00

$325.00 – 385.00

$225.00 – 300.00

$100.00 – 125.00

$100.00 – 125.00

$100.00 – 125.00

A Striking Combination of Chromium and Bronze Finish

WE'VE caught the spirit of modern times in one of the smartest groups of lighting fixtures we have ever seen. An exclusive Sears design. Sharply molded aluminum castings form the framework while Chromium plated spun brass is used for the shade holders, flared columns and other decorative parts. The background color of the framework and chains is a rich dark bronze color. Glossy ivory colored glass shades are made in a wide bowl design. Part of the light is reflected indirectly from the ceiling and part of it is diffused through the shades. The 6-light Ⓑ fixture has a glass bottom and a 4-way switch that turns on 1, 5, or 6 lights. The 5-light Ⓐ style has a 4-way switch that turns on 2, 3, or 5 lights. While essentially modern, ZEPHYR fixtures are not limited only to so-called "modern" homes. *Refer to enclosed price list for prices.*

Ⓐ 20 N 5200	Ⓑ 20 N 5201	Ⓒ 20 N 5202	Ⓓ 20 N 5199	Ⓔ 20 N 5203	Ⓕ 20 N 5204
Five-Light with 4-way Switch	Six-Light with 4-way Switch	Three-Light with Switch	Two-Light Ceiling Pull Cord Switch	One-Light Hall with Switch	One-Light Bracket with Turn Switch
Width, 20¼ in.	Width, 20¼ in.	Width, 16½ in.	Width, 12 in.	Width, 7 inches	Width, 5¾ inches
Length, 48 in.	Length, 48 in.	Length, 48 in.	Length, 8½ in.	Length, 45 inches	Length, 8½ inches

Drop fixtures have removable chain links that permit adjusting length to height of ceiling.

42][SEARS, ROEBUCK AND CO.

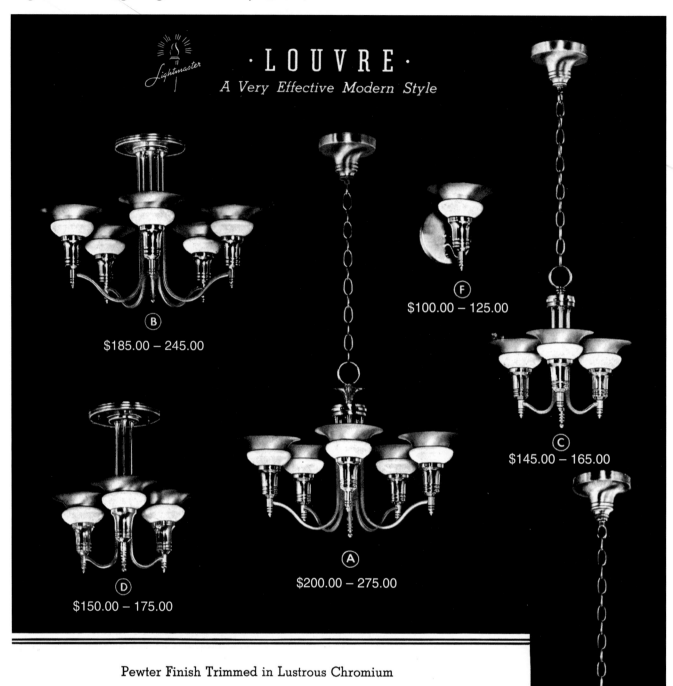

LOUVRE

A Very Effective Modern Style

Lightmaster

B
$185.00 – 245.00

F
$100.00 – 125.00

C
$145.00 – 165.00

D
$150.00 – 175.00

A
$200.00 – 275.00

E
$100.00 – 120.00

Pewter Finish Trimmed in Lustrous Chromium

ANOTHER modern group for those who like the beauty of simplicity. Stately and graceful, with pewter finish chains and tubular risers. The deep shade holders and other bright parts are polished chromium plate to furnish the needed contrast for a rich effect. Opal white glass bowl-like shades are mounted with pewter finished deflectors that spread the light more evenly about the room. Both deflectors and glass shades are easily removed for cleaning. The 5-light Ⓐ drop has a 4-way switch that turns on 2, 3 or 5 lights. Here again are fixtures to harmonize with homes that are furnished in the most modern manner. At the same time they are designed with such good taste that they harmonize beautifully with furniture in the average home of today. An exclusive Sears design. *Refer to enclosed price list for prices.*

Ⓐ 20 N 5740	Ⓑ 20 N 5741	Ⓒ 20 N 5745	Ⓓ 20 N 5744	Ⓔ 20 N 5743	Ⓕ 20 N 5742
Five-Light Drop	Five-Light	Three-Light Drop	Three-Light	One-Light	One-Light Bracket
4-way Switch	Semi-Ceiling	with Switch	Semi-Ceiling	Hall Fixture	with Turn Switch
Width, 19 inches	Width, 19 in.	Width, 12½ in.	Width, 12½ in.	Width, 9¼ in.	Width, 5¾ inches
Length, 35 inches	Length, 13½ in.	Length, 35 in.	Length, 13¼ in.	Length, 35 in.	Length, 5 inches

Drop fixtures have removable chain links that permit adjusting length to height of ceiling.

SEARS, ROEBUCK AND CO. 〖5

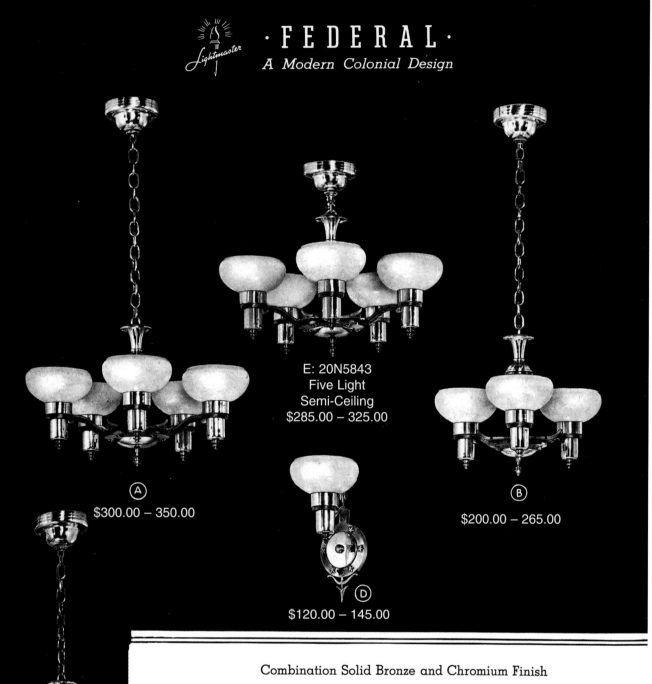

·FEDERAL·
A Modern Colonial Design

E: 20N5843
Five Light
Semi-Ceiling
$285.00 – 325.00

Ⓐ
$300.00 – 350.00

Ⓑ
$200.00 – 265.00

Ⓓ
$120.00 – 145.00

Ⓒ
$150.00 – 185.00

Combination Solid Bronze and Chromium Finish

THE stately grace and beauty of Colonial design adapted to the crisp modern lines of today. Here is one of the most effective groups for homes furnished with Modern Colonial furniture. An exclusive Sears design. The solid bronze framework of the FEDERAL group has a statuary brushed finish with a raised star design. Against this are chromium finished shade holders, ornaments and canopies to lend smart contrast to the entire ensemble. Bowl shape white opal glass shades are amber tinted inside to produce a soft pleasing light. The semi-ceiling fixture shown is the 5-light drop arranged in this manner by removing the chain. The 5-light Ⓐ drop has a 4-way switch to turn on 2, 3 or 5 lights and the 3-light Ⓑ drop an "on and off" switch. In the FEDERAL group you will find a type of design that will still be smart years after they are installed.

Refer to enclosed price list for prices.

Ⓐ 20 N 5840	Ⓑ 20 N 5841	Ⓒ 20 N 5849	Ⓓ 20 N 5842
Five-Light Drop with 4-way Switch Width, 19 inches Length, 32 inches	Three-Light Drop with "on-off" Switch Width, 15 inches Length, 32 inches	One-Light Hall Fixture with Switch Width, 8½ inches Length, 32 inches	One-Light Bracket Fixture with Turn Switch Width, 5½ inches Length, 9½ inches

Drop fixtures have removable chain links that permit adjusting length to height of ceiling.

6₂ SEARS, ROEBUCK AND CO.

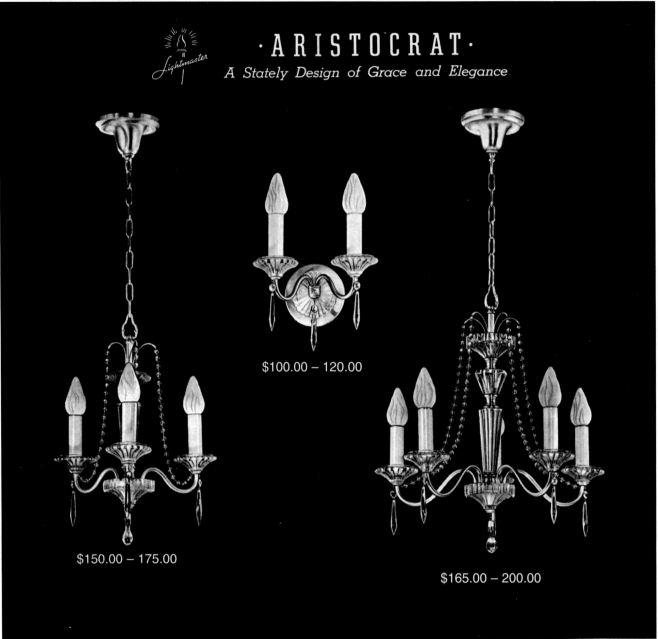

· A R I S T O C R A T ·

A Stately Design of Grace and Elegance

$100.00 – 120.00

$150.00 – 175.00

$165.00 – 200.00

Sparkling Crystal Glass and Silver Plate!

INSPIRED by the chandeliers and candelabra that furnished light for gay balls and formal dinners of Colonial statesmen. All metal parts of these fixtures are silver plated to form a fitting complement to the clear fluted crystal glass columns and ornaments. Tall white candles rest in crystal glass trays with long cut pendant drops that catch and reflect the light with their many facets. Strings of cut crystal beads drape gracefully from the center of the fixture to each light. The Aristocrat group offers unusual elegance for those who want something finer in lighting fixtures. There is also a sparkle and gaiety to them that adds much to the appearance of rooms where they are used. Their brilliance lends charm by day as well as at night. They are sold exclusively by Sears. Crystal fixtures of this type are easily cleaned by using a cloth dampened in a 10% alcohol and water solution. *Refer to enclosed price list for prices.*

20 N 5814	20 N 5811	20 N 5810
Three-Light Candle Fixture	Two-Light Bracket with Turn Switch	Five-Light Candle Fixture
Width, 14¾ inches; Length 41 inches	Width, 10¼ inches; Length, 9 inches	Width, 20¼ inches; Length, 41 inches

Drop fixtures have removable chain links that permit adjusting length to height of ceiling.

SEARS, ROEBUCK AND CO. [7

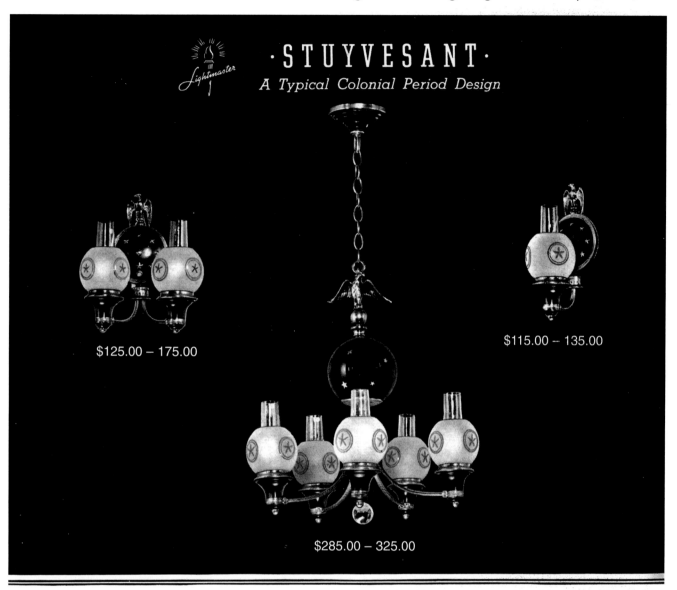

· S T U Y V E S A N T ·
A Typical Colonial Period Design

$125.00 – 175.00

$115.00 – 135.00

$285.00 – 325.00

Spun Brass Finished in Ebony and Gold Color

THOSE who appreciate true Colonial design will recognize the care with which every detail of the STUYVESANT group has been carried out. Ebony black and gold is the color scheme that has been used so effectively. Here is a style of fixture that harmonizes beautifully with all types of Colonial furnishings. The material used is spun brass, with chains, eaglet and arms that support the lights finished in a ruddy gold color. The large ebony black glass ball on the 5-light fixture is decorated with gold color stars and so are the round plaques on the bracket fixtures. The globe portion of the glass* shades is frosted and has a hand cut star design, while the chimney-like extensions are clear glass. They are authentic reproductions of the glass chimneys used on old Colonial oil lamps. If you are looking for Colonial fixtures of exceptional beauty and correctness of detail, we strongly recommend the STUYVESANT group. Whether your furnishings are Colonial or not, these beautiful fixtures will add a decorative note that will improve the appearance of your rooms. They are beautifully proportioned and well constructed throughout—excellent values in high grade fixtures. For those who are modernizing present homes or building new ones, the STUYVESANT group will be a wise choice. You will be proud of these fixtures for years to come. *Refer to enclosed price list for prices.*

*GLASS MADE IN CZECHOSLOVAKIA.

20 N 5726	20 N 5725	20 N 5727
Two-light Bracket with turn switch	Five-light drop fixture	One-light Bracket with turn switch
Width, 10 inches; length, 12 inches	Width, 19½ inches; length, 47 inches	Width, 5 inches; length, 12 inches

Drop fixtures have removable chain links that permit adjusting length to height of ceiling.

8 ┃ SEARS, ROEBUCK AND CO.

·ARGYLE·

They Possess an Air of Distinction

Ⓓ
$100.00 – 125.00

Ⓒ
$120.00 – 145.00

Ⓐ
$145.00 – 200.00

Ⓑ
$150.00 – 225.00

Gleaming Silver Plate Trimmed in Gold Color

HERE in the beautiful ARGYLE group Colonial design has been expertly employed in adapting it to present day lighting needs. There is a simple grace in every line that achieves distinction without undue ornamentation. The gracefully curved arms and the tall flared glass shades are features that make the ARGYLE fixtures one of our most outstanding groups.

The principal parts of these fixtures are spun brass, plated with pure silver. For contrast, gold color is used for the finish of the eaglets and the ornamental ball on the 5-light Ⓐ drop fixture. The shields are silver plated with a raised gold color border. Tall glass shades on the 5-light Ⓑ upright fixture and the 2-light bracket are flared at the top and frosted in a wide band. The frosted portion diffuses the light evenly to all parts of the room.

Your home need not be furnished in true Colonial period for you to enjoy the distinction of ARGYLE fixtures. They lend beauty and modern lighting efficiency wherever they are installed. You can select them and be confident that they will add to the effectiveness of your interior decorating scheme. Authentic design, excellent materials and careful workmanship are features that make these outstanding fixtures real values. *Refer to enclosed price list for prices.*

Ⓐ 20 N 5721	Ⓑ 20 N 5720	Ⓒ 20 N 5722	Ⓓ 20 N 5723
Five-light drop fixture Width, 18½ inches; length, 40½ inches	Five-light shaded candle drop style. Width, 19¾ inches; length, 40½ inches	One-light shaded candle Hall fixture (ceiling type) Width, 6½ in.; length, 13 in.	Two-light shaded candle bracket with turn switch Width, 10½ in.; lgth, 10¼ in.

Drop fixtures have removable chain links that permit adjusting length to height of ceiling.

SEARS, ROEBUCK AND CO.

·CHELSEA·
Lightmaster
Quaint New England Design

Ⓐ $185.00 – 225.00

Ⓔ $120.00 – 130.00

Ⓕ $100.00 – 115.00

Ⓓ $100.00 – 135.00

Ⓑ $175.00 – 200.00

Ⓒ $100.00 – 120.00

Spun Brass Finished in Antique Bronze

WHEN colonial craftsmen produced their work they had in mind utility and durabiiity. In producing something that served its purpose well, they also created a rugged type of beauty that has remained throughout centuries. Sold exclusively by Sears.

The CHELSEA group of fixtures are authentic Colonial designs in spun brass, finished in statuary bronze color. The glass chimneys are frosted and each one bears a hand-cut authentic grape design that further carries out the Colonial motif.

This group is unusually complete, offering two types of 5-light fixtures, one an upright style with glass chimneys and the other a simple drop light for use with decorative ball shape lamps. A 2-light dome ceiling light is also included for sunporches, breakfast rooms, halls, etc. There is a CHELSEA fixture for every downstairs room. *Refer to enclosed price list for prices.*

Ⓐ 20 N 5275	Ⓑ 20 N 5276	Ⓒ 20 N 5277	Ⓓ 20 N 5281	Ⓔ 20 N 5279	Ⓕ 20 N 5278
Five-Light Upright Style Width, 20 inches Length, 39 inches	Five-Light Drop Style Width, 18 inches Length, 39 inches	One-Light Hall Pendant Width, 9¼ in. Length, 39 in.	Two-Light Dome Type Ceiling Width, 11⅛ inches Length, 8 inches	Two-Light Bracket with Turn Switch Width, 10 inches Length, 10 inches	One-Light Bracket with Turn Switch Width, 5 inches Length, 10 inches

Drop fixtures have removable chain links that permit adjusting length to height of ceiling.

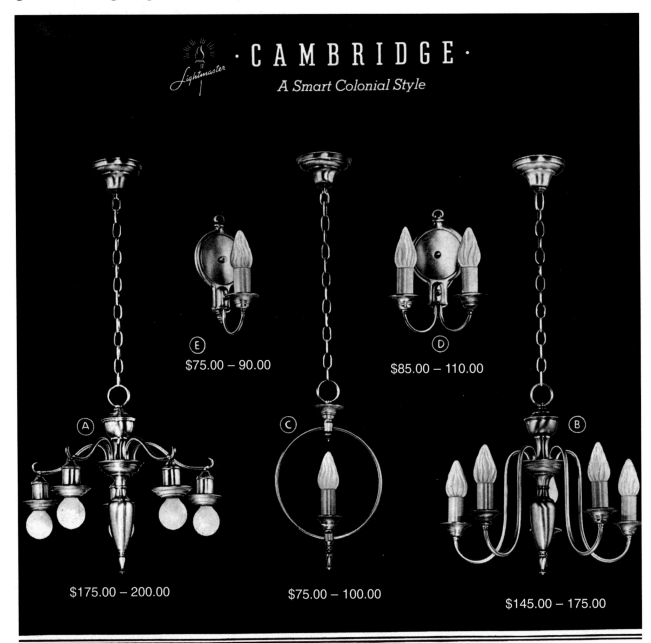

· C A M B R I D G E ·
A Smart Colonial Style

(E) $75.00 – 90.00

(D) $85.00 – 110.00

(A) $175.00 – 200.00

(C) $75.00 – 100.00

(B) $145.00 – 175.00

Brushed Pewter Finish Adds Richness

HERE is another group of Colonial fixtures that feature the beauty of simplicity with a minimum of ornamentation. Moderately priced. They are made of spun brass and finished in soft brushed pewter that harmonizes with any color scheme of interior decoration. The 5-light © candle fixture has long graceful tubular arms that support ivory color candles. The two wall brackets are of fine cast aluminum with spun brass for the round placques; both have convenient turn switches.

The CAMBRIDGE group offers many possibilities to those who want smart fixtures at a reasonable cost. They have become one of our most popular groups both for those who are modernizing and for new home builders. Why not select this smart group for refixturing your home? You will be sure of a design that will always be in good taste. *Refer to enclosed price list for prices.* Sold exclusively by Sears.

(A) 20 N 5266	(B) 20 N 5265	(C) 20 N 5267	(D) 20 N 5269	(E) 20 N 5268
Five-Light Drop for ball shape lamps Width, 18 inches Length, 41 inches	Five-Light Candle Type Fixture Width, 17¾ inches Length, 41 inches	One-Light Candle Style Hall Fixture Width, 9¼ inches Length, 41 inches	Two-Light Bracket with Turn Switch Width, 8¼ inches Length, 10 inches	One-Light Bracket with Turn Switch Width, 4⅞ inches Length, 10 inches

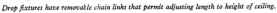

Drop fixtures have removable chain links that permit adjusting length to height of ceiling.

SEARS, ROEBUCK AND CO. [211

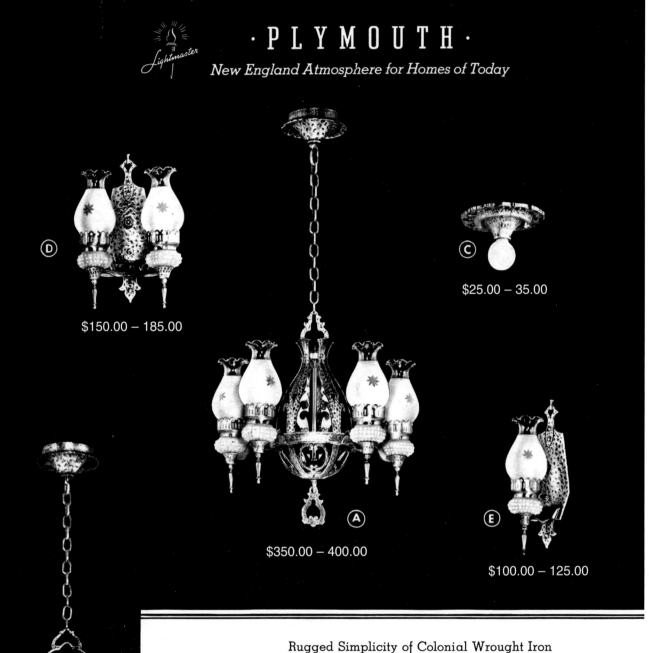

· P L Y M O U T H ·

New England Atmosphere for Homes of Today

$150.00 – 185.00

$25.00 – 35.00

$350.00 – 400.00

$100.00 – 125.00

$125.00 – 145.00

Rugged Simplicity of Colonial Wrought Iron

COLLECTORS have searched the by-ways of New England for relics like those that furnished the inspiration for this handsome group of fixtures. Sold exclusively by Sears. A design that brings back the beauty of early American hammered iron. Hand wrought iron was carefully reproduced in aluminum castings to form the sturdy framework. Frosted hob-nail glass founts, chimneys with hand cut star design and cut brass holders all serve to carry out the oil lamp motif. The 5-light fixture Ⓐ is an authentic reproduction of an oil lamp chandelier used by old Plymouth Colony settlers. Those who admire Colonial design will appreciate this group, but you don't have to own a Colonial house to enjoy these attractive fixtures. Sound quality and authentic design have made the PLYMOUTH fixtures one of our most favored groups. They are in good taste with average furniture in the home of today. *Refer to enclosed price list for prices.*

Ⓐ 20 N 5285	Ⓑ 20 N 5286	Ⓒ 20 N 5289	Ⓓ 20 N 5288	Ⓔ 20 N 5287
Five-Light Upright Style	One-Light Hall	One-Light Ceiling	Two-Light Bracket with Turn Switch	One-Light Bracket with Turn Switch
Width, 18 inches	Width, 7 inches	Width, 7½ inches	Width, 9 inches	Width, 4¾ inches
Length, 36 inches	Length, 36 inches	Length, 2 inches	Length, 13 inches	Length, 13 inches

Drop fixtures have removable chain links that permit adjusting length to height of ceiling.

12 ‖ SEARS, ROEBUCK AND CO.

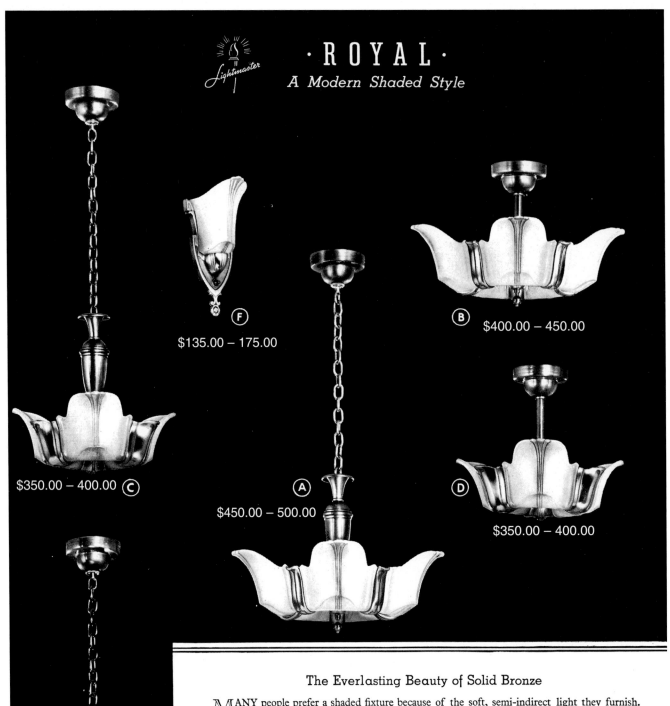

·ROYAL·

A Modern Shaded Style

F $135.00 – 175.00

B $400.00 – 450.00

C $350.00 – 400.00

A $450.00 – 500.00

D $350.00 – 400.00

E $185.00 – 235.00

The Everlasting Beauty of Solid Bronze

MANY people prefer a shaded fixture because of the soft, semi-indirect light they furnish. This group is sold exclusively by Sears. In the ROYAL series, solid cast bronze has been used effectively and an added richness is achieved by using a statuary brushed finish. Smartly designed amber tinted glass shades cast a mellow glow of light that is soft, yet ample to provide eye-saving illumination in all parts of the room. The ROYAL group of lighting fixtures fits into the average modern home and lends a welcome note of distinction. The 5-light drop has a 4-way switch, permitting you to turn on 2, 3 or 5 lights. The hall light and bracket have on and off switches. The glass shades on all fixtures in this group can be easily removed for cleaning. *See the enclosed price list for prices.*

Ⓐ 20 N 5843	Ⓑ 20 N 5844	Ⓒ 20 N 5845	Ⓓ 20 N 5846	Ⓔ 20 N 5847	Ⓕ 20 N 5848
Five-Light Drop 4-Way Switch Width, 18¼ in. Length, 34 in.	Five-Light Semi-Ceiling Fixture Width, 18¼ in. Length, 12 in.	Three-Light Drop with Switch Width, 14½ in. Length, 34 in.	Three-Light Semi-Ceiling Fixture Width, 14½ inches Length, 12¼ inches	One-Light Hall with Switch Width, 10 in. Length, 30 in.	One-Light Bracket with Turn Switch Width, 14⅜ in. Length, 10¾ in.

Removable chain links in drop fixtures permit adjusting length to height of ceiling.

14₂] SEARS, ROEBUCK AND CO.

·FLEUR-DE-LIS·

Amber Tinted Shades Soften Light

Note: Please take special notice of beautiful cut work in the metal frames. It resembles the old cut work of Battenburg lace.

Ⓒ $450.00 – 675.00

Ⓑ $550.00 – 750.00

Ⓐ $350.00 – 400.00

Ⓕ $150.00 – 200.00

Ⓓ $750.00 – 950.00

Ⓔ $225.00 – 285.00

Gold and Silver Color Tints in a Design of Great Richness

THE style of the FLEUR-DE-LIS was taken from the French Renaissance period. Rich ornamentation in metal work has been used here in a graceful and charming manner without being too ornate. The finish is polished silver effect with gold color high lights. Amber tinted glass shades, arranged for semi-indirect lighting, produce a pleasing mellow glow that is soft and at the same time conforms with the requirements of proper illumination. The FLEUR-DE-LIS is one of our most popular fixture groups—sold exclusively by Sears. Priced to save you money.

Fixture Ⓑ has a switch that controls all lights. Fixture Ⓓ has a center light that makes it especially desirable for dining rooms, and a 4-way switch permits you to turn on 1, 5 or 6 lights. *Refer to enclosed price list for prices.*

Ⓐ 20 N 5127	Ⓑ 20 N 5122	Ⓒ 20 N 5124	Ⓓ 20 N 5110	Ⓔ 20 N 5126	Ⓕ 20 N 5129
Three-Light Drop Fixture	Five-Light Drop with Switch	Five-Light Semi-Ceiling Fixture	Six-Light Drop 4-way Switch	Two-Light Drop Fixture	One-Light Bracket with Turn Switch
Width, 15 inches	Width, 19 inches	Width, 19 inches	Width, 19 inches	Width, 13¼ inches	Width, 5½ inches
Length, 48 inches	Length, 48 inches	Length, 26 inches	Length, 48 inches	Length, 48 inches	Length, 13 inches

Removable chain links in drop fixtures permit adjusting length to height of ceiling.

SEARS, ROEBUCK AND CO. ⟦15

·AMBASSADOR·
In Tune with the Modern Trend

B $375.00 – 435.00

C $300.00 – 325.00

E $125.00 – 150.00

A $475.00 – 550.00

D $175.00 – 225.00

Cast Aluminum Finished in Silver and Gold Effect

MODERN design in its more modified form has been employed in the AMBASSADOR group to gain the grace and beauty of simple lines. The metal parts are constructed of cast aluminum finished in silver effect with gold color highlighting. Softly tinted amber color glass shades are designed in harmony with the rest of the fixture. The lighting is partly indirect by reflection from the ceiling and partly direct in a cheerful diffused glow. Here is a design that harmonizes with the average home of today. The 7-light fixture Ⓐ has a glass bottom and a 4-way switch that permits lighting 2, 5 or 7 bulbs. This gives three degrees of light intensity through all five shades and the glass bottom. Those who like modern shaded fixtures will appreciate the AMBASSADOR group for richness of color and design. *Refer to the enclosed price list for prices.* Sold exclusively by Sears.

Ⓐ 20 N 5855	Ⓑ 20 N 5856	Ⓒ 20 N 5857	Ⓓ 20 N 5858	Ⓔ 20 N 5859
Seven-Light Drop with 4-way Switch Width, 18 inches Length, 36 inches	Five-Light Semi-Ceiling. No Switch Width, 18 inches Length, 14½ inches	Three-Light Drop with Switch Width, 13 inches Length, 36 inches	Two-Light Drop with Switch Width, 13 inches Length, 35 inches	One-Light Bracket with Turn Switch Width, 6 inches Length, 11 inches

Removable chain links in drop fixtures permit adjusting length to height of ceiling

16 ▐ SEARS, ROEBUCK AND CO.

· W I N D S O R ·
Beautifully Shaded · · Smartly Designed

(E) $125.00 – 145.00

(D) $400.00 – 450.00

(B) $465.00 – 550.00

(F) $125.00 – 140.00

(A) $585.00 – 675.00

(C) $425.00 – 475.00

Finished in Dull Bronze with Amber Toned Shades

HERE is another contribution to better lighting in the home—a group of lighting fixtures that combine correct illumination with decorative qualities. The castings used in the WINDSOR group are solid aluminum, sharply molded and finished in dark bronze. Highlights of a lighter toned bronze form an attractive contrast to the darker background. There is a Grecian motif in the design of the glass shades that adds a classic touch to these beautiful fixtures. Indirect light is reflected from the ceiling while a soft diffused glow is emitted from the satin finished glass shades that are tinted a delicate amber color. Fixture Ⓓ, 3-light drop, is especially desirable for small dining rooms. Fixture Ⓐ, the 6-light drop, has a glass bottom and a 4-way switch that turns on 1, 5 or 6 lights. *Refer to enclosed price list for prices.*

Ⓐ 20 N 5206	Ⓑ 20 N 5205	Ⓒ 20 N 5207	Ⓓ 20 N 5208	Ⓔ 20 N 5209	Ⓕ 20 N 5210
Six-Light Drop	Five-Light Drop	Five-Light Semi-	Three-Light Drop	One-Light	One-Light Bracket
4-way Switch	with Switch	Ceiling Fixture	with Switch and Outlet	Ceiling Fixture	with Turn Switch
Width, 18¼ in.	Width, 16¼ in.	Width, 16¼ in.	Width, 13¼ inches	Width, 9¾ in.	Width, 5 in.
Length, 48 in.	Length, 40 in.	Length, 17 in.	Length, 48 inches	Length, 9½ in.	Length, 11 in.

Removable chain links in drop fixtures permit adjusting length to height of ceiling.

SEARS, ROEBUCK AND CO.

Lightmaster

·FERNDALE·
Rugged Design ·· Graceful Proportions

(F) $135.00 – 150.00

(D) $250.00 – 300.00

(B) $325.00 – 385.00

(C) $250.00 – 300.00

(A) $250.00 – 300.00

(G) $125.00 – 145.00

(H) $85.00 – 110.00

(E) $125.00 – 145.00

A Complete Group in Beautifully Cast Solid Aluminum

STATELY and impressive—characterized by rugged wrought effect designs. The finish is silver color against a dull gold color background. Certain portions are highly polished and buffed to form contrast. The 7-light drop is well suited to large rooms. Six outside lights and one central light inside a frosted glass bowl afford ample illumination. The 3-light drop makes an ideal type for sun rooms, breakfast nooks, etc. Equipped with convenience outlet and switch that controls the lights independently of the outlet. *Refer to enclosed price list for prices.*

(A) **20 N 5575**—Five-Light Drop Fixture. Width, 16¾ inches. Length, 46 inches.

(B) **20 N 5573**—Seven-Light Drop Fixture. With 4-way switch that turns on 1, 6 or 7 lights. Width, 16¾ inches. Length, 46 inches.

(C) **20 N 5576**—Five-Light Candle Drop Fixture. Width, 16¾ inches. Length, 46 inches.

(D) **20 N 5577**—Five-Light Semi-Ceiling Fixture. Width, 17 inches. Length, 20½ inches.

(E) **20 N 5574**—Three-Light Drop Fixture. Width, 12⅛ in. Length, 46 in. Has convenience outlet and switch.

(F) **20 N 5578**—One-Light Hall Fixture. Width, 7⅜ inches. Length, 46 inches.

(G) **20 N 5580**—Two-Light Bracket Fixture. Width, 8¾ inches. Length, 11⅛ inches. Has turn switch.

(H) **20 N 5579**—One-Light Bracket Fixture. Width, 4½ inches. Length, 11⅛ inches. Has turn switch.

Removable chain links in drop fixtures permit adjusting length to height of ceiling.

SEARS, ROEBUCK AND CO. [19

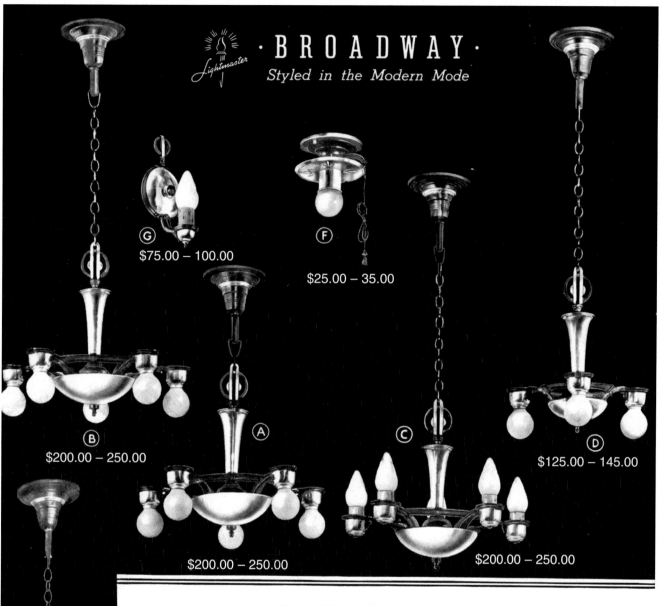

Lightmaster · B R O A D W A Y ·
Styled in the Modern Mode

G $75.00 – 100.00

F $25.00 – 35.00

B $200.00 – 250.00

A $200.00 – 250.00

C $200.00 – 250.00

D $125.00 – 145.00

E $110.00 – 125.00

Crisp, Modern Lines Lend New Charm

THE smooth flowing lines of modern design are fast becoming a part of our daily environment and true modern design is pleasing to the eye. If you like the new lines of motor cars and furniture you will like them in the BROADWAY group of lighting fixtures. These beautiful fixtures will harmonize with interior decorating schemes in any American home. If your home is furnished along modern lines, this group of fixtures will harmonize perfectly with your furniture and your entire decorative scheme. Yet the design is one that can be used with furniture of almost any period or style.

Every detail of the BROADWAY group has been carefully worked out. The framework is cast aluminum, finished in deep maroon. Other parts, such as flared columns, candle holders and large bowls in drop fixtures, are polished chromium finish.

Smart and practical, yet the BROADWAY fixtures are priced reasonably. Modernize with this charming group. Sold exclusively by Sears. (Fixture Ⓐ is the same as drop fixture Ⓑ with chain links removed. Order 20 N 5211.) *Refer to enclosed price list for prices.*

ⒶⒷ 20 N 5211	Ⓒ 20 N 5212	Ⓓ 20 N 5214	Ⓔ 20 N 5217	Ⓕ 20 N 5215	Ⓖ 20 N 5216
Five-Light Drop with Switch	Five-Light Candle Fixture with Switch	Three-Light Drop Fixture with Switch	One-Light Hall Drop Fixture Pull Switch	One-Light Ceiling Fixture Pull Switch	One-Light Bracket with Turn Switch
Explained above					
Width, 16¾ inches	Width, 16¾ inches	Width, 12⅜ inches	Width, 6¾ inches	Width, 6 inches	Width, 4½ inches
Length, 45 inches	Length, 45 inches	Length, 45 inches	Length, 37 inches	Length, 4 inches	Length, 10 inches

Drop fixtures have removable chain links that permit adjusting length to height of ceiling.

· H A R T F O R D ·

Designed in Good Taste · · Moderately Priced

Silver Highlights on a Background of Gold Color

SMART as they are, the HARTFORD group of lighting fixtures are priced low enough for those who want to modernize at a reasonable figure. In finish, design and quality of construction, these fixtures are better values than you will find in similar fixtures sold elsewhere at 50% higher prices. They are designed along simple lines with good proportions and are constructed of carefully molded aluminum castings. The design is brought out in a sharp, clean-cut manner. The HARTFORD group is attractively finished in dull gold color with accents in silver effect. The two, three and five light drop fixtures have turn switches at the bottom. The HARTFORD group offers the home and apartment owner modern lighting equipment at moderate cost. Here is an opportunity to have fixtures in your rooms that will give you correct eye-saving illumination. They will also add a new decorative note wherever they are installed. The HARTFORD is one of our most popular groups of fixtures. In design, finish and construction they are excellent values. *Refer to enclosed price list for prices.*

Ⓐ 20 N 5350 Five-Light Ceiling Fixture Width, 17½ in. Length, 5½ in.	Ⓑ 20 N 5345 Five-Light Drop with Switch Width, 17½ in. Length, 36 in.	Ⓒ 20 N 5349 Five-Light Candle Type with Switch Width, 17½ in. Length, 36 in.	Ⓓ 20 N 5346 Three-Light Drop with Switch Width, 12½ in. Length, 36 in.	Ⓔ 20 N 5351 Three-Light Ceiling Fixture Width, 12½ in. Length, 5½ in.	Ⓕ 20 N 5348 Two-Light Bracket with Turn Switch Width, 7½ in. Length, 12 in.	Ⓖ 20 N 5347 One-Light Bracket with Turn Switch Width, 4⅜ in. Length, 12 in.

Drop fixtures have removable chain links that permit adjusting length to height of ceiling.

SEARS, ROEBUCK AND CO. [21

· M A R I E T T A ·

$5.00 – 8.00

$25.00 – 35.00

$20.00 – 30.00

$30.00 – 45.00

THE MARIETTA group shown above will win your instant and lasting admiration. It is one of our most popular groups of bedroom fixtures. The finish is a dainty egg shell ivory, delicately tinted with light pastel colors Clear sharp detail in the decorations is assured by cast aluminum alloy construction which also gives unusual strength. The two and three-light fixtures are available with special pull chain arrangements permitting individual lighting of lamps. The bracket is provided with an outlet for appliances—as well as the usual switch. *Refer to enclosed price list for prices.* For illustration in natural color see inside back cover.

| One-Light Ceiling Fixture
Diameter, 5⅜ inches
Length, 3¼ inches
20 N 5332—For Wall switch
20 N 5331—Pull Chain switch | Three-Light Ceiling Fixture
Diameter, 10⅞ inches
Length, 4¼ inches
20 N 5336—For Wall switch
20 N 5335—Pull Chain switch | Two-Light Ceiling Fixture
Dimension, 13½x6½ inches
Length, 4 inches
20 N 5334—For Wall switch
20 N 5333—Pull Chain switch | One-light Bracket Fixture
With Extra Outlet
Width, 5 inches
Length, 10½ inches
20 N 5339—With Turn switch |

· S U N B U R S T ·

$7.00 – 10.00

$25.00 – 35.00

$35.00 – 50.00

$35.00 – 50.00

THE presence of these beautiful fixtures in any room of any home is constant evidence of supreme good taste. The SUNBURST group, made of long wearing, durable cast art metal, offers you a choice of two ultra-smart finishes, each a splendid example of modern art. Your choice of two finishes: plated gold color finish, or antique ivory color finish. You will find a wall bracket of the SUNBURST group in antique ivory finish illustrated on the inside page of back cover. Modernize your bedroom lighting with these smartly designed fixtures. When ordering please specify finish. *Refer to enclosed price list for prices.*

| One-Light Ceiling Fixture
Diameter, 8¼ inches
Length, 3 inches
20 N 6164—For Wall switch
20 N 6167—Pull Chain switch | Two-Light Ceiling Fixture
Dimension, 12½x9 inches
Length, 6 inches
20 N 5163—For Wall switch
20 N 5502—Pull Chain switch | Three-Light Ceiling Fixture
Diameter, 11¾ inches
Length, 6 inches
20 N 5109—For Wall switch
20 N 5503—Pull Chain switch | One-Light Bracket Fixture
Candle Type
Width, 5⅜ inches
Length, 9½ inches
20 N 6165—With Turn switch |

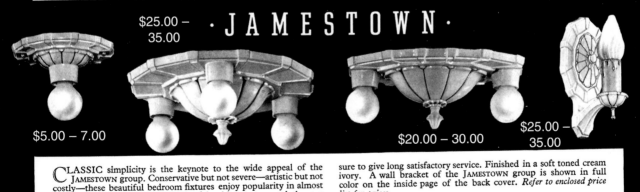

$25.00 – 35.00

· J A M E S T O W N ·

$5.00 – 7.00

$20.00 – 30.00

$25.00 – 35.00

CLASSIC simplicity is the keynote to the wide appeal of the JAMESTOWN group. Conservative but not severe—artistic but not costly—these beautiful bedroom fixtures enjoy popularity in almost every type of home. Carefully made of durable cast art metal, they are sure to give long satisfactory service. Finished in a soft toned cream ivory. A wall bracket of the JAMESTOWN group is shown in full color on the inside page of the back cover. *Refer to enclosed price list for prices.*

| One-Light Ceiling Fixture
Diameter, 7 inches
Length, 2⅜ inches
20 N 6052—For Wall switch
20 N 6053—Pull Chain switch | Three-Light Ceiling Fixture
Diameter, 13⅛ inches
Length, 4½ inches
20 N 6056—For Wall switch
20 N 6057—Pull Chain switch | Two-Light Ceiling Fixture
Dimension, 12¼x7¾ inches
Length, 4½ inches
20 N 6054—For Wall switch
20 N 6055—Pull Chain switch | One-Light Bracket Fixture
Candle Type
Width, 4¼ inches
Length, 8¼ inches
20 N 6058—With Turn switch |

Refer to enclosed price list for prices

ECONOMY

$25.00 – 35.00

$10.00 – 15.00

$20.00 – 30.00

$5.00 – 7.00

SELDOM do you see such beauty of design and color in fixtures priced so low as these—featured as the ECONOMY Group. They are typically representative of Sears outstanding fixture values. Carefully made of durable pressed steel. All except 20 N 5696 and 20 N 5697 have graceful floral designs actually pressed right into the metal—then artistically tinted in appropriate color—against a background finish of mellow old ivory color. The 20 N 5381 bracket has a convenient outlet for appliances. 20 N 5696 and 20 N 5697 are furnished in old ivory color with gold stars and spear pendant. *Refer to enclosed price list for prices.*

Two-Light Ceiling—*Round*	One-Light Bracket—*Turn Switch*	Two-Light Ceiling—*Oval*	One-Light Ceiling—*Round*
Diameter, 9 inches	Width, 5⅛ inches	Dimension, 12½x6½ inches	Diameter, 4¾ inches
Length, 5½ inches	Length, 9¾ inches	Length, 2¼ inches	Length, 3⅜ inches
20 N 5696—For Wall switch	20 N 5380—Without Outlet	20 N 5374—For Wall switch	20 N 5379—For Wall switch
20 N 5697—Pull Chain switch	20 N 5381—With Outlet	20 N 5373—Pull Chain switch	20 N 5378—Pull Chain switch

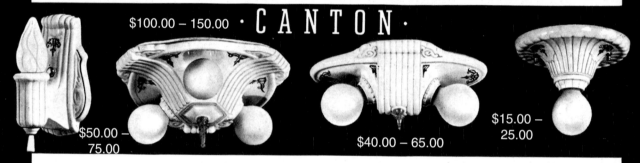

· CANTON ·

$100.00 – 150.00

$50.00 – 75.00

$40.00 – 65.00

$15.00 – 25.00

THE CANTON Group is comprised of genuine porcelain fixtures gracefully designed with an unusually pleasing underglazed decoration. These fixtures are of exceptionally fine quality with the hard ivory colored finish baked right on. They are guaranteed not to crack or craze. Each piece is washable and consequently can be kept sparkling clean and bright with little effort. Here is one of the most practical and beautiful types of fixtures you could possibly select for your bedrooms. They are priced unusually low for porcelain fixtures. See inside back cover for picture in natural color. *Refer to enclosed price list for prices.*

One-Light Bracket Fixture *For Bedroom or Bathroom*	Three-Light Ceiling Fixture	Two-Light Ceiling—*Oval*	One-Light Ceiling—*Round*
Width, 4½ inches	Diameter, 10½ inches	Dimension, 10x6 inches	Diameter, 6¾ inches
Length, 8 inches	Length, 5¼ inches	Length, 4¼ inches	Length, 2¾ inches
20 N 5506—With switch	20 N 5509—For Wall switch	20 N 5507—For Wall switch	20 N 5512—For Wall switch
	20 N 5510—Pull Chain switch	20 N 5508—Pull Chain switch	20 N 5511—Pull Chain switch

· DRESDEN ·

$50.00 – 75.00

$50.00 – 75.00

$100.00 – 150.00

$25.00 – 35.00

SIMILAR to fine china in refinement of design and appealing charm in this beautiful DRESDEN Group of genuine porcelain. The superb finish is baked on with the same precise, painstaking care that is exercised in the making of costly dinnerware. The floral motif emphasized in the decoration is shown in full color. Each piece is washable and is easily kept immaculately clean! To gain an idea of the DRESDEN's loveliness, refer to the Inside Back Cover of this catalog for picture in natural color.

One-Light Bracket Fixture *For Bedroom or Bathroom*	Two-Light Ceiling—*Oval*	Three-Light Ceiling Fixture	One-Light Ceiling—*Round*
Width, 4 inches	Dimension, 10¾x6 inches	Diameter, 10 inches	Diameter, 7 inches
Length, 7 inches	Length, 5 inches	Length, 5 inches	Length, 3 inches
20 N 5518—With switch	20 N 5516—For Wall switch	20 N 5515—For Wall switch	20 N 5517—For Wall switch
	20 N 5520—Pull Chain switch	20 N 5519—Pull Chain switch	20 N 5521—Pull Chain switch

Refer to enclosed price list for prices.

SEARS, ROEBUCK AND CO. 〖 25

· BATHROOM and KITCHEN LIGHTS ·

$10.00 – 15.00 $10.00 – 15.00 $15.00 – 25.00 $30.00 – 40.00

Chrome Candle Bracket
Will not rust, stain or tarnish. Easy to clean. Attractive design. With turn switch. Length, 7¾ inches; width, 4⅛ inches.
20 N 5481—Chrome Candle Bracket

Chrome Candle Bracket
Identical with bracket light at right except this fixture has no shade. With turn switch for light. Length, 5 inches; width, 3½ inches.
20 N 5705—Chrome Candle Bracket.

Shaded Chrome Bracket
Smart bracket with symmetrical shade of translucent white opal glass. Complete with turn switch. Length, 6⅜ inches; width, 3½ inches.
20 N 5706—Bracket and Shade.

Chrome Mirror Bracket
Chrome candle bracket with mirror—lends new charm to the bathroom. Complete with turn switch for light. Length, 9 inches; width, 4⅜ inches.
20 N 5482—Mirror Candle Bracket

$65.00 – 100.00 $50.00 – 90.00 $45.00 – 75.00 $35.00 – 60.00

Modern Chrome Bracket
The popular modern trend is artistically expressed in this graceful chrome bracket fixture. Half cylinder opal shade. A very decorative bracket and priced unusually low. With turn switch. Length, 9 in.; width, 4⅜ in.
20 N 5483—Chrome Plated Bracket; glass Shade.

Smartly Designed Bracket
Here is a striking and practical fixture that will beautify your bathroom. Chromium plated cast aluminum bracket with handsome harmonizing shade. With pull chain switch. Length, 8½ in.; width, 4¼ in.
20 N 5709—Chromium Plated Bracket; glass Shade.

Tubular Light Bracket
The latest! Chromium plated cast aluminum bracket of modern design and heavy opal tubular shade—1½ in. diameter—6½ inches long. Complete with pull chain switch for light. Length, 10½ inches; width, 3⅞ inches.
20 N 5710—Chromium Plated Bracket with Shade.

Half Shaded Bracket
Substantial chrome bracket of conventional pattern for kitchen or bathroom. Octagon shape white opal half shade. With pull chain switch for light. Length, 4⅜ in.; width, 4⅜ in. Extends 8¼ in. from wall.
20 N 8022—Chrome Bracket with Shade.
20 N 9075—Shade only for 2¼-in. holder.

(For prices of all merchandise shown on this page see enclosed price list)

$50.00 – 75.00 $65.00 – 90.00 $50.00 – 65.00

For Bathroom or Kitchen
Chromium plated brass bracket; white opal glass shade. Pull switch. Length, 5½ in.; width, 5¾ inches.
20 N 5707—Chromium Plated Bracket with Glass Shade

Wide Shade Bracket
Especially good for use above sink or mirror. Chromium plated brass bracket with rich looking white opal glass shade of a very popular shape. Complete with pull chain switch. Length, 4½ inches; width, 8½ inches.
20 N 5708—Chromium Bracket with Glass Shade.

Modern Dome Light—Chromium Plated
A simple but extremely handsome dome fixture for dining room, bedroom, kitchen or bathroom. White glass bowl and shade. Brass holder is finished in lustrous chromium plate. Will not rust or tarnish. For wall switch. Diameter, 8 inches. Length, 5 inches.
20 N 5746—8-in. Dome Fixture—2 Lights.

26 ‖ SEARS, ROEBUCK AND CO.

MODERN KITCHEN LIGHTS

An Abundance of Light Without Glare or Shadows

$75.00 – 100.00

$55.00 – 65.00

New Daylight Shade—Porcelain Holder

Sears offer for the first time an exclusive new shade with daylight blue glass bottom that gives daylight indoors with ordinary bulb. Shade is about 8¾ inches in diameter. Holder is made of solid white porcelain —is easy to clean and keep clean. Overall length, 9 inches.

20 N 8034—For Wall Switch
20 N 8035—With Pull Chain Switch
20 N 8036—With drop cord switch and appliance outlet
20 N 9064—Daylight shade only, for 4-inch holder

Chromium Holder—Crystal Bottom Shade

Two-piece shade with opal glass sides and crystal bottom is about 8½ inches in diameter. Close fitting chromium plated holder will not rust or tarnish. Overall length, 8½ inches.

20 N 7053—For Wall Switch
20 N 7054—With Pull Chain Switch
20 N 7055—With drop cord switch and appliance outlet
20 N 9027—Two-piece shade only, for 4-inch holder

$125.00 – 175.00

$100.00 – 150.00

Distinctive—Modern

Designed for those who want something out of the ordinary. The vertically ribbed opal glass shade is 8 inches in diameter. The holder is made of brass, chromium plated. Overall length, 11½ inches.

20 N 5718—For Wall Switch
20 N 5719—With Pull Chain Switch

New—Crystal Top Spreads Light

New crystal top shade distributes light evenly throughout room. Lower part of shade is opal white. Shade is 9¼ inches in diameter. Has a chromium plated brass holder. Overall length, 10 inches.

20 N 5714—For Wall Switch
20 N 5715—With Pull Chain Switch

Refer to enclosed price list for prices.

· REFLECTO-LIGHT ·

$100.00 – 135.00

$150.00 – 200.00

$175.00 – 250.00

Indirect Lighting for Stores and Offices

ONE of the smartest designs for lighting stores and offices. Harmonizes with modern interiors. Artistic louvres cast light upward and ceiling reflects it evenly without eye straining glare or shadows. Part of the light is deflected outward through the louvres. Strong durable construction, of spun aluminum, finished in French gray with highly polished silver color trimmings, REFLECTO LIGHT fixtures meet modern commercial lighting needs at a reasonable cost.

Refer to enclosed price list for prices.

2-Tier Louvre Ceiling Light

20 N 5693—A graceful practical fixture that will dress up any office or store. It provides soft, indirect light that improves displays—eliminates glare. Spun aluminum as described above. Has opal glass disc in bottom. Diameter, 10½ inches. Length, 9 inches.

3-Tier Louvre Wall Bracket

20 N 5691—A very smart fixture when used alone or in combination with ceiling lights shown at left and right. Very attractive when mounted on columns as well as on walls. Spun aluminum as described above. Diameter, 5¾ inches. Length, 8 inches.

3-Tier Louvre Ceiling Light

20 N 5690—Substantial and smart is this ceiling drop light. Matches fixtures shown at left. Diameter 13¼ inches. Length, 21 inches.
20 N 5692—As above except 4-tier louvre. Diameter, 19⅜ inches. Length, 25 inches.

GLASS SHADES FOR COMMERCIAL LIGHTING

$75.00 – 100.00

$100.00 – 150.00

$185.00 – 250.00

$25.00 – 30.00

Cylinder Design

Translucent opal glass shade with crystal glass bottom held to top by neat nickel plated rim. Gives excellent light—easy to clean. For 6 in. holder.
20 N 9115—2-Piece Cylinder shade for 6 inch holder. 9 inches diameter. Length, 12½ inches.
20 N 9114—Same as above with daylight blue glass bottom.

Octagon Design

Telescopic shape. Translucent opal glass decorated with attractive black painted design.
20 N 9122—1 Piece—8½ inches in diameter—7¾ inches in depth—for 4 inch holder.
20 N 9123—1 Piece—12 inches in diameter—9½ inches in depth—for 6 inch holder.

This shade matches that shown at left but is elongated.
20 N 9124—1 Piece 9½ inches in diameter—16¼ inches in depth —for 6 inch holder.

Popular Design

Quality opal glass. Standard shape.
20 N 9116—10 inch diameter; for 4 inch holder. 7 inch depth.
20 N 9117—12 inch diameter; 8½-inch depth for 6-in. holder.
20 N 9119—14 inch diameter; 9½-in. depth for 6 in. holder.
20 N 9120—16 inch diameter; 10½-in. depth for 6 inch holder.

SHADE HOLDERS
for Stores, Schools and Public Buildings

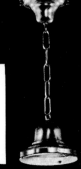

Chromium Plated Finish

Thoroughly modern in design—but not extreme—this up-to-date fixture will serve for years. The finish is of non-tarnishing chromium plate. Unusually strong construction. Drop fixtures are 36 inches long but may be shortened to length desired.
20 N 7508—Drop fixture with 6-in. shade holder.
20 N 7510—Drop fixture with 4-in. shade holder.
20 N 7528—6-in. ceiling holder. Extends 6 inches.
20 N 7530—4-in. ceiling holder. Extends 5 inches.

Bronze-Tone Finish

You will find these very sturdy and handsome fixtures unsurpassed for long satisfactory service. Substantially made of copper-face steel, finished in a rich tone of bronze. Drop fixtures are 36 inches long but may be shortened to length desired.
20 N 7500—Drop fixture with 6-in. shade holder.
20 N 7502—Drop fixture with 4-in. shade holder.
20 N 7520—6-in. ceiling holder. Extends 5¼ inches.
20 N 7522—4-in. ceiling holder. Extends 4½ inches.

SEARS, ROEBUCK AND CO. 31

$25.00 – 40.00

$30.00 – 45.00

DECORATIVE GLASS SHADES

$10.00 – 25.00

$10.00 – 25.00

$15.00 – 30.00

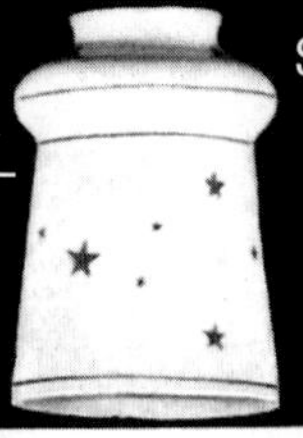

$10.00 – 25.00

$25.00 – 35.00

Lantern Shape
Attractive for drop light. Choice of White, Green, Amber or Rose. Shade is 4¼ in. in diameter at widest point, 4¼ in. deep, for 2¼ in. holder.
20 N 9051—*State color.* Lantern Shaped Shade

Bell Shape
Diameter 4½ in. at widest point. 5⅛ in. deep, for 2¼ in. holder.
20 N 9200—Plain White Glass.
20 N 9201—As illustrated with hand painted border. Choice of Blue, Green or Rose floral design. *Specify color.*

Straight Bell Shape
A simple shade of pleasing proportions, reasonably priced. Ivory colored glass. Choice of green or red decoration of unusual design. Diameter, 3⅞ in. at widest point. 5¼ in. deep. For 2¼ in. holder.
20 N 9209—Bell Shaped Shade

Straight Bell Design
Blue stars give this graceful bell-shaped white opal glass shade a smart individuality that you will admire. Diameter 3⅞ inches at widest point. 5¼ inches deep. For 2¼-inch holder.
20 N 9203—Bell Shaped Shade

Inverted Bowl Shape
Bowl shaped white opal glass shade with attractive hand painted floral design. Choice of Blue, Green or Rose decoration. Diameter, 6⅛ in. at widest point. 6 in. diameter 5-in. deep. For 2¼ in. holder.
20 N 9204—Bowl Shaped Shade

$25.00 – 35.00

$25.00 – 35.00

$75.00 – 100.00

$60.00 – 85.00

Wide Bell Shape
Harmony of design and choice of Green or Red decoration (specify color) permits wide use throughout the home for this daintily flared ivory colored glass shade. Diameter 7½ in. at widest point. 5 in. deep. For 2¼ in. holder.
20 N 9210—Wide Bell Shape

Popular Style
A style that gives a soft diffused light. Enclosed Ivory Color glass globe. Hand painted floral design in Red or Green. *State color.* 9 inch in diameter, 7 inch deep. For 4 inch holder.
20 N 9211—Globe Shaped Shade

Tapered Bowl Shape
A wide glass shade that affords plenty of light without glare. Hand painted floral and parrot decoration in natural colors. Slightly tapered white opal glass shade. Diameter 8 inches, 5⅞ inches deep. For 2¼ inch holder.
20 N 9207—Slightly Tapered Shade

Tapered Shape
A shade of popular design priced to save you money. Slightly tapered ivory colored glass shade with hand painted floral design in natural colors. Diameter 8 inches 5⅞ inches deep. For 2¼ inch holder.
20 N 9212—Slightly Tapered Shade

For Prices of All Merchandise Shown on This Page See the Enclosed Price List

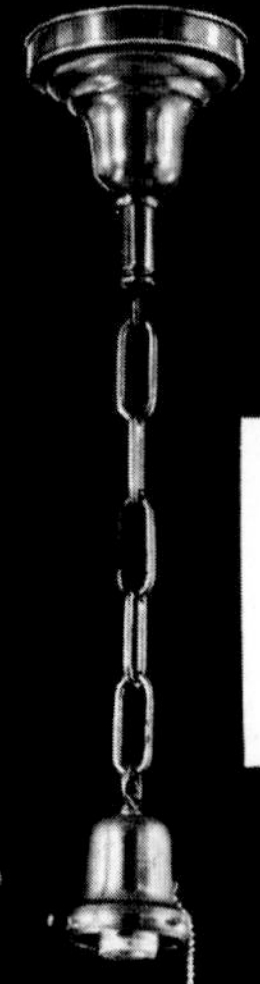

$25.00 – 35.00

$10.00 – 15.00

$10.00 – 20.00

$10.00 – 20.00

One-Light Pendant
At left one-light pendant for bedroom, bathroom, kitchen—in Ivory or Bronze. With 2¼ in. holder. For any shade with 2¼ in. opening. Length, 36 in.
20 N 7092 Pendant—Ivory Finish.
20 N 7093 Pendant—Bronze Finish.

Shade Holder
Spun steel finished in polished chrome. Has pull chain switch. May be used as ceiling fixture or wall bracket. Width, 4⅝ inch; 2¼ inch holder. Any shade on this page with 2¼ in. opening will fit this holder.
20 N 7088—Chromium finish.
20 N 7089—Same as above only white enameled finish.

Plain Bell Shade
The conventional true bell-shape that enjoys wide spread popularity because of its practicability and splendid proportions. Made of translucent white opal glass for 2¼ inch holder. Priced for economy.
20 N 9400—Bell Shade—6 inch diameter—4⅞ inch deep.
20 N 9401—Bell Shade—8 inch diameter—5⅛ inch deep.

Wide Bell Design
An inexpensive glass shade that can be used to good advantage as a simple drop light. This large ribbed white opal shade is of the reflectory type that gives unusually good lighting results. 8 inches in diameter at widest point. 4 inches deep. For 2¼ inch holder.
20 N 9056—Reflectory Type. Shade—White Opal glass.

FLOODLIGHTS

For Outdoor Use
Outdoor floodlight with powerful ribbed reflecting surface, brightly polished. Reflector 11 in. diameter at widest point. Has a convex glass lens. Gives a brilliant light. Ideal for yards, outdoor night work and sports. Use 150 or 200-Watt lamp.
20 N 7077—Outdoor Floodlight.

For Indoor Use
For brilliant indoor illumination you will find this Indoor Floodlight with 6 cellophane colored sheets (no glass lens) highly efficient. Particularly suited for basements, large halls, rooms and garages. Use 150 to 200 Watt lamp. Reflector 11 inches in diameter at widest point.
20 N 7078—Indoor Floodlight.

30₂ SEARS, ROEBUCK AND CO.

$35.00 – 50.00

WEATHERPROOF · DESIGNS ·
For Outdoor Use

$15.00 – 25.00

$35.00 – 50.00

$50.00 – 65.00

$50.00 – 65.00

Weatherproofed Ceiling Light
Sharply molded design. Rust-proof black holder; 6-in. pebbly, frosted white ball shade. 3¼-in. opening.
20 N 7032—Ceiling Light
20 N 9225—Shade only, for any 3¼-in. holder
20 N 7034—As above with **20 N 9226** Shade at right

Cast Aluminum Wall Bracket
Cast aluminum holder—black finish. 6-in. Octagon crackled amber glass shade. 3¼ in. opening.
20 N 7033—Wall Bracket
20 N 9226—Shade only, for any 3¼-in. holder
20 N 7031—As above with **20 N 9225** Shade at left

Quaint Bracket Lantern
An old English style lantern that blends with almost all types of architecture. Pressed steel finished in statuary bronze. Fitted with amber glass panels.
20 N 7000—Wall Bracket   **20 N 7002**—Ceiling

$45.00 – 60.00

$45.00 – 60.00

$30.00 – 45.00

$30.00 – 45.00

Colonial Ceiling Lantern
A simple entrance light made of rust-proof cast aluminum. Designed like old Colonial lanterns. Dull black finish with attractive glass panels. Your choice of ceiling or bracket style.
20 N 7004—Ceiling Lantern   **20 N 7003**—Bracket Lantern

Bracket Ship Lantern
Romance of old sailing days lingers in the classic design of this graceful lantern. A distinct improvement for any entrance. Dull copper finish with clear crystal glass shade.
20 N 7005—Bracket Lantern   **20 N 7006**—Ceiling Lantern

For prices of all fixtures on this page see price list enclosed.

$60.00 – 85.00

$60.00 – 85.00

$35.00 – 50.00

$40.00 – 55.00

$40.00 – 55.00

Cast Aluminum Bracket Lantern
This quaint light casts a glow of welcome on any entrance. Weather resisting cast aluminum. Arabian steel finish. Amber glass shade. Two styles.
20 N 7009—Bracket Lantern
20 N 7010—Ceiling Lantern

Coach Bracket Lantern
Dignity and distinction identify this attractively designed lantern. Strongly made of weatherproof cast aluminum, finished in statuary bronze. For wall mounting.
20 N 7007—Coach Bracket Lantern

Colonial Wall Bracket Lantern
An artistic lantern of authentic Colonial design with beautiful "hobnail" glass shade. Will improve the appearance of any entrance. Cast aluminum. Finished in weathered bronze color.
20 N 5541—Wall Bracket Lantern
20 N 5540—Ceiling Lantern

$25.00 – 35.00

$20.00 – 30.00

$30.00 – 45.00

$30.00 – 40.00

Solid Bronze Wall Lantern
Trimmed in Red, Black and Gold color. Ribbed glass half-shade.
20 N 7015—Wall Lantern

Gooseneck Reflector Bracket
For rear entrances, barns, garages, etc. Weatherproof. Made of heavy galvanized steel with substantial highly polished 10 in. reflector. Extends 22 in.
20 N 7062—Outdoor Bracket

Cast Aluminum Bracket
Rustproof—built to last a lifetime. Graceful design—black finish. Arm extends 16 in. Polished 10-in. reflector.
20 N 7039—Outdoor Bracket.

Cast Aluminum Ceiling Light
Cast aluminum—natural finish. Has amber tint glass panels on six sides and one on bottom. Extends 4½ inches from ceiling.
20 N 7008—Ceiling Fixture

32₃ ‖ SEARS, ROEBUCK AND CO.

MARKEL
10000 LINE

10141

10142

10155

No. 10141
ONE-LIGHT BRACKET
Wall Plate 5½" Diam.; Extends 6"
Finish: Chromium
Wired: Canopy Switch
Standard Quantity: Ten
Code: Leander

$145.00 — 175.00

No. 10155
FIVE-LIGHT DROP FIXTURE
Length 48"; Spread 18"
Finish: Chromium
Wired: Keyless Sockets
Standard Quantity: Five
Code: Learning

$425.00 — 500.00

No. 10142
TWO-LIGHT BRACKET
Wall Plate 5½" Diam.; Extends 5"
Finish: Chromium
Wired: Canopy Switch
Standard Quantity: Five
Code: Lector

$200.00 — 235.00

THE 10000 LINE

The pinnacle of lighting splendor is reached by these Markel Crystal Fixtures. Dignified in design, elegant in finish and colorful in effect, they provide a sparkling brilliance impossible to achieve with any other type fixture. The return to a more gracious spirit of living is greatly increasing the appreciation for crystal fixtures. The numbers in this line are traditionally correct in design and thoroughly in good taste in modern homes as in the salons of Louis XIV.

Additional Glass Shades No. G-433

MARKEL
10000 LINE

No. 10145
FIVE-LIGHT DROP FIXTURE
Length 48"; Spread 18"
Finish: Chromium
Wired: Keyless Sockets
Standard Quantity: Five
Code: Leak
   $400.00 – 500.00

No. 10133
THREE-LIGHT DROP FIXTURE
Length 48"; Spread 13"
Finish: Butler Silver
Wired: Keyless Sockets
Standard Quantity: Five
Code: Leach
   $350.00 – 400.00

THE 10000 LINE

For centuries Crystal fixtures have been preferred in homes where fine things and gracious living go hand in hand. By day or by night, no other type of lighting equipment is so lovely to look at, so thoroughly in good taste. They have the quality of adding distinction to any home that passing fads and fancies in lighting can never destroy. Note that these Markel Crystal Fixtures possess the added beauty of Crystal Cut Frosted Shades.

Additional Glass Shades for 10133—No. G-449
Additional Glass Shades for 10145—No. G-433

MARKEL
10000 LINE

10171

10172

10175

No. 10171
ONE-LIGHT BRACKET
Wall Plate 8'' x 4''; Extends 6''
Finish: Butler Silver
Wired: Canopy Switch
Standard Quantity: Ten
Code: Ligneous

$135.00 – 185.00

No. 10175
FIVE-LIGHT DROP FIXTURE
Length 48''; Spread 17''
Finish: Butler Silver
Wired: Keyless Sockets
Standard Quantity: Five
Code: Lignite

$450.00 – 525.00

No. 10172
TWO-LIGHT BRACKET
Wall Plate 8'' x 4''; Extends 4½''
Finish: Butler Silver
Wired: Canopy Switch
Standard Quantity: Ten
Code: Lignose

$215.00 – 260.00

THE 10000 LINE

These fixtures present the splendor of crystal at its best. Dignified in design, elegant in finish and colorful in effect — they meet every need of the increasing demand for crystal fixtures. The Crystal Cut frosted chimneys add to the charm of these fixtures, harmonizing beautifully into the general effect. Homes that demand unquestioned good taste in every decorative detail can do no better than to select crystal fixtures from this complete line.

Additional Glass Shades—No. G-449

MARKEL
10000 LINE

10131

10132

10136

No. 10131
ONE-LIGHT BRACKET
Wall Plate 6'' x 3¼''; Extends 6''
Finish: Butler Silver
Wired: Canopy Switch
Standard Quantity: Ten
Code: Ligula

$125.00 – 175.00

No. 10136
SIX-LIGHT DROP FIXTURE
Length 48''; Spread 19''
Finish: Butler Silver
Wired: Keyless Sockets
Standard Quantity: Five
Code: Lloyd

$450.00 – 525.00

Additional Glass Shades—No. G-449

No. 10133
THREE-LIGHT DROP FIXTURE
(Not Illustrated)
Length 48''; Spread 13''
Finish: Butler Silver
Wired: Keyless Sockets
Standard Quantity: Five
Code: Leach

$350.00 – 400.00

No. 10132
TWO-LIGHT BRACKET
Wall Plate 6'' x 3¾''; Extends 5''
Finish: Butler Silver
Wired: Canopy Switch
Standard Quantity: Ten
Code: Loath

$200.00 – 245.00

MARKEL
8500 LINE

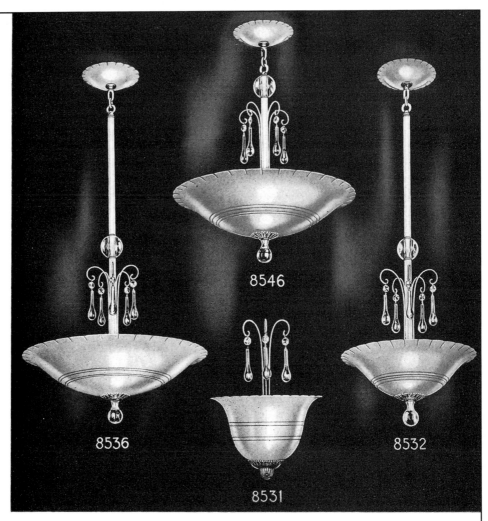

No. 8536
THREE-LIGHT DROP FIXTURE
Length 42"; Spread 16"
Finish: Empire White and Gold
Wired: Keyless Sockets for Three 100 Watt Bulbs; with Four-way Switch — Tassel Controlled
Standard Quantity: Five
Code: Faneuil
$225.00 – 295.00

No. 8546
THREE-LIGHT SEMI-CEILING FIXTURE
Length 21"; Spread 16"
Finish: Empire White and Gold
Wired: Keyless Sockets for Three 100 Watt Bulbs
Standard Quantity: Five
Code: Foote
$225.00 – 285.00

No. 8531
TWO-LIGHT BRACKET
Wall Plate 9" x 12"; Extends 5"
Finish: Empire White and Gold
Wired: For Two 40 Watt Bulbs; with Canopy Switch
Standard Quantity: Ten
Code: Fawks
$195.00 – 215.00

No. 8532
TWO-LIGHT DROP FIXTURE
Length 36"; Spread 12"
Finish: Empire White and Gold
Wired: Keyless Sockets for Two 75 Watt Bulbs
Standard Quantity: Five
Code: Fitch
$200.00 – 235.00

THE 8500 LINE
Combines the beauty and dignity of the Empire Period with modern indirect lighting to give the best in decorative, efficient illumination. Made of Spun Aluminum, finished in Empire White and Gold to fit into the popular vogue for white in all types of house furnishings.

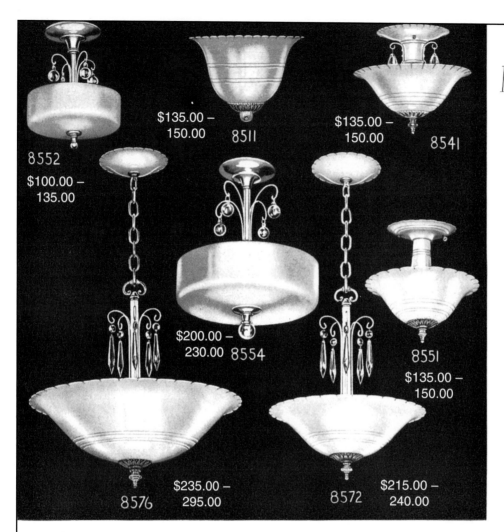

MARKEL
8500 LINE

$135.00 – 150.00 8511

$135.00 – 150.00 8541

8552
$100.00 – 135.00

$200.00 – 230.00 8554

8551
$135.00 – 150.00

$235.00 – 295.00
8576

$215.00 – 240.00
8572

No.	Lights	Finish	Code	Bulb Size	Wall Plate	Extends	Std. Qty.
8511	Two-Light Bracket	Empire White and Gold	Ferrule	Two 40 Watt	9" x 6½"	5"	10
					Length	Spread	
8541	One-Light Ceiling Fixture	Empire White and Gold	Frey	One 75 Watt	8¾"	9"	5
8542	Two-Light Semi-Ceiling Fixture	Empire White and Gold	Fell	Two 75 Watt	13"	12"	5
8551	One-Light Semi-Ceiling Fixture	Empire White and Gold	Feather	One 100 Watt	10"	9½"	5
8552	Two-Light Semi-Ceiling Fixture	Empire White and Gold	Fence	Two 60 Watt	10"	8"	5
8553	Two-Light Semi-Ceiling Fixture	Empire White and Gold	Fend	Two 75 Watt	10"	10"	5
8554	Three-Light Semi-Ceiling Fixture	Empire White and Gold	Fern	Three 75 Watt	15½"	12"	5
8555	Three-Light Semi-Ceiling Fixture	Empire White and Gold	Ferret	Three 100 Watt	15½"	14"	5
8558	One-Light Semi-Ceiling Fixture	Empire White and Gold	Federal	One 150 Watt	12½"	12½"	5
8572	Two-Light Drop Fixture	Empire White and Gold	Favor	Two 75 Watt	42"	12"	5
8576	Three-Light Drop Fixture	Empire White and Gold	Fay	Three 100 Watt	42"	16"	5

MARKEL
8300 LINE

No. 8336
FIVE-LIGHT DROP FIXTURE
Length 42"; Spread 21"

Finish:	Code:
French Bronze and Gold	Linden
Ivory Crackle and Gold	Lindsay

Wired: Keyless Sockets with Four-way Switch Control
Standard Quantity: Five

$200.00 – 255.00

THE 8300 LINE

In these fixtures better light for better sight is admirably combined with smart styling in the contemporary manner. Note particularly the Opal Glass Bottoms in fixtures Nos. 8336 and 8346 for downward diffusion of soft glowing light—a feature especially desirable in dining room lighting. Here may be used bulbs up to 150 watts for complete illumination of the table. Finished in French Bronze or Ivory Crackle and Gold with Pearl Iridescent Glass Shades.

No. 8346
FIVE-LIGHT SEMI-CEILING FIXTURE
Length 14"; Spread 21"

Finish:	Code:
French Bronze and Gold	Lineage
Ivory Crackle and Gold	Lineal

Wired: Keyless Sockets
Standard Quantity: Five

$200.00 – 245.00

No. 8331
ONE-LIGHT BRACKET
Wall Plate 10½" x 4½"; Extends 7½"

Finish:	Code:
French Bronze and Gold	Liberal
Ivory Crackle and Gold	Liberty

Wired: Canopy Switch
Standard Quantity: Ten

$100.00 – 125.00

Additional Glass Shades No. G-4261
Glass Bottom No. G-453

MARKEL
8300 LINE

8343
8345

8335

8333

No. 8335
FIVE-LIGHT DROP FIXTURE
Length 42"; Spread 20"

Finish:	Code:
French Bronze and Gold	Linen
Ivory Crackle and Gold	Linger

Wired: Keyless Sockets with Four-way Switch—Tassel Controlled
Standard Quantity: Five

$200.00 – 250.00

No. 8341
ONE-LIGHT HALL FIXTURE
(Not illustrated)
Length 36"; Spread 9"
Finish: French Bronze and Gold
Wired: Keyless Sockets
Standard Quantity: Five
Code: Loin

$100.00 – 135.00

No. 8345
FIVE-LIGHT SEMI-CEILING FIXTURE
Length 15"; Spread 20"

Finish:	Code:
French Bronze and Gold	Lingo
Ivory Crackle and Gold	Link

Wired: Keyless Sockets
Standard Quantity: Five

$200.00 – 240.00

No. 8343
THREE-LIGHT SEMI-CEILING FIXTURE
(Not Illustrated)
Length 15"; Spread 15"

Finish:	Code:
French Bronze and Gold	Linn
Ivory Crackle and Gold	Lisbon

Wired: Keyless Sockets
Standard Quantity: Five

$165.00 – 185.00

Additional Glass Shades No. G-4261

No. 8333
THREE-LIGHT DROP FIXTURE
Length 42"; Spread 15"

Finish:	Code:
French Bronze and Gold	Linseed
Ivory Crackle and Gold	Litter

Wired: Keyless Sockets
Standard Quantity: Five

$175.00 – 195.00

MARKEL
7800 LINE

Note the description and the use of plastic. Shade panels are plastic.

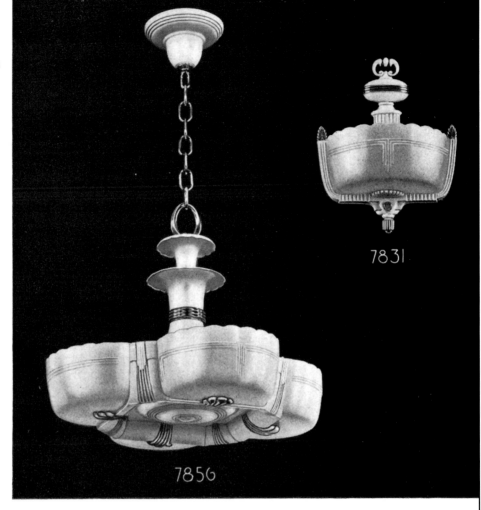

7831

7856

No. 7856
FIVE-LIGHT DROP FIXTURE
Length 42''; Spread 17½''

Finish:	Code:
Empire White and Gold	Lucania
French Bronze and Gold	Lucan

Wired: Keyless Sockets with Four-way Switch

Standard Quantity: Five

$200.00 – 250.00

THE 7800 LINE

Constructed of plastic and metal, with glass bottom in No. 7856 for downward diffusion of light. These fixtures are as modern as tomorrow in materials, design, efficiency and beauty. They reduce surface glare to a minimum without sacrificing high light output. Note the harmony of line and design in every element of these fixtures. They are widely adapted for many rooms in the home and are especially desirable for dining room illumination. The plastic panels are in Ivory and the fixtures are finished in Empire White and Gold or French Bronze and Gold.

No. 7831
ONE-LIGHT BRACKET
Wall Plate 10'' x 8½''; Extends 4¼''

Finish:	Code:
Empire White and Gold	Lubricity
French Bronze and Gold	Lubricator

Wired: Canopy Switch
Standard Quantity: Ten

$85.00 – 110.00

Additional Shades No. G-480 Bottom Bowl
Additional Shades No. GP-448 Pocket

MARKEL
7800 LINE

Note: Shade panels
are made of plastic.

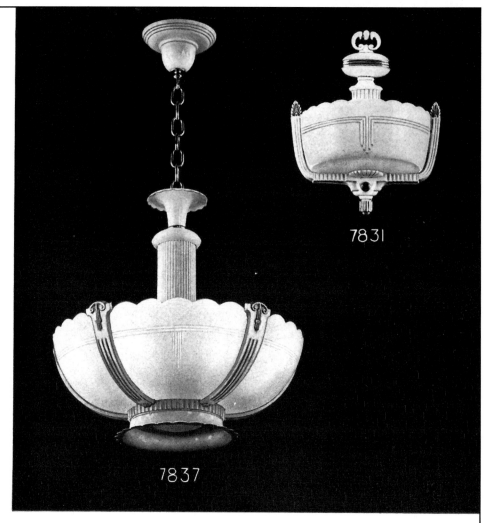

7831

7837

No. 7837
ONE-LIGHT DROP FIXTURE
Length 42"; Spread 17"

Finish:	Code:
Empire White and Gold	Ludicrous
French Bronze and Gold	Lucy

Wired: Three-way Pull Chain;
150 to 200 to 350 Watts
Standard Quantity: Five

$100.00 – 125.00

THE 7800 LINE

A new type of beauty has been designed into the fixtures of the Markel 7800 line. But of outstanding importance is the high degree of lighting efficiency these fixtures deliver. Note particularly No. 7837 with its plastic panels for wide spreading of light without glare; also the circular plastic bottom for downward diffusion of light. Finished in Empire White and Gold or in French Bronze and Gold. Plastic panels are Ivory. The scientific efficiency of this and other 7800 line fixtures is charted and analyzed on the reverse side of this page.

No. 7847
ONE-LIGHT SEMI-CEILING FIXTURE
(Not illustrated)
Length 20"; Spread 17"

Finish:	Code:
Empire White and Gold	Lullaby
French Bronze and Gold	Luke

Wired: Three-way Pull Chain;
150 to 200 to 350 Watts
Standard Quantity: Five

$100.00 – 125.00

No. 7831
ONE-LIGHT BRACKET
Wall Plate 10" x 8½"; Extends 4¼"

Finish:	Code:
Empire White and Gold	Lubricity
French Bronze and Gold	Lubricator

Wired: Canopy Switch
Standard Quantity: Ten

$85.00 – 110.00

Additional Shades No. GP-429 Panel
Additional Shades No. GP-448 Pocket
Additional Shades No. GP-457 Bottom

MARKEL
7800 LINE

Note: Shade panels are made of plastic.

No. 7835
FIVE-LIGHT DROP FIXTURE
Length 42"; Spread 17"

Finish:	Code:
Empire White and Gold	Lucent
French Bronze and Gold	Lucarne

Wired: Keyless Sockets with Four-way Switch — Tassel Controlled
Standard Quantity: Five
$190.00 — 235.00

No. 7845
FIVE-LIGHT SEMI-CEILING FIXTURE
(Not illustrated)
Length 16½"; Spread 17"

Finish:	Code:
Empire White and Gold	Lugger
French Bronze and Gold	Luggage

Wired: Keyless Sockets
Standard Quantity: Five
$190.00 — 215.00

No. 7862
TWO-LIGHT SEMI-CEILING FIXTURE
Length 12½"; Spread 9½"

Finish:	Code:
Empire White and Gold	Lucrative
French Bronze and Gold	Lucky

Wired: Keyless Sockets
Standard Quantity: Five
$100.00 — 125.00

No. 7852
TWO-LIGHT DROP FIXTURE
(Not illustrated)
Length 36"; Spread 9½"

Finish:	Code:
Empire White and Gold	Lucid
French Bronze and Gold	Lucerne

Wired: Keyless Sockets
Standard Quantity: Five
$125.00 — 150.00
Additional Shades No. GP-429 Panel
Additional Shades No. GP-448 Pocket

No. 7853
THREE-LIGHT DROP FIXTURE
Length 36"; Spread 13"

Finish:	Code:
Empire White and Gold	Luciger
French Bronze and Gold	Lucifer

Wired: Keyless Sockets
Standard Quantity: Five
$165.00 — 200.00

No. 7863
THREE-LIGHT SEMI-CEILING FIXTURE
(Not illustrated)
Length 13"; Spread 13"

Finish:	Code:
Empire White and Gold	Lucretia
French Bronze and Gold	Lucre

Wired: Keyless Sockets
Standard Quantity: Five
$135.00 — 165.00

MARKEL
7770 LINE

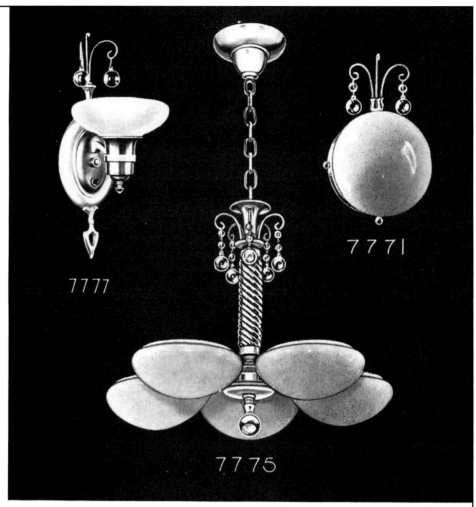

7777

7771

7775

No. 7777
ONE-LIGHT BRACKET
Wall Plate 13½" x 4½"; Extends 7"
Finish: Butler Silver and Satin Gold
Wired: Canopy Switch
Standard Quantity: Ten
Code: Lard

$115.00 – 145.00

No. 7775
FIVE-LIGHT DROP FIXTURE
Length 42"; Spread 20"
Finish: Butler Silver and Satin Gold
Wired: Keyless Sockets with Four-way Tassel
Standard Quantity: Five
Code: Labellum
$225.00 – 285.00

No. 7771
ONE-LIGHT BRACKET
Wall Plate 6¾" dia.; Extends 3½"
Finish: Butler Silver and Satin Gold
Wired: Canopy Switch
Standard Quantity: Ten
Code: Laban

$120.00 – 150.00

THE 7770 LINE

A brilliant line, new, beautiful and decidedly in good taste for all interiors. Note the twisted columns in crystal glass with the glass ball drops which reflect light, color and sparkling elegance. The new beige color glassware —unusual in shape and highly efficient for better light for better sight, adds a modern note of distinction. Finished in Butler Silver and Satin Gold. Shades are held firmly in place by spring clamps, patents applied for.

Additional Shades No. G-466
Shade for No. 7777—No. G-4941

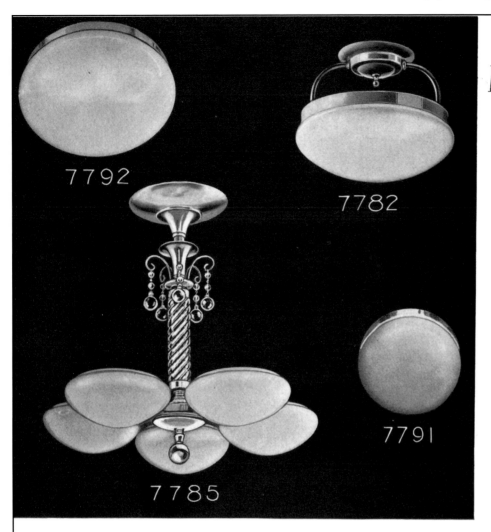

MARKEL
7770 LINE

7792

7782

7791

7785

No. 7792
TWO-LIGHT CEILING FIXTURE
Length 4½"; Spread 11½"

Finish:	Code:
Butler Silver	Louis
Fumed Brass	Louvain
French Bronze	Lout

Wired: Keyless Sockets
Standard Quantity: Five

$40.00 – 50.00

No. 7785
FIVE-LIGHT SEMI-CEILING FIXTURE
Length 18"; Spread 20"
Finish: Butler Silver and Satin Gold
Wired: Keyless Sockets
Standard Quantity: Five
Code: Lobial

$225.00 – 285.00

No. 7782
TWO-LIGHT SEMI-CEILING FIXTURE
Length 10"; Spread 11½"

Finish:	Code:
Butler Silver and Satin Gold	Louise
French Bronze and Chromium	Lounge

Wired: Keyless Sockets
Standard Quantity: Five

$85.00 – 100.00

No. 7791
ONE-LIGHT CEILING FIXTURE
Length 3½"; Spread 6¾"
Finish: Fumed Brass
Wired: Keyless Socket
Standard Quantity: Ten
Code: Loud

$25.00 – 35.00

No. 7791-C
ONE-LIGHT CEILING FIXTURE
Length 3½"; Spread 6¾"
Finish: Chromium
Wired: Keyless Socket
Standard Quantity: Ten
Code: Louse

$25.00 – 35.00

Additional Shades No. G-466
Shades for 7782 - 92—No. G-481

MARKEL
6370 LINE

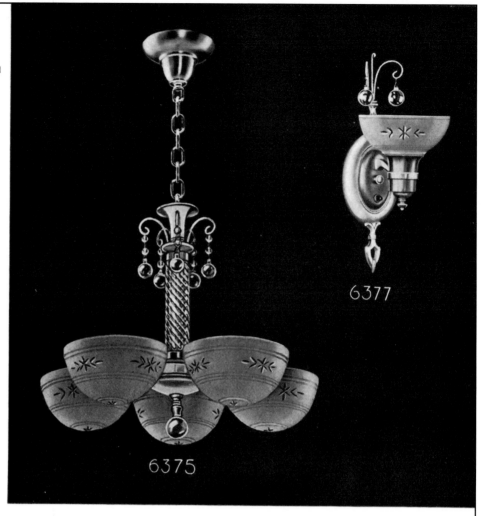

6377

6375

No. 6375
FIVE-LIGHT DROP FIXTURE
Length 42"; Spread 19"
Finish: Butler Silver and Satin Gold
Wired: Keyless Sockets with Four-way
       Switch — Tassel Controlled
Standard Quantity: Five
Code: Manakin
    $250.00 – 295.00

No. 6377
ONE-LIGHT BRACKET
Wall Plate 13½" x 4½"; Extends 7"
Finish: Butler Silver and Satin Gold
Wired: Canopy Switch
Standard Quantity: Ten
Code: Manage
    $100.00 – 135.00

THE 6370 LINE
A line that is strikingly new in conception and freedom of design. Note the sparkling brilliance of the twisted glass columns and the interesting note provided by the crystal balls. The glassware is cut crystal and frosted to reduce surface brightness. Finished in Butler Silver and Satin Gold — a new color combination of unusual quality.

Additional Shades No. G-4703
Shades for 6377—No. G-4913

MARKEL
6370 LINE

6392

6382

6385

No. 6382
TWO-LIGHT SEMI-CEILING FIXTURE
Length 10"; Spread 11½"

Finish:	Code:
Butler Silver and Satin Gold	Landor
Colonial Brass	Love

Wired: Keyless Sockets
Standard Quantity: Five

$125.00 – 145.00

No. 6385
FIVE-LIGHT SEMI-CEILING FIXTURE
Length 18"; Spread 19"
Finish: Butler Silver and Satin Gold
Wired: Keyless Sockets
Standard Quantity: Five
Code: Mandarin

$250.00 – 285.00

No. 6392
TWO-LIGHT CEILING FIXTURE
Length 4½"; Spread 11½"

Finish:	Code:
Butler Silver	Lowell
Colonial Brass	Lower

Wired: Keyless Sockets
Standard Quantity: Five

$95.00 – 110.00

Additional Shades for 6385—No. G-4703
Additional Shades for 6382-92—No. G-4811

MARKEL
6350 LINE

6357

6355

No. 6357
ONE LIGHT BRACKET
Wall Plate 10¾" x 4¼"; **Extends** 6½"
Finish: Colonial Brass
Wired: Canopy Switch
Standard Quantity: Ten
Code: Aorta

$75.00 — 95.00

No. 6355
FIVE-LIGHT DROP FIXTURE
Length 42"; **Spread** 19"
Finish: Colonial Brass
Wired: Keyless Sockets with Four-way
Switch — Tassel Controlled
Standard Quantity: Five
Code: Apex

$225.00 — 250.00

THE 6350 LINE
The Colonial influence in the designing of this new Markel line has been modernized to adapt it with perfect harmony in Empire, Provincial and Modern interiors as well as Colonial settings. Note the graceful proportion of the molded spindle and the pleasing use of crystal glassware, beautifully cut and frosted to reduce glare. Finished in Colonial Brass, beautifully polished. The shades are attached by a special clamp, Patent Applied For.

Additional Shades No. G-4703
Shade for 6357—No. G-4913

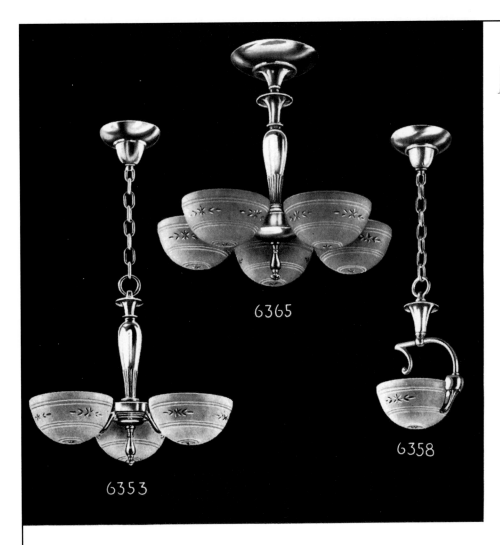

6365

6353

6358

MARKEL
6350 LINE

No. 6353
THREE-LIGHT DROP FIXTURE
Length 42"; Spread 16½"
Finish: Colonial Brass
Wired: Keyless Sockets
Standard Quantity: Five
Code: Apache
$165.00 – 190.00

No. 6365
FIVE-LIGHT SEMI-CEILING FIXTURE
Length 18"; Spread 19"
Finish: Colonial Brass
Wired: Keyless Sockets
Standard Quantity: Five
Code: Apple
$220.00 – 240.00

No. 6358
ONE-LIGHT DROP FIXTURE
Length 36"; Spread 7½"
Finish: Colonial Brass
Wired: Keyless Sockets
Standard Quantity: Five
Code: Apricot
$125.00 – 150.00

No. 6363
THREE-LIGHT SEMI-CEILING FIXTURE
(Not illustrated)
Length 18"; Spread 16½"
Finish: Colonial Brass
Wired: Keyless Sockets
Standard Quantity: Five
Code: Apostle
$150.00 – 180.00

No. 6361
ONE-LIGHT SEMI-CEILING FIXTURE
(Not illustrated)
Length 12"; Spread 7½"
Finish: Colonial Brass
Wired: Keyless Sockets
Standard Quantity: Five
Code: Apiary
$85.00 – 100.00

Additional Shades No. G-4703

MARKEL
6330 LINE

6331

6335

No. 6335
FIVE-LIGHT DROP FIXTURE
Length 42"; Spread 19"
Finish: French Bronze and Chromium
Wired: Keyless Sockets with Four-way
      Switch — Tassel Controlled
Standard Quantity: Five
Code: Ankle

    $185.00 – 215.00

No. 6331
ONE-LIGHT BRACKET
Wall Plate 9" x 4½"; Extends 7"
Finish: French Bronze and Chromium
Wired: Canopy Switch
Standard Quantity: Ten
Code: Animal

    $65.00 – 85.00

THE 6330 LINE

Modern designing without severity characterizes this new Markel line to adapt it to contemporary decorative themes as well as many period rooms. The beautifully proportioned iridescent glassware delivers glowing colorful light without glare for restful seeing and eye protection. The fluted columns, banded in Chromium, the graceful trumpets and loops with Chromium finish are fine interpretations of the modern influence in designing. Finished in French Bronze and Chromium. The shades are attached by a special clamp, Patent Applied For.

Additional Shades No. G-4702

MARKEL
6330 LINE

No. 6333
THREE-LIGHT DROP FIXTURE
Length 42"; Spread 16½"
Finish: French Bronze and Chromium
Wired: Keyless Sockets
Standard Quantity: Five
Code: Anise
    $150.00 – 175.00

No. 6345
FIVE-LIGHT SEMI-CEILING FIXTURE
Length 12"; Spread 19"
Finish: French Bronze and Chromium
Wired: Keyless Sockets
Standard Quantity: Five
Code: Anthem
    $175.00 – 200.00

No. 6338
ONE-LIGHT DROP FIXTURE
Length 36"; Spread 7½"
Finish: French Bronze and Chromium
Wired: Keyless Sockets
Standard Quantity: Five
Code: Annual
    $125.00 – 150.00

No. 6343
THREE-LIGHT SEMI-CEILING FIXTURE
(Not illustrated)
Length 12"; Spread 16½"
Finish: French Bronze and Chromium
Wired: Keyless Sockets
Standard Quantity: Five
Code: Anode
    $150.00 – 175.00

No. 6341
ONE-LIGHT SEMI-CEILING FIXTURE
(Not illustrated)
Length 12"; Spread 7½"
Finish: French Bronze and Chromium
Wired: Keyless Sockets
Standard Quantity: Five
Code: Angora
    $85.00 – 100.00

Additional Shades No. G-4702

MARKEL
6000-6050 LINE

6026   6066

6016   6056   6001 6051

No. 6016
SIX-LIGHT DROP
Length 42"; Spread 20"
Finish: Natural Forge
Wired: Keyless Sockets with Four-way Switch Control
Standard Quantity: Five
Glassware: Frosted Crystal
Code: Target
$300.00 – 400.00
No. 6056
Same as 6016 except Antique Bronze finish with Amber Glass shades and Frosted Crystal Bottom.
Code: Tarnish

No. 6001
ONE-LIGHT BRACKET
Wall Plate $9\frac{1}{4}$" x $4\frac{1}{2}$"; Extends $5\frac{7}{8}$"
Finish: Natural Forge
Wired: Canopy Switch
Standard Quantity: Ten
Glassware: Frosted Crystal
Code: Templar
$100.00 – 135.00
No. 6051
Same as 6001 except Antique Bronze finish with Amber Glass shade.
Code: Tendon

Additional Glass Shades Crystal No. G-446
Amber No. G-4461
Additional Bottom Bowl Crystal No. G-441

No. 6026
SIX-LIGHT SEMI-CEILING
Length $15\frac{1}{2}$"; Spread 20"
Finish: Natural Forge
Wired: Keyless Sockets
Standard Quantity: Five
Glassware: Frosted Crystal
Code: Tartar
$300.00 – 390.00
No. 6066
Same as 6026 except Antique Bronze finish with Amber Glass Shades and Frosted Crystal Bottom.
Code: Teetor

THE 6000—6050 LINES
These fixtures recall pioneer days in their primitive beauty, and sturdy massiveness. Authentic in design, they reflect the best in Early American designing and beautifully harmonize with Old English and Provincial interiors. Note that the 6000 series is finished in Natural Forge with glassware in Frosted Crystal; the 6050 series is finished in Antique Bronze with Amber Glass Shades. Note also the Frosted Crystal Bottoms in the six light fixtures. Cast in Aluminum.

MARKEL
6000-6050 LINE

6025   6065
$290.00 – 325.00

6015   6055
$295.00 – 335.00

6013   6053
$250.00 – 275.00

No.	Lights	Finish	Code	Length	Spread	Std. Qty.
6013	3 Lt. Drop	Natural Forge	Temple	42"	15"	5
*6015	5 Lt. Drop	Natural Forge	Tennis	42"	20"	5
**6023	3 Lt. Semi-Ceil.	Natural Forge	Terrace	15½"	15"	5
6025	5 Lt. Semi-Ceil.	Natural Forge	Teuton	15½"	20"	5
**6041	1 Lt. Hall	Natural Forge	Loft	36"	8"	5
6053	3 Lt. Drop	Antique Bronze	Texan	42"	15"	5
*6055	5 Lt. Drop	Antique Bronze	Textile	42"	20"	5
**6063	3 Lt. Semi-Ceil.	Antique Bronze	Thesis	15½"	15"	5
6065	5 Lt. Semi-Ceil.	Antique Bronze	Thicket	15½"	20"	5
**6071	1 Lt. Hall	Antique Bronze	Log	36"	8"	5

*All wired with Keyless Sockets except Nos. 6015 and 6055 which are equipped with Four-way Switch Tassel Controlled.

**Not illustrated.

Additional Glass Shades Crystal No. G-446
Amber No. G-4461

Additional Bottom Bowl Crystal No. G-441

MARKEL
5530 LINE

5531

5535

No. 5535
FIVE-LIGHT DROP FIXTURE
Length 42''; Spread 19''
Finish: French Bronze and Chromium
Wired: Keyless Sockets with Four-way
Switch — Tassel Controlled
Standard Quantity: Five
Code: Bauble

$250.00 – 285.00

No. 5531
ONE-LIGHT BRACKET
Wall Plate 8¼'' x 4¼''; Extends 6''
Finish: French Bronze and Chromium
Wired: Canopy Switch
Standard Quantity: Ten
Code: Barrage

$95.00 – 115.00

THE 5530 LINE

The twisted glass columns of these fixtures provide sparkling elegance and the gracefully sweeping curves of the arms give modern rhythm and symmetry that is thoroughly in good taste in nearly all kinds of decorative schemes. Note also the interesting shape and harmony of line in the glassware. Finished in French Bronze and Chromium with glassware in French Crystal, frosted to reduce glare and cut with modern design.

Additional Shades No. G-4861

MARKEL
5530 LINE

5545

5533

5538

No. 5533
THREE-LIGHT DROP FIXTURE
Length 42"; Spread 17"
Finish: French Bronze and Chromium
Wired: Keyless Sockets
Standard Quantity: Five
Code: Battery
$200.00 – 235.00

No. 5545
FIVE-LIGHT SEMI-CEILING FIXTURE
Length 17"; Spread 19"
Finish: French Bronze and Chromium
Wired: Keyless Sockets
Standard Quantity: Five
Code: Bethany
$240.00 – 275.00

No. 5543
THREE-LIGHT SEMI-CEILING FIXTURE
(Not illustrated)
Length 17"; Spread 17"
Finish: French Bronze and Chromium
Wired: Keyless Sockets
Standard Quantity: Five
Code: Beaker
$190.00 – 220.00

Additional Shades No. G-4861

No. 5538
ONE-LIGHT DROP FIXTURE
Length 36"; Spread 9½" x 6"
Finish: French Bronze and Chromium
Wired: Keyless Sockets
Standard Quantity: Five
Code: Beacon
$100.00 – 125.00

MARKEL
5200 LINE

5256

5246

5251

No. 5246
SIX-LIGHT DROP FIXTURE
Length 42"; Spread 18"
Finish: English Bronze and Gold
Wired: Keyless Sockets with Four-way Control Switch
Standard Quantity: Five
Code: Dabble

$465.00 – 525.00

No. 5256
SIX-LIGHT SEMI-CEILING FIXTURE
Length 16½"; Spread 18"
Finish: English Bronze and Gold
Wired: Keyless Sockets
Standard Quantity: Five
Code: Dahlia

$450.00 – 500.00

No. 5251
ONE-LIGHT BRACKET
Wall Plate 9¼" x 5½"; **Extends** 4½"
Finish: English Bronze and Gold
Wired: Canopy Switch
Standard Quantity: Ten
Code: Dacker

$120.00 – 140.00

Additional Shades—No. G-4051
Shade for 5251—No. G-4561
Bottom Bowl—No. G-3763

THE 5200 LINE
Modern designing without severity characterizes this beautiful Markel 5200 Line. Note the massive effect achieved by the use of fluted Glass Shades and the marbleized composition columns. The metal parts are finished in English Bronze with gold toned hylites and the shades are Ivory color to harmonize with the columns. These fixtures are especially beautiful when illuminated, delivering an abundance of soft shaded light without glare to meet today's standards of better light for better sight.

MARKEL
5200 LINE

No. 5245
FIVE-LIGHT DROP FIXTURE
Length 42''; Spread 18''
Finish: English Bronze and Gold
Wired: Keyless Sockets with Four-way
       Switch—Tassel Controlled
Standard Quantity: Five
Code: Daisy

$425.00 – 455.00

No. 5241
ONE-LIGHT HALL FIXTURE
Length 36''; Spread 8½''
Finish: English Bronze and Gold
Wired: Keyless Sockets
Standard Quantity: Five
Code: Dandy

$135.00 – 150.00

No. 5255
FIVE-LIGHT SEMI-CEILING FIXTURE
Length 15''; Spread 18''
Finish: English Bronze and Gold
Wired: Keyless Sockets
Standard Quantity: Five
Code: Damask

$400.00 – 435.00

Additional Shades—No. G-4051
Shade for 5241—No. G-3911

MARKEL
4650 LINE

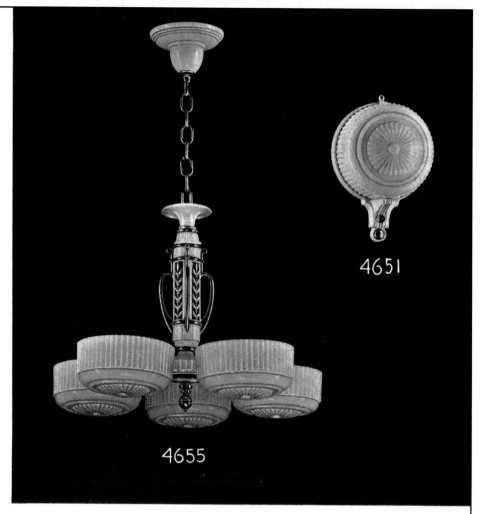

4651

4655

No. 4655
FIVE-LIGHT DROP FIXTURE
Length 42''; Spread 19''

Finish:	Code:
Empire White and Gold	Cactus
French Bronze and Gold	Caddy

Wired: Keyless Sockets with Four-way
Switch—Tassel Controlled
Standard Quantity: Five

$200.00 – 240.00

No. 4651
ONE-LIGHT BRACKET
Wall Plate 9½'' x 6¼''; Extends 2¾''

Finish:	Code:
Empire White and Gold	Bryan
French Bronze and Gold	Bunyan

Wired: Canopy Switch
Standard Quantity: Ten

$95.00 – 115.00

THE 4650 LINE

A strikingly new interpretation of modernism, based on conventionalized classic motifs. The glassware with its Doric flutings is particularly effective and in complete harmony with the general design of these fixtures. A line that is destined for wide popularity because of its unusual beauty and the massive display of soft, colorful, well diffused light. Finished in Empire White and Gold or French Bronze and Gold.

Additional Shades No. G-471

MARKEL
4650 LINE

4661

4653

4665

No. 4653	**No. 4665**	**No. 4661**
THREE-LIGHT DROP FIXTURE	**FIVE-LIGHT SEMI-CEILING FIXTURE**	**ONE-LIGHT SEMI-CEILING FIXTURE**
Length 42"; Spread 17"	Length 13"; Spread 19"	Length 11"; Spread 7¼"

No. 4653

Finish: / **Code:**
Empire White and Gold — Cabbage
French Bronze and Gold — Cabin
Wired: Keyless Sockets
Standard Quantity: Five

$150.00 – 185.00

No. 4665

Finish: / **Code:**
Empire White and Gold — Camphor
French Bronze and Gold — Canker
Wired: Keyless Sockets
Standard Quantity: Five

$200.00 – 240.00

No. 4661

Finish: / **Code:**
Empire White and Gold — Calcium
French Bronze and Gold — Caldron
Wired: Keyless Sockets
Standard Quantity: Five

$110.00 – 125.00

No. 4663
THREE-LIGHT SEMI-CEILING FIXTURE
(Not illustrated)
Length 13"; Spread 17"

Finish: / **Code:**
Empire White and Gold — Caliber
French Bronze and Gold — Calvert
Wired: Keyless Sockets
Standard Quantity: Five

$150.00 – 185.00

Additional Shades No. G-471

No. 4658
ONE-LIGHT DROP FIXTURE
(Not illustrated)
Length 36"; Spread 7¼"

Finish: / **Code:**
Empire White and Gold — Burne
French Bronze and Gold — Burton
Wired: Keyless Sockets
Standard Quantity: Five

$125.00 – 135.00

MARKEL
4500 LINE

4501
$50.00 –
85.00

$175.00
– 195.00   4525

4502
$100.00
– 135.00

$225.00
– 265.00   4515

$145.00
– 195.00   4512
4513

No.	Description	Finish	Code	Wiring	Wall Plate	Extends	Std. Qty.
4501	1 Lt. Bracket	Herald Brown and Silver Ivory and Gold	Tangent Tangerine	Canopy Switch	10" x 4¼"	3"	10
4502	2 Lt. Bracket	Herald Brown and Silver Ivory and Gold	Tapster Tardy	Canopy Switch	10" x 4¼"	3½"	10
					Length	Spread	
4512	2 Lt. Drop	Herald Brown and Silver	Tantrum	Keyless Sockets	36"	12" x 7"	5
4513	3 Lt. Drop	Herald Brown and Silver	Tapioca	Keyless Sockets	36"	13"	5
4515	5 Lt. Drop	Herald Brown and Silver	Tannic	Keyless Sockets	42"	16"	5
*4515S	5 Lt. Drop	Herald Brown and Silver	Thegn	Keyless Sockets	42"	16"	5
4525	5 Lt. Semi-Ceil.	Herald Brown and Silver	Tautog	Keyless Sockets	11"	16"	5

*4515S same as **4515** except wired with Keyless Sockets and Four-way Switch-Tassel Controlled.

THE 4500 LINE

The charm of French elegance of the 18th century is recreated in these beautiful fixtures for modern American homes. A complete line providing just the right fixture for every room in the home. Cast in Ferro Metal, finished in Herald Brown and Silver with brackets and one, two and three light ceiling fixtures also finished in Ivory and Gold.

MARKEL
4400-A LINE

Note: We called these "horn of plenty" shades because of the shape.

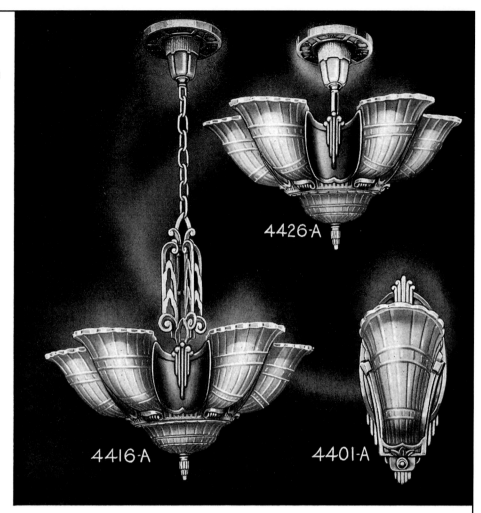

4426-A

4416-A

4401-A

No. 4416-A
SIX-LIGHT DROP FIXTURE
Length 42"; Spread 20"
Finish: Herald Brown and Silver
Wired: Keyless Sockets with Four-way Switch Control
Standard Quantity: Five
Code: Tercel

$565.00 – 725.00

No. 4426-A
SIX-LIGHT SEMI-CEILING FIXTURE
Length 15"; Spread 20"
Finish: Herald Brown and Silver
Wired: Keyless Sockets
Standard Quantity: Five
Code: Tenet

$550.00 – 700.00

No. 4401-A
ONE-LIGHT BRACKET
Wall Plate 11½" x 5"; Extends 4¼"
Finish: Herald Brown and Silver
Wired: Canopy Switch
Standard Quantity: Ten
Code: Tench

$200.00 – 235.00

Additional Shades No. G-3951
Glass Bottom Bowl No. G-4021

THE 4400-A LINE

This unusual line of Markel fixtures features a mass of glowing, colorful light diffused through gracefully designed Brown Shaded Ivory Colored Glassware. Note the harmony of line and design in all elements of these fixtures. Their beauty and efficiency in delivering soft shaded light for better sight adapt them to all types of interiors where present day standards of modern lighting are desired. Cast in Ferro Metal and finished in Herald Brown and Silver.

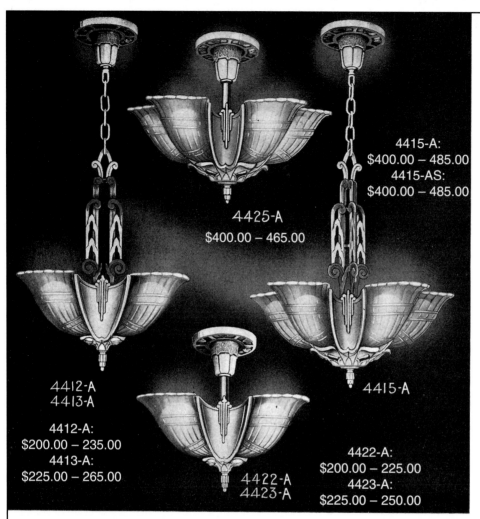

MARKEL
4400-A LINE

4415-A:
$400.00 – 485.00
4415-AS:
$400.00 – 485.00

4425-A
$400.00 – 465.00

4412-A
4413-A

4412-A:
$200.00 – 235.00
4413-A:
$225.00 – 265.00

4415-A

4422-A
4423-A

4422-A:
$200.00 – 225.00
4423-A:
$225.00 – 250.00

No.	Lights	Finish	Code	Length	Spread	Std. Qty.
4412-A	2 Lt. Drop	Herald Brown and Silver	Teraph	36"	13½" x 6"	5
4413-A	3 Lt. Drop	Herald Brown and Silver	Terbium	36"	16"	5
4415-A	5 Lt. Drop	Herald Brown and Silver	Tensil	42"	19"	5
*4415-AS	5 Lt. Drop	Herald Brown and Silver	Tipster	42"	19"	5
4422-A	2 Lt. Semi-Ceil.	Herald Brown and Silver	Tensor	12½"	13½" x 6"	5
4423-A	3 Lt. Semi-Ceil.	Herald Brown and Silver	Tentie	12½"	16"	5
4425-A	5-Lt. Semi-Ceil.	Herald Brown and Silver	Tendril	13"	19"	5

4415-AS same as **4415-A** except wired with Four-way Switch-Tassel Controlled.

Additional Shades No. G-3951

MARKEL
3800 LINE

Note: The shade cups
are made of plastic.

3801
$75.00 – 100.00

3815
$185.00 – 200.00

No. 3815
FIVE-LIGHT DROP FIXTURE
Length 42"; Spread 20"

Finish:	Code:
Empire White and Gold	Marmion
French Bronze and Gold	Marmot

Wired: Keyless Sockets with Four-way
Switch — Tassel Controlled
Standard Quantity: Five

No. 3801
ONE-LIGHT BRACKET
Wall Plate 8¼" x 4¼"; Extends 6"

Finish:	Code:
Empire White and Gold	Manuscript
French Bronze and Gold	Maple

Wired: Canopy Switch
Standard Quantity: Ten

THE 3800 LINE

A delightful combination of the modified Colonial spindle with modern arms, shade cups and Ivory toned plastic shades. This new line of Markel fixtures possesses wide adaptability in line, design and decorative characteristics to fit it to the needs of all types of interiors, either period or modern. Finished in Empire White and Gold or French Bronze and Gold.

Additional Shades No. GP-454

MARKEL
3800 LINE

Note: The shade cups
are made of plastic.

No. 3813
THREE-LIGHT DROP FIXTURE
Length 42''; Spread 18''

Finish:	Code:
Empire White and Gold	Mariner
French Bronze and Gold	Market

Wired: Keyless Sockets
Standard Quantity: Five
$135.00 – 175.00

No. 3825
FIVE-LIGHT SEMI-CEILING FIXTURE
Length 16''; Spread 20''

Finish:	Code:
Empire White and Gold	Meadow
French Bronze and Gold	Measure

Wired: Keyless Sockets
Standard Quantity: Five
$175.00 – 195.00

No. 3818
ONE-LIGHT DROP FIXTURE
Length 36''; Spread 10½'' x 6''

Finish:	Code:
Empire White and Gold	Medley
French Bronze and Gold	Melody

Wired: Keyless Sockets
Standard Quantity: Five
$100.00 – 125.00

No. 3823
THREE-LIGHT SEMI-CEILING FIXTURE
(Not Illustrated)
Length 16''; Spread 18''

Finish:	Code:
Empire White and Gold	Master
French Bronze and Gold	Matron

Wired: Keyless Sockets
Standard Quantity: Five
$135.00 – 165.00

No. 3821
ONE-LIGHT SEMI-CEILING FIXTURE
(Not illustrated)
Length 14½''; Spread 10½'' x 6''

Finish:	Code:
Empire White and Gold	Marshall
French Bronze and Gold	Marten

Wired: Keyless Sockets
Standard Quantity: Five
$75.00 – 100.00

Additional Shades No. GP-454

MARKEL
3630 LINE

Note: The shade cups
are made of plastic.

3643

3635

3631

No. 3635
FIVE-LIGHT DROP FIXTURE
Length 42"; Spread 19½"
Finish: Pearl Ivory and Gold
Wired: Keyless Sockets with Four-way
    Switch—Tassel Controlled
Standard Quantity: Five
Code: Steuben

$200.00 – 250.00

THE 3630 LINE

Beautiful colonial fixtures, tempered in design to modern decorative requirements. Note the graceful sweep of the arms and the symmetry of the
body elements — also the fitness of the shades to general design of the
fixtures. These fixtures are finished in Pearl Ivory and Gold — beautifully
harmonizing with the trend for simplicity in colonial treatments. The shades
are of Ivory plastic, practically unbreakable and produce a soft diffused
light for better sight and eye protection.

No. 3643
THREE-LIGHT SEMI-CEILING FIXTURE
Length 16"; Spread 17½"
Finish: Pearl Ivory and Gold
Wired: Keyless Sockets
Standard Quantity: Five
Code: Stewart

$100.00 – 150.00

No. 3631
ONE-LIGHT BRACKET
Wall Plate 6" x 3¼"; Extends 6¾"
Finish: Pearl Ivory and Gold
Wired: Canopy Switch
Standard Quantity: Ten
Code: Stoner

$85.00 – 100.00

Additional Shades—No. G. P. 424

MARKEL
3630 LINE

3645

3633

3641

Note: The shades are made of plastic.

No. 3633
THREE-LIGHT DROP FIXTURE
Length 42"; Spread 17½"
Finish: Pearl Ivory and Gold
Wired: Keyless Sockets
Standard Quantity: Five
Code: Stubbs

$125.00 – 175.00

No. 3641
ONE-LIGHT HALL FIXTURE
Length 42"; Spread 8"
Finish: Pearl Ivory and Gold
Wired: Keyless Socket
Standard Quantity: Five
Code: Sussex

$100.00 – 125.00

No. 3645
FIVE-LIGHT SEMI-CEILING FIXTURE
Length 16"; Spread 19½"
Finish: Pearl Ivory and Gold
Wired: Keyless Sockets
Standard Quantity: Five
Code: Sumer

$200.00 – 225.00

Additional Shades—No. G. P. 424

MARKEL
3470 LINE

3472
$100.00 – 125.00

3478
$125.00 – 135.00

3479
$135.00 – 150.00

3477
$145.00 – 175.00

No.	Description	Finish	Code	Wired	Length	Spread	Std. Qty.
3471	Two-Light Ceiling Fixture (Same as 3472)	Nuchrome	Salvage	Keyless Sockets	5"	12¼"	5
3472	Two-Light Ceiling Fixture	Empire White and Gold	Samson	Keyless Sockets	5"	12¼"	5
3477	Two-Light Semi-Ceiling Fixture	Blonde and Gold	Sanctum	Keyless Sockets	12"	10½"	5
3478	Two-Light Semi-Ceiling Fixture	Empire White and Gold	Sandall	Keyless Sockets	13"	10½"	5
3479	Two-Light Drop Fixture	Empire White and Gold	Satin	Keyless Sockets	36"	10½"	5

Glassware—G-488 for 3472-77-78-79 Ivory toned
G-4881 for 3471 White Opal

THE 3470 LINE

The fixtures in this new Markel line utilize a modernization of the fluted Doric motif in a strikingly new and beautiful manner. Note the harmony in line and design between the fluted columns and the moulded glass bottoms of these fixtures. Though created in the modern manner these fixtures are equally well adapted to period interiors. No. 3471 finished in Nuchrome with White Opal Glass Bowl. No. 3477 finished in Blonde and Gold with Ivory toned Glass Bowl. All others finished in Empire White and Gold with Ivory toned Glass Bowl.

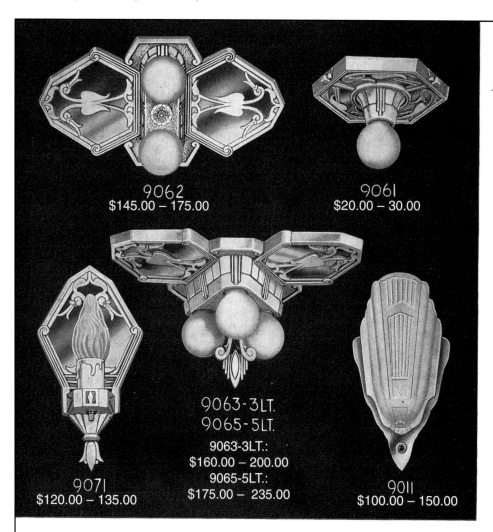

MARKEL
9000 LINE

9062
$145.00 – 175.00

9061
$20.00 – 30.00

9063-3LT.
9065-5LT.

9063-3LT.:
$160.00 – 200.00
9065-5LT.:
$175.00 – 235.00

9071
$120.00 – 135.00

9011
$100.00 – 150.00

No.	Lights	Finish	Wired	Code	Wall Plate	Extends	Std. Qt.
9011	One-Light Bathroom Bracket	Chromium	Canopy Switch	Abrest	9½" x 5¼"	4½"	Ten
9071	One-Light Bracket	Old Ivory with Chromium	Turn Knob Socket	Accord	10" x 5½"	3"	Ten
					Length	Spread	
9061	One-Light Ceiling Fixture	Old Ivory with Chromium	Keyless Socket	Absurd	2½"	7½"	Ten
9062	Two-Light Ceiling Fixture	Old Ivory with Chromium	Keyless Sockets	Acclimate	6"	13" x 6¾"	Ten
9063	Three-Light Ceiling Fixture	Old Ivory with Chromium	Keyless Sockets	Academy	6"	15"	Ten
9065	Five-Light Ceiling Fixture	Old Ivory with Chromium	Keyless Sockets	Abelard	6"	18"	Five

THE 9000 LINE

An unusual line of ceiling and bracket fixtures in which chromium insert plates, producing a beautiful mirror like effect, are an outstanding feature. Their low price and wide adaptability have made these fixtures especially popular.

Additional Shades for 9011 Chromium Bracket G-3502, French Crystal

MARKEL
3420 LINE

3421
$35.00 – 40.00

3427
$50.00 – 75.00

3422
$100.00 – 125.00

3424
$150.00 – 185.00

3423
$135.00 – 175.00

No.	Description	Finish	Code	Wired	Length	Spread	Std. Qty.
3421	One-Light Ceiling Fixture	Empire White and Gold / Antique Brown and Gold	Metric Mold	Keyless Sockets	3½"	6¾"	10
3422	Two-Light Ceiling Fixture	Empire White and Gold / Antique Brown and Gold	Migrate Mongrel	Keyless Sockets	3½"	15" x 6¾"	10
3423	Three-Light Ceiling Fixture	Empire White and Gold / Antique Brown and Gold	Mission Morrow	Keyless Sockets	3½"	15¼"	10
3424	Four-Light Ceiling Fixture	Empire White and Gold / Antique Brown and Gold	Modiste Morse	Keyless Sockets	3½"	18"	5
					Wall Pl.	Extds.	
3427	One-Light Bracket	Empire White and Gold / Antique Brown and Gold	Molar Mort	Canopy Switch	6¾"	3½"	10

All of the above fixtures furnished with pull chain switch at slight additional cost. When ordering, designate by letter P as 3421P.

THE 3420 LINE

These fixtures are completely new in conception and as modern as tomorrow. Closely fitting to ceiling and walls they provide flush type lighting at low cost and can be mounted directly on outlet box. They are strikingly beautiful and thoroughly in keeping with the advanced idea of decorative lighting and better light for better sight. Finished in Empire White and Gold or Antique Brown and Gold. Designed for 25, 30 or 40 watt bulbs. Shades attached by Spring Clamps, Patents applied for.

Additional Shades No. G-466

MARKEL
3410 LINE

3414
$100.00 – 125.00

3411
$110.00 – 135.00

$110.00 – 125.00
3412

$115.00 – 135.00
3413

No. 3414
ONE-LIGHT SEMI-CEILING FIXTURE
Length 11"; Spread 11½"
Finish: Empire White and Gold
Wired: Keyless Socket
Size Bulb: 100 or 150 Watts
Standard Quantity: Five
Code: Message

No. 3412
ONE-LIGHT SEMI-CEILING FIXTURE
Length 11"; Spread 10¾"
Finish: Empire White and Gold
Wired: Keyless Socket
Size Bulb: 100 Watts
Standard Quantity: Five
Code: Merger

No. 3411
ONE-LIGHT SEMI-CEILING FIXTURE
Length 10"; Spread 11"

Finish:	**Code:**
Empire White and Gold	Mental
Blonde and Gold	Mercury

Wired: Keyless Socket
Size Bulb: 100 or 150 Watts
Standard Quantity: Five

No. 3413
ONE-LIGHT SEMI-CEILING FIXTURE
Length 11"; Spread 9"
Finish: Empire White and Gold
Wired: Keyless Socket
Size Bulb: 100 Watts
Standard Quantity: Five
Code: Merit

Additional Shades No. G-466

THE 3410 LINE

This new Markel line provides an interesting variety of ceiling fixtures to meet the rapidly growing demand for reflected light. Numbers 3411 and 3413 are equipped with Ivory toned glass bottoms for downward diffusion of light. These fixtures are especially adapted to the lighting needs of kitchens, halls, bathrooms, nurseries, etc. Finished in Empire White and Gold; Number 3411 also in Blonde and Gold.

MARKEL
3100 LINE

3146

3136

3131

Note: The shades are made of plastic.

No. 3136
SIX-LIGHT DROP FIXTURE
Length 42''; Spread 19''
Finish: Empire White and Gold
Wired: Keyless Sockets with Four-way Switch Control
Standard Quantity: Five
Code: Licorice

$250.00 – 295.00

No. 3146
SIX-LIGHT SEMI-CEILING FIXTURE
Length 18''; Spread 19''
Finish: Empire White and Gold
Wired: Keyless Sockets
Standard Quantity: Five
Code: Lilt

$235.00 – 275.00

No. 3131
ONE-LIGHT BRACKET
Wall Plate 8⅜'' x 4½''; Extends 6¾''
Finish: Empire White and Gold
Wired: Canoy Switch
Standard Quantity: Ten
Code: Lichen

$85.00 – 110.00

Additional Shades—GP-424
Glass Bottom Bowl—G-4042

THE 3100 LINE

Contemporary designing, combining traditional and modern motifs characterize these beautiful fixtures. A highly popular line interpreting the better tastes of the vast majority of home-makers. Cast in Ferro Metal and finished in Empire White and Gold. The shades are of cream color plastic, practically unbreakable, and easily cleaned. They deliver soft, completely diffused light that meets the advanced standards of better lighting for better sight.

MARKEL
3100 LINE

3143
3145

3135

3133

Note: The shades are
made of plastic.

No. 3135
FIVE-LIGHT DROP FIXTURE
Length 42"; Spread 19"
Finish: Empire White and Gold
Wired: Keyless Sockets with Four-way
Switch—Tassel Controlled
Standard Quantity: Five
Code: Limit
$225.00 — 265.00

No. 3145
FIVE-LIGHT SEMI-CEILING FIXTURE
Length 16½"; Spread 19"
Finish: Empire White and Gold
Wired: Keyless Sockets
Standard Quantity: Five
Code: Livery
$225.00 — 250.00

No. 3133
THREE-LIGHT DROP FIXTURE
Length 42"; Spread 14½"
Finish: Empire White and Gold
Wired: Keyless Sockets
Standard Quantity: Five
Code: Limber
$195.00 — 220.00

No. 3143
THREE-LIGHT SEMI-CEILING FIXTURE
(Not illustrated)
Length 16½"; Spread 14½"
Finish: Empire White and Gold
Wired: Keyless Sockets
Standard Quantity: Five
Code: Lizard
$185.00 — 210.00

Additional Shades—GP-424

MARKEL
3000 LINE

No. 3016
SIX-LIGHT DROP FIXTURE
Length 42"; Spread 17½"
Finish: **Code:**
Silver Grey and Gold   Calf
Empire White and Gold   Cambrie
Wired: Keyless Sockets with Four-way
Switch Control
Standard Quantity: Five

$475.00 – 550.00

No. 3026
SIX-LIGHT SEMI-CEILING FIXTURE
Length 15"; Spread 17½"
Finish: **Code:**
Silver Grey and Gold   Cameo
Empire White and Gold   Camera
Wired: Keyless Sockets
Standard Quantity: Five

$450.00 – 500.00

No. 3011
ONE-LIGHT BRACKET
Wall Plate 5½" x 10¼"; Extends 4¼"
Finish: **Code:**
Silver Grey and Gold   Camp
Empire White and Gold   Canard
Wired: Canopy Switch
Standard Quantity: Ten

$115.00 – 135.00

THE 3000 LINE

Gracefully sweeping glassware to provide glowing, shaded light, now being demanded for better seeing, provides the dominating note of beauty in these fixtures. Finished in Empire White and Gold or Silver Grey and Gold. Cast in Ferro Metal. The glassware is satin finish, Peach-Glo in color, diffusing mellow, colorful light. These fixtures are especially desirable for modernizing and refixturing. The two popular finishes harmonize with nearly every decorative plan.

Additional Shades No. G-3351
Glass Bottom Bowl No. G-4041

MARKEL
3000 LINE

No. 3015
FIVE-LIGHT DROP FIXTURE
Length 42"; Spread 17½"

Finish:	Code:
Silver Grey and Gold	Canary
Empire White and Gold	Candid

Wired: Keyless Sockets
Standard Quantity: Five

$465.00 — 525.00

No. 3025
FIVE-LIGHT SEMI-CEILING FIXTURE
Length 12"; Spread 17½"

Finish:	Code:
Silver Grey and Gold	Cane
Empire White and Gold	Cannel

Wired: Keyless Sockets
Standard Quantity: Five

$425.00 — 465.00

No. 3013
THREE-LIGHT DROP FIXTURE
Length 42"; Spread 16"

Finish:	Code:
Silver Grey and Gold	Cannister
Empire White and Gold	Cannon

Wired: Keyless Sockets
Standard Quantity: Five

$385.00 — 425.00

No. 3023
THREE-LIGHT SEMI-CEILING FIXTURE
Length 10½"; Spread 16"

Finish:	Code:
Silver Grey and Gold	Canoe
Empire White and Gold	Canteen

Wired: Keyless Sockets
Standard Quantity: Five

$365.00 — 400.00

Additional Shades No. G-3351
Glass Bottom Bowl No. G-4041

No. 3015-S
FIVE-LIGHT DROP FIXTURE
(Not Illustrated)
Exactly the same as No. 3015 Except
with Four-way Switch—Tassel Controlled

Finish:	Code:
Silver Grey and Gold	Candor
Empire White and Gold	Candy

$465.00 — 525.00

MARKEL

2925
$435.00 – 475.00

2982
$200.00 – 250.00

2941
$150.00 – 185.00

$500.00 – 585.00 2936

$485.00 – 550.00 2915

NO.	LIGHTS	FINISH	CODE	LENGTH	SPREAD	STD. QTY.
2915	5 Lt. Drop	Old Gold	Campus	36″	17½″	5
2925	5 Lt. Semi-Ceil.	Old Gold	Casement	12″	17½″	5
2936	6 Lt. Drop	Old Gold	Chalice	42″	17½″	5
2941	1 Lt. Drop	Old Gold	Chuckle	36″	6″	5
2982	2 Lt. Ceiling	Old Gold	Chant	10″	13¼″	5
		Ivory and Orchid	Chime			

The 2900 Line

EMPHASIZING the modern beauty of Shaded Light. These fixtures are cast in metal and finished in Old Gold with Tan Iridescent Glass Shades. Ivory and Orchid numbers are furnished with Orchid Glass. See Glass-wear specifications on following page.

Note: Ivory and orchid fixtures furnished with orchid shades.

M A R K E L

2922:
$225.00 – 250.00
2923:
$365.00 – 400.00

2922
2923

2996
$450.00 – 500.00

2901
$115.00 – 135.00

2976
$475.00 – 525.00

2912:
$250.00 – 325.00
2913:
$350.00 – 400.00

2912
2913

NO.	LIGHTS	FINISH	CODE	WALL PLATE	EXTENDS	STD. QTY.
2901	1 Lt. Bracket	Old Gold	Cabinet	10½″ x 5½″	4½″	10
		Ivory and Orchid	Cackle			
				LENGTH	SPREAD	
2912	2 Lt. Drop	Old Gold	Cajole	36″	16″ x 6½″	5
		Ivory and Orchid	Calender			
2913	3 Lt. Drop	Old Gold	Callow	36″	16″	5
		Ivory and Orchid	Calomel			
2922	2 Lt. Semi-Ceil.	Old Gold	Canyon	10½″	16″ x 6½″	5
		Ivory and Orchid	Caprice			
2923	3 Lt. Semi-Ceil.	Old Gold	Caravan	10½″	16″	5
		Ivory and Orchid	Cardiac			
2976	6 Lt. Drop	Old Gold	Cabaret	42″	18½″	5
2996	6 Lt. Semi-Ceil.	Old Gold	Cafe	18″	18½″	5

Additional Shades No. G335   Column Shade for Nos. 2936, 2941—No. G334

Bowl for No. 2982—No. G330   Bottom Bowl for Nos. 2976, 2996—No. G3521

MARKEL
2300 LINE

2301

2315

No. 2301
ONE-LIGHT BRACKET
Wall Plate 9" x 4¼"; Extends 7"
Finish: Antique Gold
Wired: Canopy Switch
Standard Quantity: Ten
Code: Tailor

$200.00 – 250.00

No. 2315
FIVE-LIGHT DROP FIXTURE
Length 42"; Spread 19½"
Finish: Antique Gold
Wired: Keyless Sockets with Four-way
Switch—Tassel Controlled
Standard Quantity: Five
Code: Talcum

$450.00 – 500.00

THE 2300 LINE
Modern in design and modern in the effective way they deliver better light for better sight — these fixtures are flatteringly decorative in any interior. The Tan Iridescent Glassware gives a pleasing note of color that harmonizes beautifully with the Antique Gold finish. Cast in Ferro Metal.

Additional Glass Shades—No. G-3731

MARKEL
2300 LINE

2325

2313

2312

No. 2313
THREE-LIGHT DROP FIXTURE
Length 42''; Spread 15¼''
Finish: Antique Gold
Wired: Keyless Sockets
Standard Quantity: Five
Code: Tank
$400.00 – 450.00

No. 2325
FIVE-LIGHT SEMI-CEILING FIXTURE
Length 14''; Spread 19''
Finish: Antique Gold
Wired: Keyless Sockets
Standard Quantity: Five
Code: Tandem
$400.00 – 435.00

No. 2323
THREE-LIGHT SEMI-CEILING FIXTURE
Not Illustrated
Length 14''; Spread 15¼''
Finish: Antique Gold
Wired: Keyless Sockets
Standard Quantity: Five
Code: Taper
$385.00 – 425.00

No. 2312
TWO-LIGHT DROP FIXTURE
Length 36''; Spread 14½''
Finish: Antique Gold
Wired: Keyless Sockets
Standard Quantity: Five
Code: Tangle
$250.00 – 300.00

Additional Glass Shades—No. G-3731

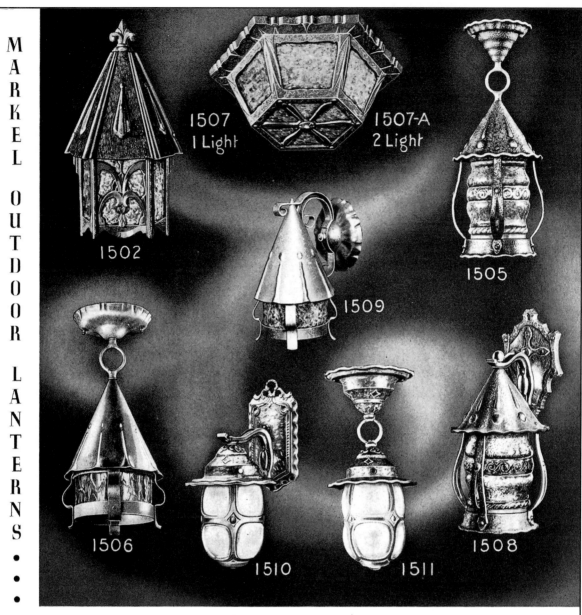

These will cost from $100.00 – 150.00 depending
on metal used and ornateness.

MARKEL OUTDOOR LANTERNS

On this page and its reverse side is illustrated and described a wide variety of outdoor lanterns de-
signed to conform to practically all architectural styles.   Several of these lanterns are cast in Ferro
Metal or Aluminum; others are fashioned of weatherproofed Sheet Metal. The Glassware is Cracked
Amber excepting numbers 1510, 1511, 1512 which are furnished with Pearl Iridescent Globes.

SEE REVERSE SIDE FOR COMPLETE SPECIFICATIONS

Extra Globes for 1510, 1511 and 1512 Lanterns No. G-315—Pearl Iridescent.
All lanterns are wired with Keyless Receptacles.
Packed one in carton and five in standard quantity.

MARKEL
1420 Series
RESIDENTIAL LUMINAIRES

BETTER LIGHT FOR BETTER SIGHT

DESIGNED to conform to the principles of I. E. S. Better Light—Better Sight Lamps, to solve the problem of providing decorative light for those many places that are so difficult to adequately and scientifically illuminate.

Markel Residential Luminaires possess every desirable feature for eye comfort, sight protection; proper light distribution; elimination of glare and general room illumination.

Especially for
DINING ROOMS
DINETTES
NURSERIES
BEDROOMS
LIBRARIES
HALLS — STUDIES

MARKEL Residential Luminaires are finished in French Bronze or Empire White and Gold to harmonize with any type of furnishing. Equipped with a choice of Silk pleated, Parchment, Rayon covered or Metal Shades. The efficient glass diffusing bowls provide maximum light output. Note wall sconce which is very decorative as well as efficient. A unit which will meet the needs of the entire family.

MARKEL

1428-B
$85.00 – 100.00

1422-B
$100.00 – 135.00

1424-E
$125.00 – 150.00

NO.	FINISH	LIST PRICE	CODE	SHADE		GLASS REFLECTOR	BULB SIZE
1422A	French Bronze	$14.25	Legation	20″	Parchment	10″	G-30–100–200–300 Watt
1422B	French Bronze	16.50	Legible	20″	Rayon	10″	G-30–100–200–300 Watt
1422C	French Bronze	17.85	Legislate	20″	Champagne Silk	10″	G-30–100–200–300 Watt
1424E	Empire White and Gold	27.00	Legume	20″	Aluminum	10″	G-30–100–200–300 Watt
1428A	Old Ivory	5.25	Lemur	10½″	Parchment	6″	100 Watt
	Herald Brown and Gold	5.25	Lena	10½″	Parchment	6″	100 Watt
1428B	Old Ivory	6.75	Leoline	10½″	Rayon	6″	100 Watt
	Herald Brown and Gold	6.75	Lens	10½″	Rayon	6″	100 Watt

All Drop Fixtures 48″ long   Standard Quantity—Five

Parchment Shades—Decoration as illustrated on 1422A

Silk Pleated Shades—Rayon Lined as illustrated on 1423C

Tan Rayon Shades—Paper Lined as illustrated on 1422B

M A R K E L

1422-A

$115.00 – 150.00

1423-C

$125.00 – 150.00

NO.	FINISH	LIST PRICE	CODE	SHADE	GLASS REFLECTOR	BULB SIZE
1422A	French Bronze	$14.25	Legation	20″ Parchment	10″	G-30–100–200–300 Watt
1423C	Empire White and Gold	19.50	Leopold	20″ Champagne or Ivory Silk	10″	G-30–100–200–300 Watt
1423D	French Bronze	19.50	Leper	20″ Gold Silk	10″	G-30–100–200–300 Watt
1423E	Empire White and Gold	24.00	Lessing	20″ Aluminum	10″	G-30–100–200–300 Watt
1426A	Old Ivory	8.25	Leporin	18″ Parchment	8″	150 Watt
	French Bronze	8.25	Leroy	18″ Parchment	8″	150 Watt
1426B	Old Ivory	9.75	Leprosy	18″ Rayon	8″	150 Watt
	French Bronze	9.75	Lesson	18″ Rayon	8″	150 Watt
1427A	Empire White and Gold	11.25	Lethal	16″ Parchment	8″	100 Watt
	French Bronze	11.25	Lettuce	16″ Parchment	8″	100 Watt
1427B	Empire White and Gold	13.50	Levant	16″ Rayon	8″	100 Watt
	French Bronze	13.50	Levity	16″ Rayon	8″	100 Watt
1429A	Old Ivory	6.75	Lexicon	12″ Parchment	6″	100 Watt
	French Bronze	6.75	Liability	12″ Parchment	6″	100 Watt
1429B	Old Ivory	8.25	Liar	12″ Rayon	6″	100 Watt
	French Bronze	8.25	Libel	12″ Rayon	6″	100 Watt

NOS. 1426-1427-1429 ILLUSTRATED ON FOLLOWING PAGE

MARKEL

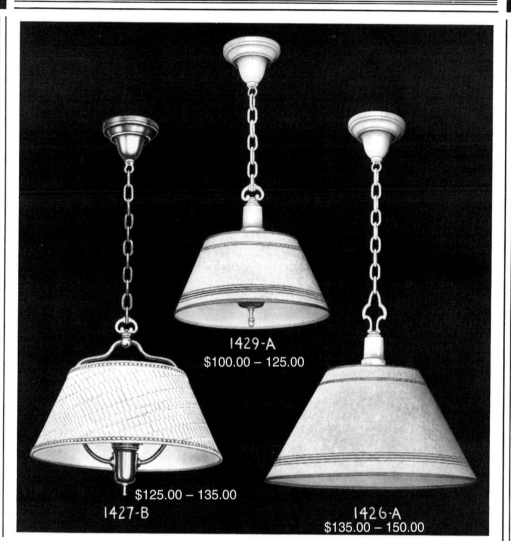

1429-A
$100.00 – 125.00

$125.00 – 135.00
1427-B

1426-A
$135.00 – 150.00

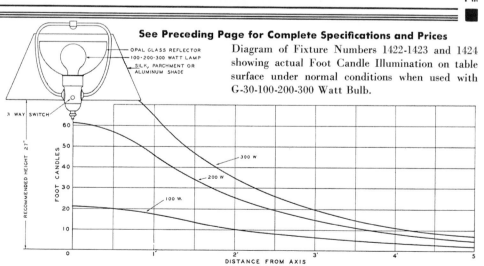

See Preceding Page for Complete Specifications and Prices

OPAL GLASS REFLECTOR
100-200-300 WATT LAMP
SILK, PARCHMENT OR ALUMINUM SHADE

3 WAY SWITCH

RECOMMENDED HEIGHT 27"

Diagram of Fixture Numbers 1422-1423 and 1424 showing actual Foot Candle Illumination on table surface under normal conditions when used with G-30-100-200-300 Watt Bulb.

FOOT CANDLES

300 W
200 W
100 W.

DISTANCE FROM AXIS

MARKEL
CHROMIUM
LINE

1433:
$85.00 – 115.00
1436:
$125.00 – 150.00
1438:
$125.00 – 140.00
1439:
$100.00 – 120.00
1466:
$35.00 – 50.00
1467:
$50.00 – 65.00
1468P:
$125.00 – 165.00
1470P:
$100.00 – 120.00
1522:
$65.00 – 75.00
1545:
$40.00 – 60.00
1579:
$100.00 – 120.00

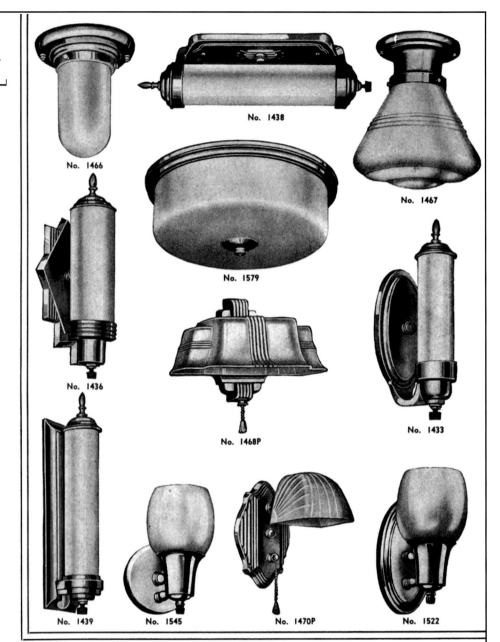

No. 1466
No. 1438
No. 1467
No. 1579
No. 1436
No. 1433
No. 1468P
No. 1439
No. 1545
No. 1470P
No. 1522

No.	Finish	Code	Wall Plate	Extends	Glass	No.	Finish	Code	Wall Plate	Extends	Glass
1433	Chromium	Kaiser	3¼" x 5¾"	3½"	No. G-442	1469P	Chromium	Kennel	4¼" x 6½"	8"	No. G-447
1436	Chromium	Kanaka	4¼" x 6¼"	3¼"	No. G-445		Same as 1470 except with Convenience Outlet				Pull Chain
1438	Chromium	Karnak	2¾" x 7½"	3¼"	No. G-448	1470	Chromium	Keno	4¼" x 6½"	8"	No. G-447
1439	Chromium	Katrine	3" x 9"	2½"	No. G-443						Keyless
1466	Chromium	Keel	Length 7"	Fitter 3¼"	No. G-440	1470P	Chromium	Kent	4¼" x 6½"	8"	No. G-447
1467	Chromium	Kelt	Length 11"	Fitter 4"	No. G-416						Pull Chain
1467P	Chromium	Karala	Length 11"	Fitter 4"	No. G-416	1522	Chromium	Kiosk	3" x 4¼"	5"	No. G-495
					Pull Chain	1545	Chromium	Kazen	4" dia.	3½"	No. G-495
			Wall Plate	Extends		1577	Nuchrome	Kean			
1468	Chromium	Kemp	4" x 6½"	5"	No. G-434		Two-Light Keyless Ring Diam. 9" Glass Diam. 8"				No. G-4351
					Keyless	1578	Nuchrome	Kearney			
1468P	Chromium	Kayak	4" x 6½"	5"	No. G-434		Two-Light Keyless Ring Diam. 11" Glass Diam. 10"				No. G-4361
					Pull Chain	1579	Nuchrome	Keats			
1469	Chromium	Kendal	4¼" x 6½"	8"	No. G-447		Three-Light Keyless Ring Diam. 13" Glass Diam. 12"				No. G-4371
					Keyless	1580	Nuchrome	Kebble			
	Same as 1470 except with Convenience Outlet						Three-Light Keyless Ring Diam. 15" Glass Diam. 14"				No. G-4381

Brackets wired with individual switch control
Standard Quantity—Ten   Bulbs not included

MARKEL
HEETAIRES
BUILT-IN WALL TYPE
NEO-GLO
ELEMENTS

●

$50.00+

NEW MARKEL HEETAIRE No. 182
Double Element

● Two separate elements, 500 watts each with individual switch control. Beautifully designed and finished. Tested and approved by Underwriters' Laboratories of the National Board of Fire Underwriters.

● Markel Neo-Glo Heetaires, inset wall type, provide the comfort and convenience of electric heat as an integral part of the home. Built into the wall—they are out of the way—ready to deliver volumes of heat at the click of a switch. Markel built-in Heetaires are a permanent addition to the home. The modern solution of auxiliary heating problems. Efficient, economical, practical for old homes or new. They increase the value of the property far beyond their cost. They provide that touch of modern convenience that stamps the home as especially desirable—either to live in, to rent or sell. Being electric, there are no fumes, dirt or dust to soil the walls or create unhealthful odors. They are today the most advanced note in auxiliary heating equipment.

MARKEL HEETAIRES ARE EASY TO INSTALL IN NEW WALLS OR OLD

Markel Heetaires can be readily installed by any electrician, either in a new or an old building.

The operations are the same as when installing a convenience outlet.

Heetaire grills overlap sufficiently so that rough edges of openings do not show.

MARKEL ELECTRIC PRODUCTS, Inc., BUFFALO, N. Y.

PRINTED IN U.S.A.

Gill Glass and Fixture Company, 1938

COMMERCIAL LIGHTING

GLASSWARE
AND
LIGHTING
FIXTURES

RESIDENTIAL LIGHTING

R. E. BAUM
REPRESENTATIVE
163 SECOND STREET
SAN FRANCISCO   CALIFORNIA

CATALOG
NO. 24

Gill Glass and Fixture Company
PHILADELPHIA

Hyperion Glass

The word "HYPERION" connotes the same standard of efficiency and excellence, in illuminating glassware, as "SEVRES" does in china or as "STERLING" does in silver. That is to say, it does more than stand for a "PRODUCT"—it signifies efficiency and unequaled "SERVICE".

Let us consider for a moment the type and character of service performed by "HYPERION." The glaringly brilliant illumination generated by an electric bulb is precipitated in keen daggers of light, hardly to be sustained by the human eye—there is an obvious need of shading, of merging, of coalescing the glittering bayonets of light to make them more serviceable and more practicable. This need is met more completely and thoroughly by a luminaire made of "HYPERION" glass. The glare is transmuted into a soft and pleasing mass of light diffused in luminous ways on the working plane below. The quality of the light, and its character are both affected by the transformation—it is softened into a glareless illumination, innocuous to the human eye.

Efficiency, however, means more than diffusion of the proper kind of illumination. It means also the percentage of light generated by the lamp, ultimately utilized by the luminaire. Using "HYPERION" as the diffusive agency, the largest percentage of light is precipitated on the working plane. Photometric tests of "HYPERION" glass show it to have an average efficiency of 88%—an amazing recommendation of its outstanding qualifications as a luminaire.

WHEN YOU SHADE LIGHT—SHADE IT WITH "HYPERION."
IT IS A GOOD AGENCY—AND THE BEST.

"Waverly" Line

Design by Aglow

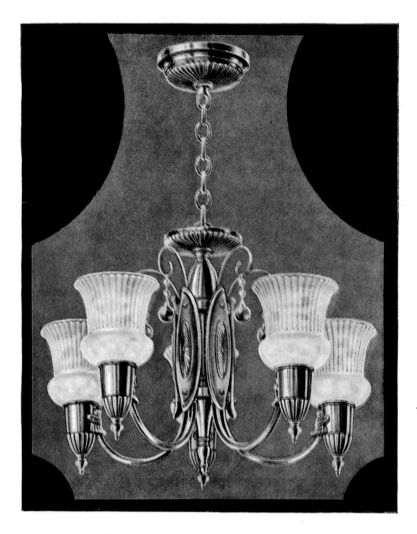

The fixture above illustrates the combination
of Pewter and Iridescent Pearl Glassware.

$250.00 – 300.00

"Waverly" Line

Choice of Finishes

Pewter with Pearl
Iridescent Glassware.
Stained Bronze with Gold
Iridescent Glassware.

No. 1435 [5 Lights]

Length Overall.........................42 inches
Spread................................21 inches

For 5 Light Fixtures wired with 3 circuit turn switch in
bottom centre, add **$1.50** list.

$250.00 — 300.00

No. 1401 [1 Light Bracket]

Backplate.........................7 x 3½ inches
Extension from wall....................8 inches

[With Canopy Turn Switch]

$100.00 — 125.00

Listed under Label Service of Underwriters' Laboratories, Inc.

"Waverly" Line

No. 1425 [5 Lights]

Length Overall.........................17 inches
Spread...............................21 inches

For 5 Light fixtures wired with 3 circuit turn switch in
bottom centre, add **$1.50** list.

$225.00 — 285.00

No. 1421 [1 Light]

Length Overall.....16½ inches
Spread.............7¾ inches

$110.00 — 135.00

No. 1423 [3 Lights]

Length Overall......................14½ inches
Spread...............................18 inches

$195.00 — 225.00

Listed under Label Service of Underwriters' Laboratories, Inc.

"Windsor" Line

Design by Aglow

The fixture above illustrates the combination of Colonial Brass and Crystal Frosted Glassware.

$200.00 — 250.00

"Windsor" Line

Choice of Finishes
Colonial Brass.
Stained Bronze.
Iridescent Gold Glassware.
Crystal Glass with Frosting.
[as illustrated.]

No. 1935 [5 Lights]

Length Overall.........................42 inches
Spread.................................18 inches

For 5 Light fixtures wired with 3 circuit turn switch in bottom centre, add **$1.50** List.

$200.00 – 250.00

No. 1901 [1 Light Bracket]

Backplate........ 6 x 3¼ inches
Extension from wall.....6 inches

[With Canopy Turn Switch]

$85.00 – 100.00

For extra lengths of chain on pendant fixtures, add **45c** List per foot or fraction of a foot.

Listed under Label Service of Underwriters' Laboratories, Inc.

"Windsor" Line

No. 1925 [5 Lights]
Length Overall........................18 inches
Spread................................18 inches

For 5 Light fixtures wired with 3 circuit turn switch in
bottom centre, add **$1.50** List.

$195.00 – 225.00

No. 1921 [1 Light]
Length Overall.....16½ inches
Spread.............6¾ inches

$100.00 – 115.00

No. 1923 [3 Lights]
Length Overall........................17 inches
Spread................................15 inches

$150.00 – 175.00

Listed under Label Service of Underwriters' Laboratories, Inc.

"Jefferson" Line

Design by Orth

The fixture above illustrates the combination of Antique Bronze
and Chrome with Pearl Iridescent Glassware.

$275.00 – 325.00

"Jefferson" Line

Choice of Finishes

Antique Bronze and Chrome
with Pearl Iridescent
Glassware.
Antique Bronze with
Gold Iridescent Glassware.

No. 1835 [5 Lights]

Length Overall.........................42 inches
Spread.................................18 inches

$275.00 – 325.00

For extra lengths of chain on pendant
fixtures, add **45c** List per foot or fraction
of a foot.

No. 1801 [1 Light]

Backplate.......4¾ x 4¾ inches
Extension from wall...6½ inches
[With Canopy Turn Switch]

$100.00 – 125.00

Listed under Label Service of Underwriters' Laboratories, Inc.

"Jefferson" Line

No. 1825 [5 Lights]

Length Overall.......................14 inches
Spread...............................18 inches

$265.00 — 300.00

No. 1821 [1 Light]

Length Overall.......15 inches
Spread.............7½ inches

$115.00 — 135.00

No. 1823 [3 Lights]

Length Overall.......................12 inches
Spread...............................14½ inches

$200.00 — 250.00

Listed under Label Service of Underwriters' Laboratories, Inc.

"Belgrade" Line
Design by Aglow

The fixture above illustrates the combination of
*Carat Gold and Iridescent Gold Glassware.

$200.00 – 250.00

*Carat Gold is a beautiful rich gilt finish, which looks like real Gold Plate.

"Belgrade" Line

Choice of Finishes
Carat Gold.
Bone White & Gold.
Glassware is Iridescent
Gold.

No. 2435 [5 lights]
Length Overall.........................42 inches
Spread.................................20 inches
For 5 Light fixtures wired with 3 circuit turn switch
in bottom centre, add **$1.50** List.

$200.00 — 250.00

For extra lengths of chain on pendant
fixtures, add **45c** List per foot or fraction
of a foot.

No. 2401 [1 Light Bracket]
Backplate........ 7¼ x 4 inches
Extension from wall.. 7½ inches

[With Canopy Turn Switch.]

$85.00 — 115.00

Listed under Label Service of Underwriters' Laboratories, Inc.

"Belgrade" Line

No. 2425 [5 Lights]
Length Overall........................18 inches
Spread................................20 inches

For 5 Light fixtures wired with 3 circuit switch in bottom centre, add **$1.50** List.

$200.00 – 225.00

No. 2421 [1 Light]
Length Overall.....16½ inches
Spread.............7¾ inches

$100.00 – 115.00

No. 2423 [3 Lights]
Length Overall........................16 inches
Spread................................18 inches

$195.00 – 225.00

Listed under Label Service of Underwriters' Laboratories, Inc.

"Delaware" Line
Design by Aglow

An attractive line of Lighting Fixtures, in a choice of beautiful
finishes and with Colonial type glass shades in lustrous
ivory iridescence

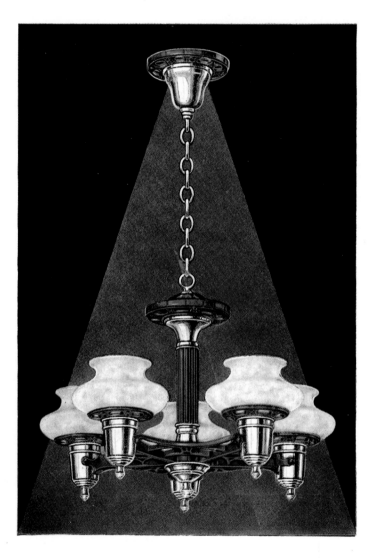

The fixture above illustrates the combination of Maroon and
Chrome with Iridescent Ivory Glass Shades

$250.00 — 300.00

"Delaware" Line
Design by Aglow

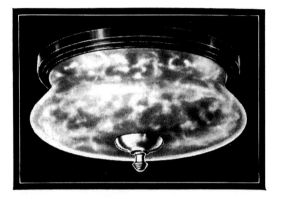

No. 3410 [2 Lights]

Diameter of Glassware................10 inches
Diameter of Metal Band...............10 inches

$100.00 – 125.00

No. 3412 [2 Lights]

Diameter of Glassware................12 inches
Diameter of Metal Band...............12 inches

No. 3435 [5 Lights]

Length overall........................42 inches
Spread..............................19 inches

$250.00 – 300.00

No. 3421 [1 Light]

Length overall..........16½ inches
Spread................ 8 inches

$140.00 – 165.00

For fixtures wired with 3-circuit turn switch in bottom centre, add **$1.50** list extra.

For extra lengths of chain on pendant fixtures, add **45c** List per foot or fraction of a foot.

"Delaware" Line
Design by Aglow

No. 3425 [5 Lights]

Length overall ....17½ inches
Spread............................19 inches

$240.00 – 285.00

For fixtures wired with 3-circuit switch in bottom centre, add **$1.50** list extra.

Note—

Special 3-circuit switches are supplied only on No. 3435 and No. 3425, and only when requested.

❮❮

When ordering fixtures, please give fixture number and finish required.

Choice of Finishes

Maroon and Chrome
Maroon and Gold
Bone White and Gold

❮❮

Glassware is Iridescent Ivory

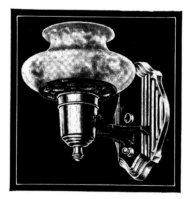

No. 3401 [1 Light Bracket]

Backplate.............6½ x 4¼ inches
Extension from wall...........7½ inches

[With Canopy Turn Switch]

$100.00 – 125.00

Listed under Label Service of Underwriters' Laboratories, Inc.

"Delaware" Line
Design by Aglow

No. 3433 [3 Lights]
Length overall.....................42 inches
Spread...........................16 inches
$200.00 – 250.00

Choice of Finishes

Maroon and Chrome
Maroon and Gold
Bone White and Gold

≫

Glassware is Iridescent Ivory

No. 3431 [1 Light]
Length overall......................42 inches
Spread............................ 8 inches
$150.00 – 175.00

When ordering, please give fixture number and finish required

≫

All fixtures are furnished wired complete with approved wiring devices and heat-resisting wire

No. 3423 [3 Lights]
Length overall...................17½ inches
Spread.........................16   inches
$200.00 – 235.00

Listed under Label Service of Underwriters' Laboratories, Inc.

"Sherwood" Line
Design by Orth

A line of Residential Lighting Fixtures, with Ornamental Filigree motif, beautifully finished and furnished with lustrous Iridescent Glass Shades.

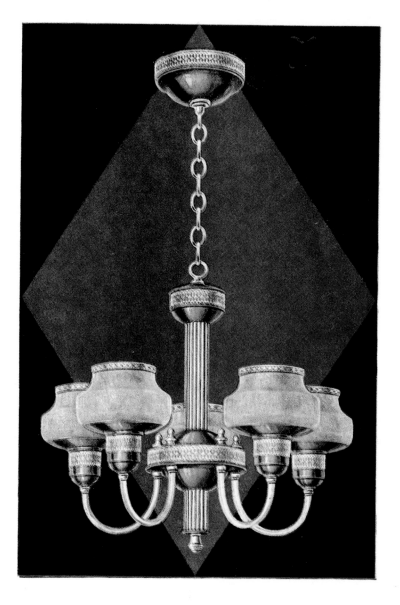
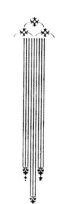

The fixture above illustrates the combination of Copper Bronze and Chrome with Iridescent Stippled Gold Glass Shades.

$285.00 – 335.00

"Sherwood" Line
Design by Orth

No. 9441 [1 Light]
Diameter .... 12 Inches
Length .... 13 Inches
[Will take up to a 100-watt lamp]
No. 9441 Can also be furnished in
Bone White and Gold

$125.00 – 150.00

All fixtures are furnished wired complete with approved wiring devices and heat-resisting wire

Note —

Special 3-circuit switches are supplied only on No. 9435 and No. 9425, and only when requested

No. 9421 [1 Light]
Length overall .... 18 inches
Spread .... 7 inches

$100.00 – 125.00

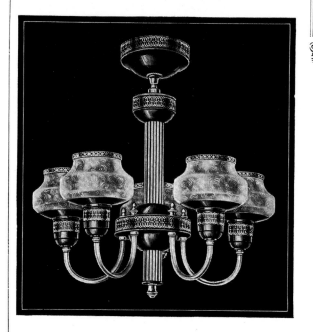

No. 9425 [5 Lights]
Length overall .... 18 inches
Spread .... 18 inches

For fixtures wired with 3-circuit turn switch in bottom centre, add **$1.50** list extra.

$275.00 – 325.00

Listed under Label Service of Underwriters' Laboratories, Inc.

"Sherwood" Line
Design by Orth

Finish

Fixtures
   Copper Bronze and Chrome

Glassware
   Iridescent Stippled Gold

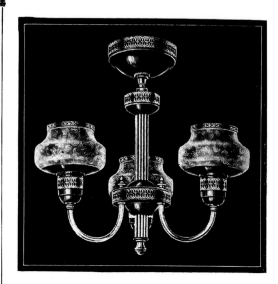

No. 9423 [3 Lights]

Overall length . . . . 16 inches
Spread . . . . 16 inches

$235.00 – 260.00

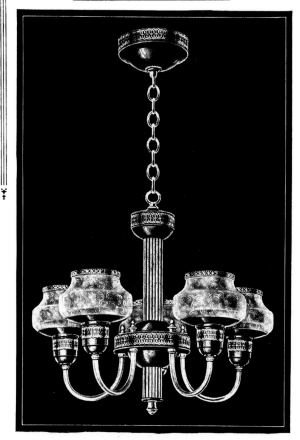

No. 9435 [5 Lights]

Overall length . . . . 42 inches
Spread . . . . 18 inches
For fixtures wired with 3-circuit turn switch in bottom
centre, add **$1.50** list extra.

$300.00 – 350.00

All fixtures are furnished wired complete
with approved wiring devices and heat-
resisting wire

No. 9401 [1 Light Wall Bracket]

Back plate . . . . 4⅝ inches
Extension from wall . . . . 7½ inches
[Furnished with Canopy Turn Switch]

$125.00 – 145.00

Listed under Label Service of Underwriters' Laboratories, Inc.

"Radcliffe" Line
Design by Aglow

Colonial Style fixtures, with a slight modern touch. Complete with beautiful iridescent white onyx glass shades and cut crystals.

The fixture above illustrates the combination of Stained Bronze and Chrome with Iridescent White Onyx Glass Shades

$250.00 – 300.00

"Radcliffe" Line
Design by Aglow

Choice of Finishes

Stained Bronze and Chrome
Polished Chrome

Glassware is Iridescent White Onyx
finish

No. 8423 [3 Lights]
Overall length 13 inches—Spread 15 inches
$200.00 — 235.00

No. 8435 [5 Lights]
Overall length 42 inches—Spread 18 inches
For fixtures wired with 3-circuit turn switch in bottom centre,
add **$1.50** list extra.
$250.00 — 300.00

For extra lengths of chain on pendant
fixtures, add **45c** List per foot or fraction
of a foot.

No. 8401 [1 Light Bracket]
Back Plate . . . . 6½ x 4¼ inches
Extension from wall . . . . 7½ inches
$100.00 — 115.00

All fixtures are furnished wired complete
with approved wiring devices and heat-
resisting wire

Listed under Label Service of Underwriters' Laboratories, Inc.

"Radcliffe" Line
Design by Aglow

All fixtures are furnished wired complete
with approved wiring devices and heat-
resisting wire

Choice of Finishes

Stained Bronze and Chrome
Polished Chrome

❧

Glassware is Iridescent White Onyx
finish

No. 8431 [1 Light]

Length overall.........42 inches
Spread...............9½ inches

$110.00 – 130.00

No. 8433 [3 Lights]

Length overal 42 inches—Spread 15 inches

$200.00 – 245.00

Listed under Label Service of Underwriters' Laboratories, Inc.

"Bellecourt"
Residential Lighting Fixtures

The fixture above illustrates the combination of Carat Gold,
with Iridescent Gold Glassware.

$200.00 – 250.00

"Bellecourt"
Residential Lighting Fixtures

No. 6741 [1 Light]

Overall length........................13 inches
Diam. of Bowl.........................12 inches

Wired with medium base socket for lamps up to 150 watts.

$185.00 – 200.00

Metal Finishes
    Carat Gold
    Bone White and Gold

Finish of Glassware
    Stippled Iridescent Gold

Carat Gold is a beautiful rich gilt finish, which looks very much like real gold plate.

No. 6731 [1 Light]

Overall length.............42 inches
Spread.................... 9 inches

Wired with medium base socket.

$125.00 – 145.00

For extra chain add **45** cents list per foot
or fraction of a foot

Listed under Label Service of Underwriters' Laboratories, Inc.

"Bellecourt"
Residential Lighting Fixtures

All fixtures are wired complete with approved wiring devices and heat-resisting wire.

No. 6716 [1 Light]

Overall length . . . . 42 inches
Diameter of Bowl . . . . 16 inches

Wired with medium base socket for lamps up to 300 watts.

$200.00 – 250.00

For extra chain add **45** cents list per foot or fraction of a foot

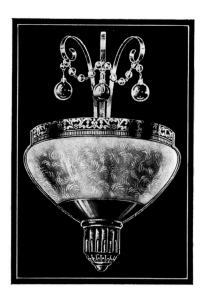

No. 6711 [1 Light]

Overall length . . . . 12 inches
Width . . . . 8 inches

Wired with medium base socket

[Add **45c** list for canopy turn switch.]

$135.00 – 165.00

Listed under Label Service of Underwriters' Laboratories, Inc.

See other side.

"Belleville"
Residential Lighting Fixtures

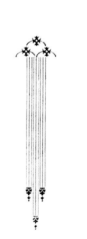

The fixture above illustrates the combination of Carat Gold,
with Iridescent Gold Glassware.

$200.00 – 250.00

"Belleville"
Residential Lighting Fixtures

Finishes of fixtures
Carat Gold
Bone White and Gold

Glassware
Iridescent Stippled Gold

Carat Gold is a beautiful rich gilt finish, which looks very much like real gold plate.

No. 9716 [1 Light]

Overall length.........................42 inches
Diameter of Bowl......................16 inches

Wired with medium base socket for lamps up to 300 watts.

$200.00 – 250.00

For extra chain add **45** cents list per foot or fraction of a foot

No. 9711 [1 Light]

Overall length..............12 inches
Width.................... 8 inches

Wired with medium base socket

[Add **45c** list for canopy turn switch.]

$125.00 – 150.00

Listed under Label Service of Underwriters' Laboratories, Inc.

"Belleville"
Residential Lighting Fixtures

No. 9741 [1 Light]

Overall length.........................12 inches
Diam. of Bowl.........................13 inches

Wired with medium base socket for lamps up to 150 watts.

$195.00 – 225.00

No. 9731 [1 Light]

Overall length.............42 inches
Diam. of Bowl............8¼ inches

Wired with medium base socket for lamps up to 150 watts.

For extra chain add **45** cents list per foot or fraction of a foot

$100.00 – 135.00

All fixtures are wired complete with approved wiring devices and heat-resisting wire

Listed under Label Service of Underwriters' Laboratories, Inc.

"Bellefont"
Residential Semi-Indirect Lighting Fixtures

No. 7716 [3 Lights]

Length......42 inches   Spread......17 inches

$195.00 – 250.00

Finishes:
Copper Bronze & Chrome
with
Blue & White Decoration
on Glassware.

Stained Bronze
with
Brown & Ivory Decoration
on Glassware.

Front View

*No. 7711 [1 Light Wall Bracket]

Overall length............11½ inches
Diameter of Glass............7 inches

$130.00 – 165.00

[With Turn Switch]
For use with one 30 watt lamp.

*Note: This is an "Edgelite" type of Bracket. The light which is hidden in the bracket filters through the edge of the glass disc, and produces a very novel and beautiful effect.

When ordering, please mention number and finish required.

Listed under Label Service of Underwriters' Laboratories, Inc.

For extra lengths of chain on pendant fixtures, add **45c** list per foot or fraction of a foot.

Novel Lighting Fixtures

The fixtures illustrated below were especially designed for the better type of Tavern, Rathskeller, Beer Parlor and Taproom and are so unique in construction, that the originality of their design is second only to the pleasing and mellow illumination, produced by the glass kegs.

The fixtures and keg-supporting brackets, which are made of cast aluminum are true reproductions of real wood carving, and the antique wood finish applied is so realistic as to challenge detection.

No. 8101 (1 Light Bracket)
Length. . . . . .8½ inches
Extension . . . . .7½ inches
(With Canopy Switch)

$200.00+

Glass kegs furnished are regular
No. 2706:—
  Diameter. . . . . . . .5 inches
  Length. . . . . .6 inches
  Fitter. . . . . .3¼ inches

$500.00+

No. 8135 (5 Lights)
Overall Length. . . . . .42 inches
Spread. . . . . .20 inches

Listed under Label Service of Underwriters' Laboratories, Inc.

Novel Lighting Luminaires

in
Antique Wood Finish
As illustrated in Color on the
reverse side of this sheet.

$200.00 –
350.00

No. 136-2700
(Crystal Bottom)

No. 123-2706
$100.00 – 135.00

No. 136-2710
$200.00 – 300.00

Note:—All metal fixture Parts
are furnished in Antique Wood
finish and are wired complete.

Glassware is furnished in
"Oak Color."

$200.00 –
285.00

No. 126-2710

$200.00 –
335.00

No. 126-2700
(Crystal Bottom)

Number	Luminaire Overall length	Glass Dimensions Width	Length	Fitter	Standard Package Luminaire Complete	Standard Package Glassware only
136-2700	42 Inches	10"	x 12"	x 6"	1	1
126-2700	16 Inches	10"	x 12"	x 6"	1	1
136-2710	40 Inches	10"	x 10"	x 6"	1	1
126-2710	14 Inches	10"	x 10"	x 6"	1	1
123-2706	9 Inches	5"	x 6"	x 3¼"	1	12

*Price of No. 2706. Barrel with metal Spigot $2.55 List. (As illustrated on the reverse side of this sheet.)
Listed under Label Service of Underwriters' Laboratories, Inc.

Novel Lighting Units

for

Beer Gardens — Taverns — Tap Rooms

No. 2700
With Clear Crystal Bottom
and Metal Connecting Ring

$200.00 — 300.00

Units can be furnish-
ed in Oak Color or
"Hyperion" White.

Specify color
desired.

No. 2710 10" x 10" x 6 "
No. 2706 5" x 6" x 3¼"
With Closed Bottom

$200.00 — 285.00

Number	Finish	Diameter	Dimensions Length	Fitter	Standard Carton	Weight Standard Carton
2700	Oak Color	10"	x 12"	x 6 "	1	6 lbs.
2700	"Hyperion" White	10"	x 12"	x 6 "	1	6 lbs.
2710	Oak Color	10"	x 10"	x 6 "	1	5½ lbs.
2710	"Hyperion" White	10"	x 10"	x 6 "	1	5½ lbs.
2706	Oak Color	5"	x 6"	x 3¼"	12	20 lbs.
2706	"Hyperion" White	5"	x 6"	x 3¼"	12	20 lbs.

Ceiling Lights

for

BEDROOM · SUN PARLOR · DINETTE

Glassware furnished in Gold Iridescence.

———

No. 4412-Fixture furnished in Ivory.

No. 4412

Diameter - 12 inches

$150.00 – 200.00

All fixtures furnished wired complete, ready to install. (We recommend lamp bulbs from 50 to 150 watts).

No. 4412-2

Diameter - 12 inches.

For attachment to any standard base socket.

$150.00 – 200.00

Listed under Label Service of Underwriters' Laboratories, Inc.

Novel Ceiling Lights

for

Bedroom—Sun Parlor—Dinette

No. 9441 [1 Light]

[Wired Complete]

Diameter....................12 inches
Overall Length..............13 inches

[Will take up to 100-watt lamp]

$200.00 – 250.00

Choice of Finishes

Fixtures

Polished Chrome and Gilt
Bone White and Gold

Glassware

Iridescent Stippled Gold

Novel Ceiling Lights

for

Bedroom - Sun Parlor - Dinette

No. 5441 (1 Light)

Wired Complete

Will take up to 100 Watt Lamp
Length - 11 inches
Diameter - 10¼ inches

$150.00 — 175.00

Finishes:—
Toned Ivory and Gold.
Plum Bronze and Gold.
Bone White and Gold.
Polished Chrome.

Glassware:—
Irridescent Opal.

Novel Ceiling Lights

for

BEDROOM • SUN PARLOR • DINETTE

No. 5442 (1 Light)

Wired Complete

Will take up to 100 Watt Lamp
Length - 11 inches
Diameter - 10¼ inches

$185.00 — 250.00

Finishes:—
    Toned Ivory and Gold
    Plum Bronze and Gold.
    Bone White and Gold.
    Polished Chrome.

Glassware:—
    Iridescent Opal.

Novel Ceiling Lights

for

BEDROOM • SUN PARLOR • DINETTE

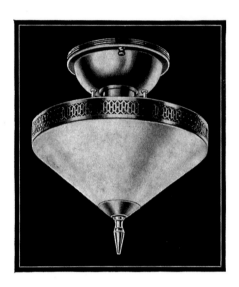

No. 5443 (1 Light)

Wired Complete

Will take up to 100 Watt Lamp
Length - 11 inches
Diameter - 10¼ inches

$200.00+

Finishes:—
    Toned Ivory and Gold.
    Plum Bronze and Gold.
    Bone White and Gold.
    Polished Chrome

Glassware:—
    Iridescent Opal.

Bedroom, Sun Parlor and Breakfast Room

B. 101 [1 Light]

Diameter .... 10½ inches
Depth .... 6½ inches

$185.00 — 235.00

Glassware will be furnished in
HONEY color only

FIXTURES are all furnished in
IVORY finish

B. 201 [1 Light]

Diameter .... 9½ inches
Length .... 10 inches

$195.00 — 250.00

Bathroom and Kitchen
Wall Brackets

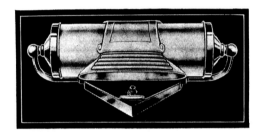

B.150 [1 Light]
Wired Complete with Pull Switch
Diameter of Glass Cylinder..................2⅞ inches
Overall length of Bracket ....12 inches

$150.00+

Finish:
    Polished Chrome

Glassware:
    White "Hyperion"

Note: The B.150 Wall Bracket can be installed in both positions as illustrated.

The glass cylinder can be turned, so that the opening faces any position desired.

Ideal for shaving.

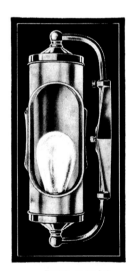

B.150 [1 Light]
Wired Complete with Pull Switch

Listed under Label Service of Underwriters' Laboratories, Inc.

Bathroom and Kitchen
Chromium Plated Wall Brackets, complete with Glassware
(Wired Complete with Turn Button Switches)

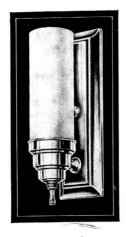

When Ordering

All Glassware shown, can be supplied with any and all of the brackets illustrated — therefore mention both the bracket number and glass number required.

Glass Numbers

G.1. Plain White Cylinder.
G.1.E. Crystal Etched Striped Cylinder.
G.1.S. Silver Striped White Cylinder.
G.2. Modernistic Striped Cylinder.
G.3. Plain White Shade.

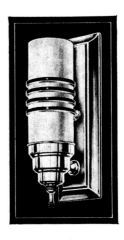

B.145—G.1.

Shown with Plain White Cylinder.

Wired Complete with Turn Switch.

Backplate—9" x 3"
Cylinder—6" x 2½"

$140.00 – 175.00

B 145—G 2.

Shown with White Modernistic Cylinder and Black Raised Stripes.

Wired Complete with Turn Switch.

Backplate—9" x 3"
Cylinder—6" x 2½"

$150.00 – 200.00

B.146—G.1E

Shown with Crystal Etched Striped Cylinder.

Wired Complete with Turn Switch.

Note: White Cylinder with Silver Stripes, can also be furnished at the same price.

(Glass Number G.1.S.)

$150.00 – 200.00

B.146—G.3.

Shown with Plain White Shade.

Wired Complete with Turn Switch.

Backplate—6¼" x 3¾"
Glassware—4½" x 3½" x 2½" fitter.

$135.00 – 165.00

B.147—G.3.

Shown with Plain White Shade.

Wired Complete with Turn Switch.

Backplate—6" long x 6" wide
Glassware—4½" x 3½" x 2½" fitter.

$100.00 – 115.00

Listed under Label Service of Underwriters' Laboratories, Inc.

Bathroom and Kitchen

Chromium Plated Wall Brackets, complete with Glassware

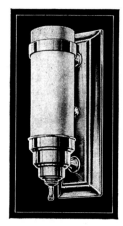

Brackets are furnished with "Hyperion" white cylinders and wired complete with Turn-Button Switches, for individual control.

B.148—G.1
Wired Complete
Backplate—9" x 3"
Cylinder—6" x 2½"
(Complete with Turn Button Switch)

$140.00 – 175.00

B.155
Wired Complete with
Convenience Outlet
Backplate—6" x 3¼"

B 155½
without Convenience Outlet
(Complete with Turn Button Switch)

$95.00 – 115.00

B.149—G.1
Wired Complete
Backplate—9" x 3"
Cylinder—6" x 2½"
(Complete with Turn Button Switch)

$150.00 – 200.00

Listed under Label Service of Underwriters' Laboratories, Inc.

Please mention Bracket Number, when ordering

Bathroom and Kitchen
[CHROMIUM PLATED WALL BRACKETS]

ALL BRACKETS are furnished wired
with approved wiring materials,
and packed complete with glassware in individual cartons.

B. 143 [2 Lights]

Length of Bracket Back.. 5¼ inches
Width of Glass Shade..12¾ inches
Extension from Wall.... 6¼ inches

[With Canopy Switch]

$165.00 — 225.00

**Can also be furnished with
Pull Chain Switch.**

Illustrating Wall Brackets of distinction, for
Medicine Cabinets and over
Kitchen Sinks.

———

Highly polished CHROMIUM with genuine
"VELVA" glassware.

B. 142 [1 Light]

Length of Bracket Back..5¾ inches
Width of Bracket Back....4¼ inches
Extension from Wall......6¾ inches

[Pull Chain]

$100.00 — 135.00

Listed under Label Service of Underwriters' Laboratories, Inc.

Series F-100

Indirect Lighting Fixtures for
Offices, Stores, Showrooms, Schools, Hospitals, etc.

Indirect Lighting
Wall Bracket

(Made of Aluminum only—without Glass)

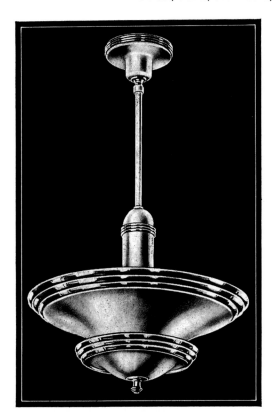

No. 4011—(75-100 watt)

Width.........................9½ inches
Length........................7½ inches
Wired Medium Base Socket.
Price........................**$8.25** ea. list

Canopy Turn Button Switch can be supplied
at 45c list extra.

$125.00 – 150.00

F 116—(150-200 watt)

Diameter—16 inches.........Overall Length—30 inches
Wired with Medium Base Socket.
Price................................**$12.75** ea. list

F 118—(300-500 watt)

Diameter—18 inches.........Overall Length—33 inches
Wired with Mogul Base Socket.
Price................................**$14.25** ea. list

F 122—(750-1000 watt)

Diameter—22 inches.........Overall Length—36 inches
Price................................**$19.50** ea. list

For additional overall lengths, add 75c list per foot, or
fraction of a foot.

$150.00 – 250.00

For fixtures wired to take 3-Light Lamps:
Add $3.00 List for 3 circuit socket and switch.
Add $1.50 List for 3 circuit socket only—
without switch.

Fixtures are made of Spun
Aluminum and are finished in
Sprayed **CHROMALUSTRE**
with Polished Aluminum
Highlights.

Sprayed **GOLDLUSTRE**
with Polished Gold
Highlights.

When ordering, please mention
Number and Finish required.

Inside of reflectors are
finished in hard White
Porcelain effect Enamel.

Listed under Label Service of Underwriters' Laboratories, Inc.

Series F-300
Semi-Indirect Lighting Fixtures
Combining a Plurality of Aluminum Louvres with
Opal Glass Disc in the bottom.
For Showrooms, Reception Rooms, Stores, Private Offices, etc.

F 318—(300-500 watt)
With Four Louvres as illustrated
Diameter—18 inches.........Overall Length—32 inches
Wired with Mogul Base Socket
Price..................................**$24.75** ea. list

F 322—(750-1000 watt)
With Five Louvres
Diameter—22 inches.........Overall Length—35 inches
Wired with Mogul Base Socket
Price..................................**$32.25** ea. list
For additional overall lengths, add 75c list per foot, or
fraction of a foot.

$250.00+

For fixtures wired to take 3-Light Lamps:
Add $3.00 List for 3 circuit socket and switch.
Add $1.50 List for 3 circuit socket only—
no switch.

Indirect Lighting
Wall Bracket
(Made of Aluminum only—without Glass)

No. 4011—(75-100 watt)
Width........................9½ inches
Length........................7½ inches
Wired Medium Base Socket.
Price........................**$8.25** ea. list
Canopy Turn Button Switch can be supplied
at 45c list extra.

$125.00 – 150.00

Fixtures are made of Spun
Aluminum and are finished in
Sprayed **CHROMALUSTRE**
with Polished Aluminum
Highlights.

Sprayed **GOLDLUSTRE**
with Polished Gold
Highlights.

When ordering, please mention
Number and Finish required.

Listed under Label Service of Underwriters' Laboratories, Inc.

Series F-4000

Efficient Luminaires of Artistic Design
for
Indirect and Semi-Indirect Illumination for
Stores, Showrooms, Reception Rooms, Banks and Lobbies

INDIRECT LIGHTING

Finishes:—
   Sprayed Chromalustre with
   Polished Aluminum Highlights

   Sprayed Goldlustre with
   Polished Gold Highlights

SEMI-INDIRECT LIGHTING
with
Opal Glass Dish

No. 4018—(300-500 watt)
Diameter—18 inches...........Overall length—32 inches
Wired Complete with Mogul Socket
Price...........................**$16.50** ea. list

No. 4022—(750-1000 watt)
Diameter—22 inches...........Overall length—35 inches
Wired Complete with Mogul Socket
Price...........................**$20.25** ea. list

$300.00+ ———

For additional overall lengths, add 75c list per foot, or
fraction of a foot.

———

For fixtures wired to take 3-light lamps:
Add $3.00 List for 3 circuit socket and switch.
Add $1.50 List for 3 circuit socket only—without switch.

Listed under Label Service of Underwriters' Laboratories, Inc.

No. 4018-G—(300-500 watt)
Diameter—18 inches...........Overall length—32 inches
Wired Complete with Mogul Socket
Price...........................**$18.00** ea. list
No. 4022-G—(750-1000 watt)
Diameter—22 inches...........Overall length—35 inches
Wired Complete with Mogul Socket
Price...........................**$22.50** ea. list

$300.00+

Series No. 9400

Semi-Indirect Ornamental Luminaires for
Showrooms, Lobbies, Reception Rooms, Stores

All Metal Parts
finished in
Stained Bronze
or
Ivory and Gold

❖

Glassware
furnished in
**Iridescent
Stippled Gold
(NuGold)**

For fixtures wired
to take 3-Light
Lamps.
Add $3.00 list
for 2 - circuit
socket & switch.
Add $1.50 list
for 2 - circuit
socket only,
when no switch
is required

Number	Dimensions		Type of Socket Furnished	Recommended Wattage
	Overall Length	Diam. of Glass		
9412	31 inches	12 inches	Medium	100
9414	32 inches	14 inches	Medium	100–150
9416	33 inches	16 inches	Medium	150–300
9418	35 inches	18 inches	Mogul	300–500

For additional overall lengths, add 75c list per foot, or fraction of a foot.

Listed under Label Service of Underwriters' Laboratories, Inc.

$250.00+

See other side of this sheet.

Series No. 9400

Semi-Indirect Ornamental Luminaires

No. 9422 to No. 9428 (1 Light)
$200.00 – 235.00

No. 9441 (1 Light)
$200.00 – 235.00

All Metal Parts are finished in
STAINED BRONZE
or
IVORY and GOLD
❖
Glassware is furnished in
**IRIDESCENT
STIPPLED GOLD**

No. 9411 (1 Light Wall Bracket)
(Canopy turn switch can be furnished
at 45c list extra.)
$100.00 – 135.00

Numbers	Dimensions		Type of Socket Furnished	Recommended Wattage
	Overall Length	Diam. of Glass		
9411	8½ inches	8 inches	Medium	75
9422	17 inches	12 inches	Medium	100
9424	18 inches	14 inches	Medium	100–150
9426	19 inches	16 inches	Medium	150–300
9428	21 inches	18 inches	Mogul	300–500
9441	13 inches	12 inches	Medium	100

When ordering, please mention **Number** and **Finish** required.

Listed under Label Service of Underwriters' Laboratories, Inc.

Series No. 9000

Semi-Indirect Ornamental Luminaires for
Banks, Showrooms, Lobbies, Stores, Reception Rooms

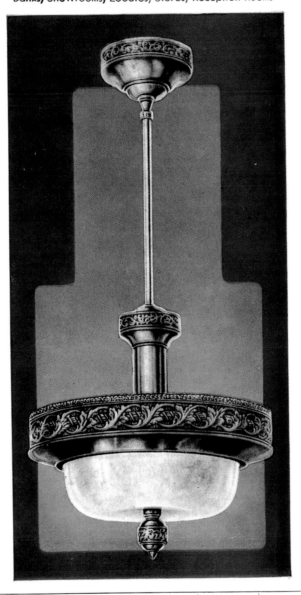

All Metal Parts
finished in
Stained Bronze

Glassware fur-
nished in
**Iridescent
Stippled Gold**

❖❖

Fixtures can also
be furnished in

**Polished or Dull
Chrome**

[Dull Chrome is
Satin-Finished
Chrome.]

For fixtures wired
to take the new
3-Light Lamps.

Add $3.00 list for
the special 2-cir-
cuit socket and
switch. Add
$1.50 list for the
2-circuit socket
only, when no
switch is re-
quired.

Number	Dimensions			Type of Socket Furnished	Recommended Wattage
	Overall Length	Diam. of Band	Diam. of Glass		
9014	33 inches	14 inches	10 inches	Medium	100–150
9016	35 inches	16 inches	12 inches	Medium	150–200
9019	36 inches	19 inches	14½ inches	Mogul	300–500
9030	42 inches	30 inches	20 inches	Mogul	750–1500

For additional overall lengths, add 75c list per foot or fraction of a foot.

Listed under Label Service of Underwriters' Laboratories, Inc.

$250.00+

Series No. 9000
Semi-Indirect Ornamental Luminaires

No. 9024 [1 Light]
No. 9026 [1 Light]
No. 9029 [1 Light]
$200.00 – 235.00

> All Metal Parts are finished in
> **STAINED BRONZE**
> Glassware is furnished in
> **IRIDESCENT STIPPLED GOLD**

> Fixtures can also be furnished in Polished
> or Dull Chrome.
> [Dull Chrome is Satin-Finished Chrome.]

No. 9011 [1 Light Wall Bracket]
[Canopy Turn Switch can be furnished at 45c list, extra.]
$125.00 – 150.00

No. 9044 [2 Lights]
No. 9046 [2 Lights]
No. 9049 [3 Lights]
$145.00 – 165.00

Number	Dimensions			Type of Socket Furnished	Recommended Wattage
	Overall Length	Diam. of Band	Diam. of Glass		
9011	8 inches	....	8 inches	Medium Base	75–100
9024	20 inches	14 inches	10 inches	Medium Base	100–150
9026	22 inches	16 inches	12 inches	Medium Base	150–200
9029	23 inches	19 inches	14½ inches	Mogul Base	300–500
9044	12 inches	12 inches	10 inches	Two Medium	Two 60 watt
9046	14 inches	14 inches	12 inches	Two Medium	Two 75 watt
9049	17 inches	17 inches	14½ inches	Three Medium	Three 75 watt

Listed under Label Service of Underwriters' Laboratories, Inc.

"Filigree"

A novel and practical Semi-Indirect Luminaire for
Offices, Showrooms, Stores, Banks, etc.

"Filigree" luminaires produce a maximum of downwardly concentrated glareless illumination, in addition to an adequate amount of diffused light around the walls and on the ceiling.

For fixtures wired to take the new 3-Light Lamps.

Add $3.00 list for the special 2-circuit socket and switch. Add $1.50 list for the 2-circuit socket only, when no switch is required.

The standard finish of metal parts is **IVORY.**

[Prices will be furnished, on request, for other special finishes.]

Glassware is "**Hyperion**" **white.**

No. 8046
Overall length—36 inches.
Diameter of Glass Bowl—16 inches.

$300.00+

Wired with medium base porcelain socket for 200-watt lamp
For additional overall lengths, add $2.40 List per foot or fraction of a foot.
Add 45¢ List for mogul socket for 300-watt lamp.

Listed under Label Service of Underwriters' Laboratories, Inc.

"Filigree"

For Offices, Showrooms, Stores, Banks, etc.

A Semi-Indirect luminaire, producing a maximum of downwardly concentrated glareless illumination—in addition to an adequate amount of diffused light around the walls and on the ceiling.

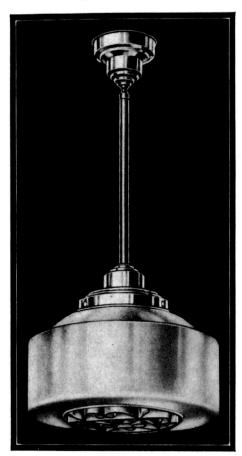

No. 726—8166

Overall length—15 inches
Diameter of Glass bowl—16 inches
Glass fitter size—6 inches
Wired with medium base porcelain socket
Mogul Socket 45c list extra.

$120.00 – 145.00

For fixtures wired to take 3-light lamps.
Add $3.00 list for the special 2-circuit socket and switch.
Add $1.50 list for the 2-circuit socket only, when no switch is required.

——————◆——————

GLASS AND GRILL ONLY

No. 716—8166

Overall length—38 inches
Diameter of Glass bowl—16 inches
Glass fitter size—6 inches
Wired with medium base porcelain socket

$165.00 – 200.00

For extra overall lengths, add 75c list per foot or fraction of a foot.

Glassware is white **"HYPERION"**

Fixtures are furnished in a Brushed Aluminum Finish.

Cast Grills are furnished in Ivory Finish.

No. 8166

Diameter—16 inches
Depth—10 inches   Fitter—6 inches

$50.00+

Listed under Label Service of Underwriters' Laboratories, Inc.

"Filigree"

Semi-Indirect Luminaire for

Offices—Showrooms—Stores—Banks—Accounting Rooms.

The standard finish of metal parts is **IVORY**.
[Prices will be furnished, on request, for other special finishes.]
Glassware is **"Hyperion" white.**

No. 8026
Overall length—14 inches.
Diameter of Glass Bowl—16 inches.
Wired with medium base porcelain socket
for 200-watt lamp
(Add 45c List for mogul socket for 300-watt Lamp.)
$125.00 – 150.00

No. 8016
Overall length—36 inches.
Diameter of Glass Bowl—16 inches.
Wired with medium base porcelain socket
for 200-watt lamp
Add 45¢ List for mogul socket for 300-watt Lamp.
$150.00+

For fixtures wired to take the new 3-Light Lamps.
Add $3.00 list for the special 2-circuit socket and switch.
Add $1.50 list for the 2-circuit socket only, when no switch
is required.

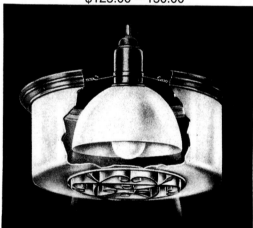

This is an illustration of the inner construction of the unit.

1. The large outer glass bowl is suspended in the metal band, which is held by the three hooks and chains fastened to the socket cover.
2. The glass reflector shade is also attached to the socket cover, by means of thumb-screws.
3. The metal grill made of Aluminum, is arranged to protrude through the hole in the bottom of the glass bowl, and is suspended from the glass by means of four side lugs, which are fastened to the metal grill.

For additional overall lengths on **No. 8016** add 75¢ list per foot or fraction of a foot.

Listed under Label Service of Underwriters' Laboratories, Inc.

See other side.

"Style-lux"

A Beautiful Semi-Indirect Luminaire

for

Showrooms, Lobbies, Banks, Stores, Reception Rooms

Patent Applied for

For fixtures wired to take the new 3-Light Lamps.

Add $3.00 list for the special 2-circuit socket and switch. Add $1.50 list for the 2-circuit socket only, when no switch is required.

All Metal Parts finished in **Stained Bronze**

Glassware furnished in **Iridescent Stippled Gold**

❖❖

Fixtures can also be furnished in: Ivory and Gold and Dull Chrome at the same Prices.

Number	Dimensions		Type of Socket Furnished	Recommended Wattage
	Overall Length	Diam. of Bowl		
6012	30 inches	12 inches	Medium Base	100- 150
6014	32 inches	14 inches	Medium Base	150- 200
6016	33 inches	16 inches	Medium Base	- 200
6018	35 inches	18½ inches	Mogul Base	300- 500
6020	36 inches	20½ inches	Mogul Base	500-1000

For additional overall lengths, add 75c list per foot, or fraction of a foot.

Listed under Label Service of Underwriters' Laboratories, Inc.

$200.00+

"Style-lux"

A Beautiful Semi-Indirect Luminaire for
Showrooms, Lobbies, Banks, Stores, Reception Rooms
Patent Applied for

All metal parts are finished in
STAINED BRONZE
Glassware is furnished in
IRIDESCENT STIPPLED GOLD

Fixtures can also be furnished in:
IVORY and GOLD
and DULL CHROME
at the same Prices.

No. 6022 to No. 6030 [1 Light]
$195.00+

No. 6721 [1 Light]
Overall length.............14 inches
Spread.................... 9 inches
Wired with medium base socket
$135.00 — 150.00

No. 6011 (1 Light)
Overall Extension................10 inches
Backplate .... 4¾ inches Diameter
(Add 45c List for Canopy Turn Switch.)
$100.00 — 125.00

No. 6021 (1 Light)
Lenght .... 8 inches
Width .... 8 inches
(Add 45c List for Canopy Turn Switch.)
$100.00 — 135.00

Number	Dimensions		Type of Socket Furnished	Recommended Wattage
	Overall Length	Diam. of Bowl		
6011	....	7 inches	Medium Base	40- 60
6021	....	....	Medium Base	75- 100
6022	17 inches	12 inches	Medium Base	100- 150
6024	19 inches	14 inches	Medium Base	150- 200
6026	20 inches	16 inches	Medium Base	- 200
6028	22 inches	18½ inches	Mogul Base	300- 500
6030	23 inches	20½ inches	Mogul Base	500-1000
6721	14 inches	9 inches	Medium Base	40- 60

For fixtures No. 6026-6028 and 6030 to take 3 Light Lamps, add $3.00 list for the **special 2-circuit socket and switch.**
Add **$1.50 list only, for 2-circuit socket, when switch is not required.**
Listed under Label Service of Underwriters' Laboratories, Inc.

Metal parts are furnished wired complete and finished in **"Silverlustre"**—an applied and lasting finish, very similar in appearance to Brushed Aluminum.

Pendants can be furnished in **"Statuary Bronze"** finish, at 75c each list extra.

For fixtures wired to take the new 3-Light Lamps.

Add $3.00 list for the special 2-circuit socket and switch.

Add $1.50 list for the 2-circuit socket only, when no switch is required.

$200.00+

SERIES F-400

A Popular Priced Scientifically Designed Luminaire, for use in Schools, Offices, Accounting Rooms, Stores, Showrooms, Hospitals and all places where good and adequate illumination is essential.

PENDANT TYPES

No. 416—16" Diam. Bowl
Recommended Wattage—150-200.
Wired Complete with Porcelain Medium Base Socket.
Overall length...............30 inches

No. 418—18" Diam. Bowl
Recommended Wattage—300-500.
Wired Complete with Porcelain Mogul Socket.
Overall length...............33 inches

No. 420—20" Diam. Bowl
Recommended Wattage—300-500.
Wired Complete with Porcelain Mogul Socket.
Overall length...............33 inches

No. 420A—20" Diam. Bowl
Wired with Giant Mogul Socket Cover for 750-1000 Watt Lamp.
Overall length...............36 inches

No. 424—24" Diam. Bowl
Recommended Wattage—750-1500.
Wired Complete with Porcelain Mogul Socket.
Overall length...............36 inches

For overall lengths of more than standard, add 45 cents list per foot or fraction of a foot.

SEMI-FLUSH TYPES

No. 426—16" Diam. Bowl
Recommended Wattage—150-200.
Wired Complete with Medium Base Socket.
Overall length...............12 inches

No. 428—18" Diam. Bowl
Recommended Wattage—300-500.
Wired Complete with Mogul Socket.
Overall length...............14 inches

No. 430—20" Diam. Bowl
Recommended Wattage—300-500.
Wired Complete with Mogul Socket.
Overall length...............15 inches

No. 430A—20" Diam. Bowl
Wired with Giant Mogul Socket Cover for 750-1000 Watt Lamp.
Overall length...............17 inches

No. 434—24" Diam. Bowl
Recommended Wattage—750-1500.
Wired Complete with Mogul Socket.
Overall length...............19 inches

$185.00+

Listed under Label Service of Underwriters' Laboratories, Inc.

Metal parts are furnished wired complete and finished in **"Silverlustre"**—an applied and lasting finish, very similar in appearance to Brushed Aluminum.

Pendants can be furnished in **"Statuary Bronze"** finish, at 75c each list extra.

For fixtures wired to take the new 3-Light Lamps.

Add $3.00 list for the special 2-circuit socket and switch.

Add $1.50 list for the 2-circuit socket only, when no switch is required.

$250.00+

SERIES F-400

A Popular Priced Scientifically Designed Luminaire, for use in Schools, Offices, Accounting Rooms, Stores, Showrooms, Hospitals and all places where good and adequate illumination is essential.

PENDANT TYPES

No. 416E—16" Diam. Bowl
Recommended Wattage—150-200.
Wired Complete with Porcelain Medium Base Socket.
Overall length...............30 inches

No. 418E—18" Diam. Bowl
Recommended Wattage—300-500
Wired Complete with Porcelain Mogul Socket.
Overall length...............33 inches

No. 420E—20" Diam. Bowl
Recommended Wattage—300-500.
Wired Complete with Porcelain Mogul Socket.
Overall length...............33 inches

No. 420AE—20" Diam. Bowl
Wired with Giant Mogul Socket Cover for 750-1000 Watt Lamp.
Overall length...............33 inches

No. 424E—24" Diam. Bowl
Recommended Wattage—750-1500.
Wired Complete with Porcelain Mogul Socket.
Overall length...............36 inches

For overall lengths of more than standard, add 45 cents list per foot or fraction of a foot.

SEMI-FLUSH TYPES

No. 426E—16" Diam. Bowl
Recommended Wattage—150-200.
Wired Complete with Medium Base Socket.
Overall length...............12 inches

No. 428E—18" Diam. Bowl
Recommended Wattage—300-500.
Wired Complete with Mogul Socket.
Overall length...............14 inches

No. 430E—20" Diam. Bowl
Recommended Wattage—300-500.
Wired Complete with Mogul Socket.
Overall length...............15 inches

No. 430AE—20" Diam. Bowl
Wired with Giant Mogul Socket Cover for 750-1000 Watt Lamp.
Overall length...............17 inches

No. 434E—24" Diam. Bowl
Recommended Wattage—750-1500.
Wired Complete with Mogul Socket.
Overall length...............19 inches

$250.00+

Listed under Label Service of Underwriters' Laboratories, Inc.

"Gill-lite"

Maximum Lighting Efficiency—Minimum Surface Brightness

"GILL-LITE" is an All-White Glass Unit which, when illuminated, produces a Beautiful Mellow Ivory Tone—(eliminating Glare and Eye-strain)—while still retaining its Interior Whiteness, for Maximum Reflection to the ceiling. "GILL-LITE" is ideal for the illumination of Hospitals, Offices, Showrooms, Schools and all other places where adequate illumination, without eye-strain, is essential.

No. 4426—With 16" diameter "Gill-lite" Bowl
Wired with porcelain Medium Base Socket for 150-200 watt lamp.
Overall length...............12 inches

No. 4428—With 18" diameter "Gill-lite" Bowl
Wired with porcelain Mogul Base Socket for 300-500 watt lamp.
Overall length...............14 inches

No. 4430—With 20" diameter "Gill-lite" Bowl
Wired with porcelain Mogul Base Socket for 300-500 watt lamp.
Overall length...............15 inches

No. 4430A—With 20" diameter "Gill-lite" Bowl
Wired with Giant Mogul Socket Cover for 750-1000 watt lamp.
Overall length...............17 inches

200.00+

**All Fixtures are furnished in
Polished Chrome.**

$235.00+

No. 4416—With 16" diameter "Gill-lite" Bowl
Wired with porcelain Medium Base Socket for 150-200 watt lamp.
Overall length...............30 inches

No. 4418—With 18" diameter "Gill-lite" Bowl
Wired with porcelain Mogul Base Socket for 300-500 watt lamp.
Overall length...............33 inches

No. 4420—With 20" diameter "Gill-lite" Bowl
Wired with porcelain Mogul Base Socket for 300-500 watt lamp.
Overall length...............33 inches

No. 4420A—With 20" diameter "Gill-lite" Bowl
Wired with Giant Mogul Socket. Cover for 750-1000 watt lamp.
Overall length...............36 inches

For longer overall lengths, add **90c** list per
foot or fraction of a foot.

For fixtures wired to take the new 3-Light Lamps.
Add **$3.00** list for the special 2-circuit socket
and switch.

Add **$1.50** list for the 2-circuit socket only,
when no switch is required.

Listed under Label Service of Underwriters' Laboratories, Inc.

The "NEW YORKER"

A Semi-indirect Luminaire of distinctive appearance, for use in Showrooms, Offices, Schools and Accounting Rooms and all other places where good, pleasing and adequate illumination, without eye-strain, is essential.

$135.00+

No. 4526

Overall Length	13	inches
Diameter of Metal Band	18	inches
Diameter of Glass	15¼	inches

Wired with Medium base socket for
150-200 watt Lamp.

No. 4528

Overall Length	15	inches
Diameter of Metal Band	22	inches
Diameter of Glass	18½	inches

Wired with Mogul base socket for
300-500 watt Lamp.

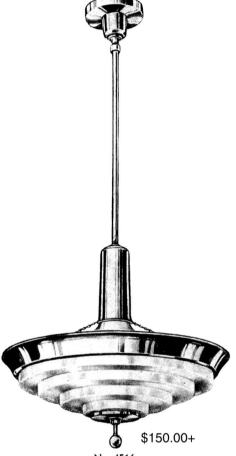

$150.00+

No. 4516

Overall Length	35	inches
Diameter of Metal Band	18	inches
Diameter of Glass	15¼	inches

Wired with medium base socket for
150-200 watt Lamp.

No. 4518

Overall Length	38	inches
Diameter of Metal Band	22	inches
Diameter of Glass	18½	inches

Wired with Mogul base socket for
300-500 watt Lamp.

———————●———————

For overall lengths of more than standard, add **90** cents list per foot or fraction of a foot.

**Finish of Metal Parts:
"Polished Chrome"**

For fixtures wired to take the new 3-Light Lamps.

Add **$3.00** list for the special 2-circuit socket and switch.

Add **$1.50** list for the 2-circuit socket only, when no switch is required.

Listed under Label Service of Underwriters' Laboratories, Inc.

"Gill-Lux"

An Indirect Lighting Unit
Combining Lighting Efficiency and Beauty

Fixtures and Brackets are furnished in **"CHROMALUSTRE"** and **"COPPERLUSTRE."**

"CHROMALUSTRE" is an applied silvery grey lustre, simulating satin chrome.

"COPPERLUSTRE" is an applied copper bronze lustre, simulating satin bronze.

The triple beaded edge of all reflectors is high polished aluminum. Reflectors are made of spun aluminum and the inside is finished bright dipped.

Glassware is Hyperion opal.

$250.00+

No. 3016—(150-200 watt)
Diameter—16 inches....................Length 30 inches
Wired medium base.

No. 3018—(300-500 watt)
Diameter—18 inches....................Length 32 inches
Wired mogul base.

No. 3022—(750-1000 watt)
Diameter—22 inches....................Length 36 inches
Wired mogul base.

For additional overall lengths, add 75c list per foot, or fraction of a foot.

For fixtures wired to take 3-light lamps:
Add $3.00 List for 3 circuit socket and switch.
Add $1.50 List for 3 circuit socket only—without switch.

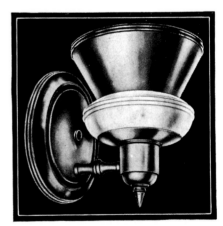

No. 3011—(100 watt)
Length..........................8½ inches
Extension.......................7 inches
(Canopy switch 45c net extra)

$125.00 – 150.00

Listed under Label Service of Underwriters' Laboratories, Inc.

Commercial Lighting Fixtures
with
"Hyperion" Glassware

Pendants are furnished in either
CHROME or CADMIUM
finishes, wired complete
with medium base
sockets

No. 816/B. 26
Length of Pendant to bottom of stem is 24 inches

If longer lengths are desired, add **90 cents** list per foot
or fraction of a foot for CHROME and **75c** list per
foot for CADMIUM

$150.00+

Number	Diameter of Glassware	Recommended Wattage
816/B. 26	16 inches	200 - 500
816/B. 24	14 "	150 - 300
816/B. 22	12 "	100 - 200

Note:- Fixtures are furnished with ¾" diam. stems, but ½" stems can be furnished if desired.
Listed under Label Service of Underwriters' Laboratories, Inc.

"Streamline"
Commercial Luminaire
with
"Hyperion" Glassware

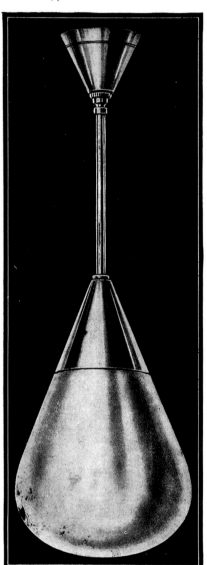

Fixtures are furnished in Polished CHROME finish, wired with medium base porcelain sockets and No. 16 heat resisting wire.

For Mogul socket, add 45c list.

No. 812/S. 12
No. 814/S. 14

$200.00+

Number	Dimensions of Unit including Metal Cone			Overall Length of Fixture Complete
	Diameter	Length	Glass Fitter	
812/S12	12" x	18" x	5"	36 inches
814/S14	14" x	22" x	6"	40 inches

Listed under Label Service of Underwriters' Laboratories, Inc.

The "Excelite" Unit

Plain White "Hyperion" Glassware with Dull Chrome Finished Fixture

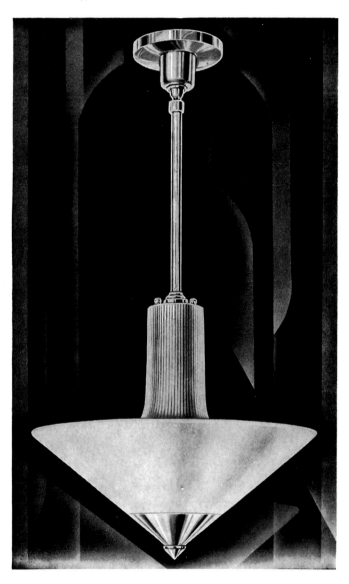

Luminaire Number	Diameter of Bowl	Overall Length of Luminaire	Standard Carton	Weight Stand. Carton	For Lamp Size
1616	16 Inches	26 Inches	1	11 lbs.	200 Watt Medium Base
1620	20 Inches	30 Inches	1	15 lbs.	300-500 Watt. Mogul Base

NOTE: It is essential that **Inside Frosted Lamps** be used to avoid unsightly ceiling striations, which are produced by clear crystal lamps

$250.00+

Listed under Label Service of Underwriters' Laboratories, Inc.

The "Excelite" Unit

Plain White "Hyperion" Glassware with Dull Chrome Finished Fixture

Metal parts furnished in
DULL CHROME
(Dull Chrome is Satin Finished Chrome)

No. 1626
Diameter........16 inches—Overall length........17 inches
For 200 watt medium base lamp
Weight Standard Carton of One..............11 lbs.

No. 1630
Diameter........20 inches—Overall length........21 inches
For 300-500 watt mogul base lamp
Weight Standard Carton of One..............15 lbs.

All fixtures furnished wired complete
$200.00+

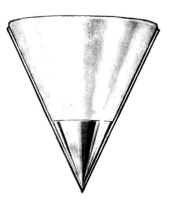

No. 1611—Wall Bracket
Length................11½ inches
Width................10¾ inches

Furnished Wired Complete, No Switch
(Add 45c List for Canopy Turn Switch)
Will take lamp sizes up to 150 watts

$125.00 – 150.00

Listed under Label Service of Underwriters' Laboratories, Inc.

Super-X-lite

For schools, offices, accounting rooms, stores, hospitals and all
places where good and adequate illumination is essential.

$150.00+

No. 2626—16" Diam. Bowl
Recommended Wattage—150-200.
Wired Complete with Porcelain Medium Base Socket
Overall length..............12 inches

No. 2628—18" Diam. Bowl
Recommended Wattage—300-500.
Wired Complete with Porcelain Mogul Socket
Overall length..............14 inches

No. 2630—20" Diam. Bowl
Recommended Wattage—300-500.
Wired Complete with Porcelain Mogul Socket
Overall length..............15 inches

No. 2630A—20" Diam. Bowl
Wired with Giant Mogul Socket cover
for 750—1000 watt lamp
Overall length..............17 inches

No. 2634—24" Diam. Bowl
Recommended Wattage—750-1500.
Wired Complete with Porcelain Mogul Socket
Overall length..............19 inches

For fixtures wired to take the new 3-light Lamps.
Add **$3.00** list for the special 2-circuit socket and switch.
Add **$1.50** list for the 2-circuit socket only, when no switch is required.
For longer overall lengths, add **90c** list per foot or fraction of a foot. Pendant Stems can be supplied in ¾" Diam. Tubing instead of Standard ½".

$150.00+

No. 2616—16" Diam. Bowl
Recommended Wattage—150-200.
Wired Complete with Porcelain Medium Base Socket
Overall length..............30 inches

No. 2618—18" Diam. Bowl
Recommended Wattage—300-500.
Wired Complete with Porcelain Mogul Socket
Overall length..............33 inches

No. 2620—20" Diam. Bowl
Recommended Wattage—300-500.
Wired Complete with Porcelain Mogul Socket
Overall length..............33 inches

No. 2620A—20" Diam. Bowl
Wired with Giant Mogul Socket Cover
for 750—1000 watt lamp
Overall length..............36 inches

No. 2624—24" Diam. Bowl
Recommended Wattage—750-1500.
Wired Complete with Porcelain Mogul Socket
Overall length..............36 inches

All Fixtures finished in "Dull Chrome"

(Dull Chrome is Satin Finished Chrome.)

No. 1611—Wall Bracket

Length..............11½ inches
Width..............10¾ inches
Furnished Wired Complete, No Switch.
(Add 45c List for Canopy Turn Switch.)
Will take lamp sizes up to 150 watts.

NOTE: Brackets are made of Cast Aluminum and are finished in Satin Aluminum, simulating Dull Chrome.

$125.00 – 150.00

Listed under Label Service of Underwriters' Laboratories, Inc.

Semi-Indirect Luminaire

for

Stores, Showrooms, Reception Rooms and Public Buildings

For fixtures wired to take 3-Light Lamps. Add $3.00 list for 2-circuit socket & switch. Add $1.50 list for 2-circuit socket only, when no switch is required.

❖

When ordering please give fixture number required.

❖

For additional overall lengths, add 90c per foot or fraction of a foot.

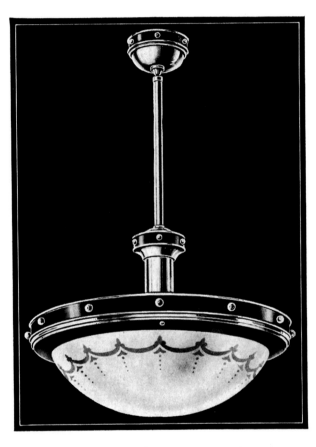

FINISHES
_____

Polished Chrome
with Ebony Trim and Opal Glass with frosted Etching.

❖

Stained Bronze
with Gold Iridescent Glassware.
(No Etching)

$200.00+

No. 7018
Diam. of Fixture.........................19 inches
Diam. of Glass Bowl....................16 inches
Overall Length of Fixture.................33 inches
Recommended Wattage..............150-200 w.

Wired with Medium Base Socket

No. 7020
Diam. of Fixture.........................21 inches
Diam. of Glass Bowl....................18 inches
Overall length of Fixture...............36 inches
Recommended Wattage..............300-500 w.

Wired with Mogul Base Socket

Listed under Label Service of Underwriters' Laboratories, Inc.

The "Ultra-Lite"

An Indirect Lighting Unit that diffuses the light, which is redirected from the ceiling to the working plane below

Beautiful in Appearance - Efficient in Illumination

Note: Overall lengths, other than shown, are not recommended, as they reduce the illumination efficiency.

If utmost efficiency is secondary to effect, fixtures can be furnished in extra lengths at an added cost of **75c** list per foot or fraction of a foot.

Note: "Ultra-Lites" are furnished wired complete with slow burning wire, and approved wiring devices.

Special white porcelain effect enamel is applied to the inside of the reflector.

The Grey outer finish is applied the same way.

$275.00+

For fixtures wired to take the new 3-Light Lamps. Add $3.00 list for the special 2-circuit socket and switch. Add $1.50 list for the 2-circuit socket only, when no switch is required.

Number	Diameter of Reflector	Finish	Overall Length	Wired	Suggested Wattage
016	16"	Chromalume and Grey	35"	Medium Base	150 - 200
020	20"	Chromalume and Grey	36"	Mogul Base	300 - 500
024	24"	Chromalume and Grey	42"	Mogul Base	750-1500

Listed under Label Service of Underwriters' Laboratories, Inc.

Glass Louvre Fixtures

for

Stores, Showrooms and Reception Rooms

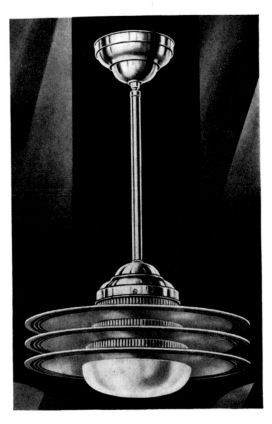

No. 926/3700

With White Glass Louvres and Clear Crystal Stripes.

No. 926/3700-C

With Crystal Clear Glass Louvres, Black Stripes and Beveled Edges.

Overall Length—16 inches.....Diam. of Louvres 17 inches

$225.00+

Diameter of Fitter - 6 inches

No. 916/3700

With White Glass Louvres and Clear Crystal Stripes.

No. 916/3700-C

With Crystal Clear Glass Louvres, Black Stripes and Beveled Edges.

Overall Length—30 inches.....Diam. of Louvres 17 inches

All fixtures are furnished wired complete with medium base sockets, and slow burning wire.
Finish of fixtures POLISHED CHROME.

$250.00+

GLASS ONLY

No. 3700

Hyperion Unit, complete with Three Glass Louvres with Clear Crystal Stripes

No. 3700-C

Hyperion Unit, complete with Three Glass Louvres with Black Stripes,

Listed under Label Service of Underwriters' Laboratories, Inc.

Moderne Louvre Luminaire

with
"Hyperion" Glassware

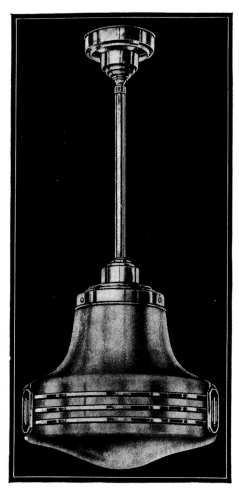

Fixtures are furnished only in CHROMAL finish, a two-tone combination of Polished Chrome on the louvres and Satin finished Aluminum on the Pendants, and Ceiling Collars.

$150.00 — 200.00

No. 724—L3309
No. 726—L3312
No. 726—L3314
No. 726—L3316
No. 726—L3318

Fixtures are furnished wired complete with No. 16 Heat Resisting Wire, and with Porcelain Medium Base Sockets. Add 45c List for Mogul Sockets.

$200.00+

No. 714—L3309
No. 716—L3312
No. 716—L3314
No. 716—L3316
No. 716—L3318

Number Fixture Complete	Number Glassware with Louvres only	Number Glassware only	Dimensions of Glassware only			Overall Length of Fixture Complete
			Diameter	Length	Fitter	
714—L3309	L3309	3309	9" x	9⅞" x	4"	36 inches
716—L3312	L3312	3312	12" x	11¼" x	6"	39 inches
716—L3314	L3314	3314	14" x	11⅜" x	6"	39 inches
716—L3316	L3316	3316	16" x	11½" x	6"	39 inches
716—L3318	L3318	3318	18" x	12½" x	6"	40 inches
724—L3309	....	....	9" x	9⅞" x	4"	14 inches
726—L3312	....	....	12" x	11¼" x	6"	16 inches
726—L3314	....	....	14" x	11⅜" x	6"	16 inches
726—L3316	....	....	16" x	11½" x	6"	16 inches
726—L3318	....	....	18" x	12½" x	6"	17 inches

NOTE: For longer overall lengths of Pendants No. 714-716, add 75c list per foot, or fraction of a foot.

For Wall Brackets and Flush Ceiling types, see back of this sheet.

Listed under Label Service of Underwriters' Laboratories, Inc.

Moderne Louvre Luminaire

With

'Hyperion" Glassware

No. 706—L3508
No. 708—L3510
No. 710—L3512
No. 712—L3514

$125.00 – 150.00

Ceiling fixtures are furnished wired complete with metal reflectors, which do not permit the light to form halos on the ceiling.

Fixtures are furnished only in CHROMAL finish, a two-tone combination of Polished Chrome on the Louvres and Satin finished Aluminum on the Ceiling Bands and Wall Brackets.

No. 702—L3306
Overall extension from wall—9 inches.

(With Canopy Switch)
$100.00 – 165.00

Number Fixture Complete	Number Glassware with Louvres only	Number Glassware only	Dimensions of Glassware Diameter	Depth	Fitter	No. of Lights
702—L3306	L3306	3306	6" x	5⅝" x	3¼"	1 Light
706—L3508	L3508	3508	8" x	3½" x	6"	1 Light
708—L3510	L3510	3510	10" x	3⅞" x	8"	2 Lights
710—L3512	L3512	3512	12" x	4⅜" x	10"	2 Lights
712—L3514	L3514	3514	14" x	4⅜" x	12"	3 Lights

For Suspension and Ceiling Type Fixtures, see other side of this sheet

Listed under Label Service of Underwriters' Laboratories, Inc.

Moderne Louvre Luminaire

with

"Hyperion" Glassware

Fixtures are furnished only in CHROMAL finish—a two-tone combination of Polished Chrome on the louvres and Satin Finished Aluminum on the Pendants.

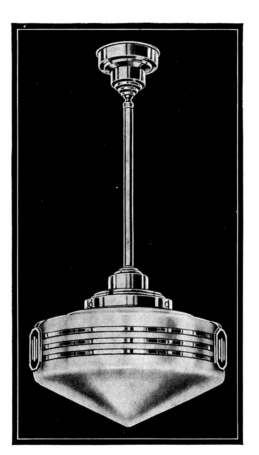

Standard Pendant length, without glassware, is 28 inches. If longer lengths are required, add 75c List per foot or fraction of a foot. Fixtures are furnished wired complete with Porcelain Medium Base Sockets. Add 45c List for Mogul Sockets.

$250.00+

No. 714—L2908
No 714—L2910
No. 716—L2912
No. 716—L2914
No. 716—L2916
No. 716—L2918

Number Fixture Complete	Number Glassware with Louvres only	Number Glassware only	Dimensions of Glassware only			Overall Length of Fixture Complete
			Diameter	Length	Fitter	
714—L2908	L2908	9908	8½" x	6⅜" x	4"	33 inches
714—L2910	L2910	2910	10" x	6½" x	4"	33 inches
716—L2912	L2912	2912	12" x	7½" x	6"	34 inches
716—L2914	L2914	2914	14" x	8⅜" x	6"	36 inches
716—L2916	L2916	2916	16" x	10" x	6"	38 inches
716—L2918	L2918	2918	18" x	11⅝" x	6" & 8"	40 inches

For Wall Bracket and Ceiling Types, see back of this sheet

Listed under Label Service of Underwriters' Laboratories, Inc.

Moderne Louvre Luminaire

with

"Hyperion" Glassware

Fixtures are furnished only in CHROMAL, a two-tone combination of Polished Chrome on the louvres and Satin Finished Aluminum on the Ceiling Collars and Brackets.

No. 724—L2908
No. 724—L2910
No. 726—L2912
No. 726—L2914
No. 726—L2916
No. 726—L2918

$200.00+

Fixtures are furnished wired complete with Porcelain Medium Base Sockets. Add 45c List, for Mogul Base Sockets on Ceiling Collars.

No. 704—L2908

Overall extension from wall 11 inches

(With Canopy Switch)

$135.00 – 185.00

Number Fixture Complete	Number Glassware with Louvres only	Number Glassware only	Dimensions of Glassware only			Overall Length of Ceiling Fixtures
			Diameter	Length	Fitter	
724—L2908	L2908	2908	8½"	x 6¾"	x 4"	12 inches
724—L2910	L2910	2910	10"	x 6½"	x 4"	12 inches
726—L2912	L2912	2912	12"	x 7½"	x 6"	13 inches
726—L2914	L2914	2914	14"	x 8½"	x 6"	14 inches
726—L2916	L2916	2916	16"	x 10"	x 6"	15 inches
726—L2918	L2918	2918	18"	x 11½"	x 6" & 8"	17 inches
704—L2908	L2908	2908	8½"	x 6¾"	x 4"	....

For Suspension Type Fixtures, see other side of sheet

Listed under Label Service of Underwriters' Laboratories, Inc.

Moderne Louvre Luminaire

with
"Hyperion" Glassware

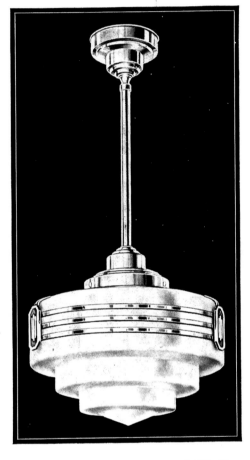

Fixtures are furnished only in CHROMAL finish—a two-tone combination of Polished Chrome on the louvres and Satin Finished Aluminum on the Pendants.

Standard Pendant length, without glassware, is 28 inches. If longer lengths are required, add 75c List per foot or fraction of a foot. Fixtures are furnished wired complete with Porcelain Medium Base Sockets. Add 45c List for Mogul Sockets.

No. 714—CL1708 $250.00+
No. 714—CL1709
No. 716—CL1712
No. 716—CL1714
No. 716—CL1716
No. 716—CL1718

Number Fixture Complete	Number Glassware with Louvres only	Number Glassware only	Dimension of Glassware only Diameter	Length	Fitter	Overall Length of Fixture Complete
714—CL1708	CL1708	1708	8″ x	6¼″ x	4″	33 inches
714—CL1709	CL1709	1709	9″ x	6½″ x	4″	35 inches
716—CL1712	CL1712	1712	12″ x	8½″ x	6″	36 inches
716—CL1714	CL1714	1714	14″ x	9¼″ x	6″	38 inches
716—CL1716	CL1716	1716	16″ x	10¾″ x	6″	39 inches
716—CL1718	CL1718	1718	18″ x	12″ x	6-8″	41 inches

Specify size of Fitter required (6″ or 8″)   For Wall Bracket and Ceiling Types, see back of this sheet

Listed under Label Service of Underwriters' Laboratories, Inc.

Moderne Louvre Luminaire

with

"Hyperion" Glassware

Fixtures are furnished only in CHROMAL, a two-tone combination of Polished Chrome on the louvres and Satin Finished Aluminum on the Ceiling Collars and Brackets.

$200.00+

No. 724—CL1708

No. 724—CL1709

No. 726—CL1712

No. 726—CL1714

No. 726—CL1716

No. 726—CL1718

Fixtures are furnished wired complete with Porcelain Medium Base Sockets. Add 45c List, for Mogul Base Sockets on Ceiling Collars.

No. 704—CL1708

Overall extension from wall 10 inches

(With Canopy Switch)

$135.00 – 185.00

Number Fixture Complete	Number Glassware with Louvres only	Number Glassware only	Dimensions of Glassware only			Overall Length of Ceiling Fixtures
			Diameter	Length	Fitter	
704—CL1708	CL1708	1708	8"	x 6¼"	x 4"	....
724—CL1708	CL1708	1708	8"	x 6¼"	x 4"	11 inches
724—CL1709	CL1709	1709	9"	x 6½"	x 4"	13 inches
726—CL1712	CL1712	1712	12"	x 8½"	x 6"	14 inches
726—CL1714	CL1714	1714	14"	x 9¼"	x 6"	15 inches
726—CL1716	CL1716	1716	16"	x 10¼"	x 6"	16 inches
726—CL1718	CL1718	1718	18"	x 12"	x 6-8"	18 inches

For Suspension Type Fixtures, see other side of this sheet

Specify size of Fitter required (6" or 8")

Listed under Label Service of Underwriters' Laboratories, Inc.

Moderne Louvre Units

Hyperion" Glassware
combined with
CHROME finished Metal Louvres

No. L601
No. L602
No. L603
No. L604

$60.00 – 125.00

Number Glassware and Louvre	Number Glassware only	Dimensions of Glassware		
		Diameter	Length	Fitter
L601	601	10" x	6¾" x	4"
L602	602	12" x	7⅜" x	6"
L603	603	14" x	8" x	6"
L604	604	16" x	8¾" x	6"

Note: Standard No. 716 Pendants can be furnished for these Louvre Units.

Moderne Louvre Luminaire

with

"Astralite" Glassware

["Astralite" is Daylight Glass]

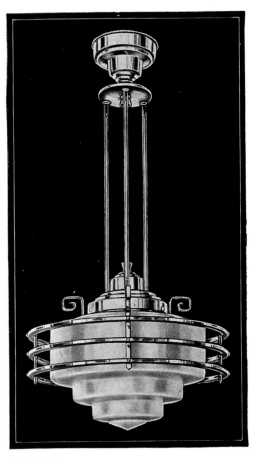

Suspension type fixtures No. 716 and No. 736 will be furnished 28 inches long —from top of canopy to bottom of holder. (Quotations will be given for special lengths other than this.)

All fixtures will be furnished with Medium Base Porcelain Sockets and No. 16 Heat Resisting Wire.

For fixtures wired with **Mogul** sockets add 45c each list.

All metal parts are finished in Chromal (CHROMAL is a Brushed Aluminum finish on the pendant and polished Chrome on the Louvres.)

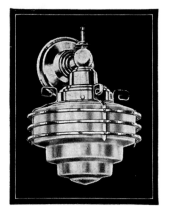

$300.00+

No. 736—L1712
No. 736—L1714
No. 736—L1716

No. 701—L1708
(With Canopy Switch)

$185.00+

Luminaire Complete	Glassware with Louvres only	Dimensions of Glassware Only		
		Diameter	Length	Fitter
716/L1712	L1712	12″ x	8½″ x	6″
726/L1712	L1712	12″ x	8½″ x	6″
736/L1712	L1712	12″ x	8½″ x	6″
716/L1714	L1714	14″ x	9¼″ x	6″
726/L1714	L1714	14″ x	9¼″ x	6″
736/L1714	L1714	14″ x	9¼″ x	6″
716/L1716	L1716	16″ x	10″ x	6″
726/L1716	L1716	16″ x	10″ x	6″
736/L1716	L1716	16″ x	10″ x	6″
701/L1708	L1708	8″ x	6¼″ x	4″

Kindly mention Fixture Number desired. Listed under Label Service of Underwriters' Laboratories, Inc.

Moderne Louvre Luminaire

with

"Astralite" Glass

["Astralite" is Daylight Glass]

No. 726—L1712
No. 726—L1714
No. 726—L1716

$250.00+

All fixtures are furnished with Porcelain Medium Base Sockets and No. 16 Heat Resisting Wire, approved by the Board of Fire Underwriters.

For fixtures wired with **Mogul** sockets add 45c each list.

Metal Parts are finished in Chromal. (CHROMAL is a Brushed Aluminum finish on the pendant and Polished Chrome on the Louvres.)

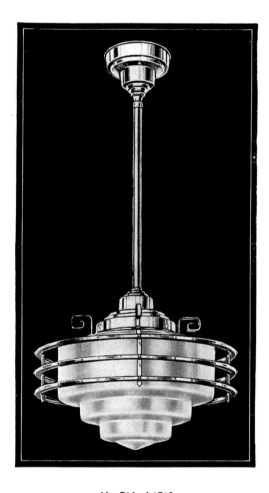

No. 716—L1712
No. 716—L1714
No. 716—L1716

$275.00+

Turn to the front of this sheet for other necessary information.

Listed under Label Service of Underwriters' Laboratories, Inc.

Moderne Louvre Luminaire

with

"Hyperion" Glass Balls

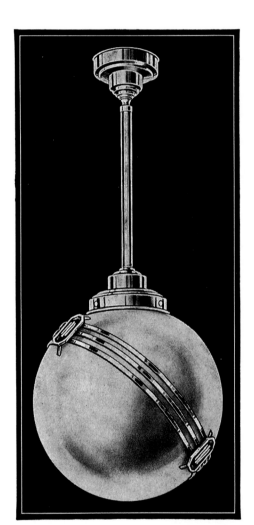

Fixtures are furnished only in CHROMAL finish—a two-tone combination of Polished Chrome on the louvres and Satin Finished Aluminum on the Pendants.

Standard Pendant length, without glassware, is 28 inches. If longer lengths are required, add 75c List per foot or fraction of a foot. Fixtures are furnished wired complete with Porcelain Medium Base Sockets. Add 45c List for Mogul Sockets.

No. 714—L57-8 No. 716—L57-14
No. 716—L57-10 No. 716—L57-16
No. 716—L57-12 No. 716—L57-18

$350.00+

Number Fixture Complete	Number Glassware with Louvre Only	Number Glassware Only	Dimensions of Glassware only Diameter	Fitter	Overall Length of Fixture Complete
714-L57-8	L57-8	57-8	8" x	4"	35 inches
716-L57-10	L57-10	57-10	10" x	6"	37 inches
716-L57-12	L57-12	57-12	12" x	6"	39 inches
716-L57-14	L57-14	57-14	14" x	6"	41 inches
716-L57-16	L57-16	57-16	16" x	6"	43 inches
716-L57-18	L57-18	57-18	18" x	6" & 8"	45 inches

For Wall Bracket and Ceiling Types, see back of this sheet
Listed under Label Service of Underwriters' Laboratories, Inc.

Moderne Louvre Luminaire

with

"Hyperion" Glass Balls

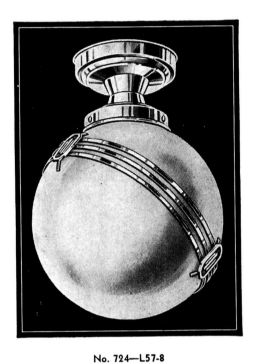

Fixtures are furnished only in CHROMAL finish, a two-tone combination of Polished Chrome on the louvres and Satin finished Aluminum on the Brackets, and Ceiling Collars.

No. 724—L57-8
No. 726—L57-10
No. 726—L57-12
No. 726—L57-14
No. 726—L57-16
No. 726—L57-18

$300.00+

Fixtures are furnished wired complete with No. 16 Heat Resisting Wire, and with Porcelain Medium Base Sockets. Add 45c **List** for Mogul Sockets.

No. 704—L57-6

Overall extension from wall 9 inches
(With Canopy Switch)

$135.00 – 185.00

Number Fixture Complete	Number Glassware with Louvre Only	Number Glassware only	Dimensions of Glassware only		Overall Length of Fixture Complete
			Diameter	Fitter	
704—L57-6	L57-6	57-6	6″ x	3¼″	....
724—L57-8	L57-8	57-8	8″ x	4″	13 inches
726—L57-10	L57-10	57-10	10″ x	6″	15 inches
726—L57-12	L57-12	57-12	12″ x	6″	17 inches
726—L57-14	L57-14	57-14	14″ x	6″	19 inches
726—L57-16	L57-16	57-16	16″ x	6″	21 inches
726—L57-18	L57-18	57-18	18″ x	6″ & 8″	23 inches

Listed under Label Service of Underwriters' Laboratories, Inc.

Moderne Louvre Luminaire
"Hyperion" Glassware
Louvres are blown in glass balls, and finished in Black

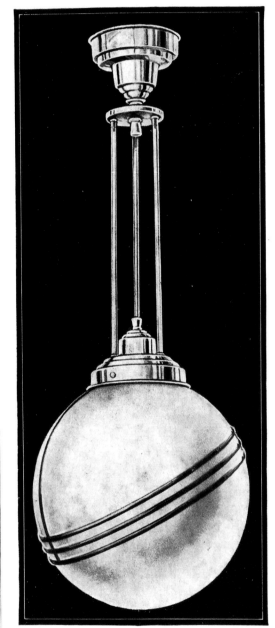

No. 726—B 814 $200.00+

Metal Parts are furnished in "BRUSHED ALUMINUM" finish.

Suspension type fixtures No. 736, will be furnished 28 inches long—from top of canopy to bottom of holder.

[Quotations will be given for special lengths.]

All fixtures will be furnished with Medium Base Porcelain Sockets and No. 16 Heat Resisting Wire.

Patents Pending on Louvre Balls

$250.00+   No. 736—B 814

No. 701—B 806
(With Canopy Switch.)
$135.00 – 165.00

When ordering B806 Glass only, please mention size of Fitter—3¼" or 4".

Number Luminaire Complete	Number Glassware Only	Dimensions of Glassware		
		Diam.	Length	Fitter
726/B 814	B814	14" x	14" x	6"
736/B 814	B814	14" x	14" x	6"
701/B 806	B806	6" x	6" x	3¼" & 4"

Listed under Label Service of Underwriters' Laboratories, Inc.

Commercial Lighting Fixtures
with
Crystal Etched Glassware

All fixtures are furnished wired complete with approved wiring material

All bands are provided with hinges for easy relamping and cleaning

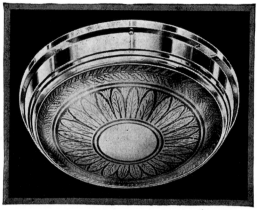

No. 80/D. E. [3 Lights]   **$150.00+**
Diameter.........15 inches   Length.........3 inches

Metal reflector inside stops any light from showing on the ceiling, around the edge of the metal band

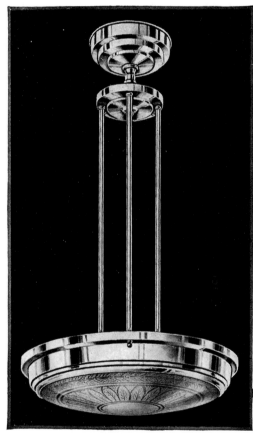

$200.00+
No. 84/D. E. [4 Lights]

Diameter....15 inches   Length...30 inches

If lengths of over 30 inches are required No. 84 will be furnished with chain between the canopy and break, at an extra cost of 45c list per foot for CHROME and 30c list per foot for CADMIUM

No. 81/D. E. [2 Lights]   **$200.00+**
Diameter.........15 inches   Length.........6 inches

No. 82/D. E. [2 Lights]   **$200.00+**
Diameter.........15 inches   Length.........8 inches

When ordering, please mention the fixture number complete

Fixture can also be furnished with plain White "Hyperion Glass" (Not Etched)

Ceiling Bowl Fixtures

Plain and Decorated

No. 708—3510
No. 710—3512
No. 712—3514
$50.00 – 75.00

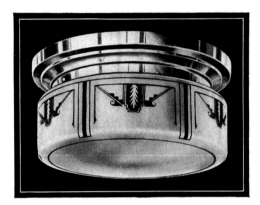

*No. 708—3510 E
*No. 710—3512 E
*No. 712—3514 E
*Etched decoration can be furnished in Black, Green or Tan. Please mention color required.
$100.00+

All fixtures are supplied wired complete, and furnished with inner metal reflectors, which do not permit the light to form halos on the ceiling.

No. 708—3510 S
No. 710—3512 S
No. 712—3514 S

$100.00+

The 'S' glassware has a Sterling Silver decoration on a lustrous irridescent background.

Metal parts can be supplied in either "CHROME" or "CHROMALUSTRE"

(Chromalustre is an applied Metalustre, giving a Satin Finish Aluminum effect.)

Number		Number Glassware Only	Dimensions of Glassware			Number of Sockets
Fixture	Glassware		Diameter	Depth	Fitter	
708—3510	3510	10"	x	3⅞"	x	8"	2 Lights
708—3510 S	3510 S	10"	x	3⅞"	x	8"	2 Lights
708—3510 E	3510 E	10"	x	3⅞"	x	8"	2 Lights
710—3512	3512	12"	x	4⅜"	x	10"	2 Lights
710—3512 S	3512 S	12"	x	4⅜"	x	10"	2 Lights
710—3512 E	3512 E	12"	x	4⅜"	x	10"	2 Lights
712—3514	3514	14"	x	4⅞"	x	12"	3 Lights
712—3514 S	3514 S	14"	x	4⅞"	x	12"	3 Lights
712—3514 E	3514 E	14"	x	4⅞"	x	12"	3 Lights

When ordering please mention Fixture and Glassware Numbers and finish desired

Listed under Label Service of Underwriters' Laboratories, Inc.

Outdoor Weatherproof Lanterns
Made of Cast Aluminum

Wired complete and packed in individual cartons with illustrated labels affixed denoting the contents.

$135.00 – 165.00

LN-110

Height overall . . . . 12 inches
Extension . . . . 7½ inches
Diameter of glass. . . . . 4½ inches
One to a Standard Package

FINISHES

Swedish Iron with Frosted Crystal glass and Clear Crystal Panels.

Antique Bronze with Frosted Amber glass and Clear Amber Panels.

$140.00 – 170.00

LN-111

Height overall . . . . 12 inches
Extension . . . . 7½ inches
Diameter of glass. . . . . 4½ inches
One to a Standard Package

FINISHES

Swedish Iron with Frosted Crystal glass and Clear Crystal Diamonds.

Antique Bronze with Frosted Amber glass and Clear Amber Diamonds.

$145.00 – 175.00

LN-112

Height overall . . . . 12 inches
Extension . . . . 7½ inches
Diameter of glass. . . . . 4½ inches
One to a Standard Package

FINISHES

Antique Copper with Frosted Amber glass and Etched Panels.

Swedish Iron with Frosted Crystal glass and Etched Panels.

$150.00 – 175.00

LN-113

Height overall . . . . 12 inches
Extension . . . . 7½ inches
Diameter of glass. . . . . 4½ inches
One to a Standard Package

FINISHES

Swedish Iron with Frosted Crystal glass and Clear Crystal Straps.

Antique Bronze with Frosted Amber glass and Clear Amber Straps.

***Specify: Number, Finish of Fixture and Finish of Glassware required

Listed under Label Service of Underwriters' Laboratories, Inc.

Outdoor Weatherproof Lanterns
Made of Cast Aluminum

Wired complete and packed in
individual cartons with illustrated
labels affixed denoting the contents.
**Length of Fixtures Overall:
36 Inches**
One to a Standard Package

LN-132
$135.00 – 150.00

LN-133
$125.00 – 140.00

LN-134
$125.00 – 150.00

LN-135
$150.00 – 175.00

STOCK FINISHES
Fixtures

Swedish Iron   Antique Bronze
Verdi Antique   Antique Copper
Bronze and Green

Glassware

Frosted Crystal with Clear Crystal
Highlights

Frosted Amber with Clear Amber
Highlights

***Specify: Number, Finish of Fixture and Finish of Glassware required

Listed under Label Service of Underwriters' Laboratories, Inc.

Outdoor Weatherproof Lanterns
Made of Cast Aluminum

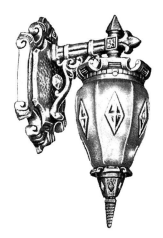

Wired complete and packed in individual cartons with illustrated labels affixed denoting the contents.

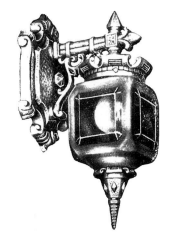

LN-114
Height overall .... 12 inches
Extension .... 7½ inches
Diameter of glass.............. 4½ inches
One to a Standard Package
$140.00 – 170.00

LN-115
Height overall .... 12 inches
Extension .... 7½ inches
Diameter of glass.............. 4½ inches
One to a Standard Package
$135.00 – 165.00

FINISHES

Swedish Iron with Frosted Crystal glass and Clear Crystal Highlights.

Verdi Antique with Frosted Crystal glass and Clear Crystal Highlights.

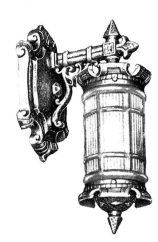

LN-117
Height overall .... 12 inches
Extension .... 7½ inches
Diameter of glass.............. 4½ inches
One to a Standard Package
$150.00 – 175.00

LN-118
Height overall .... 12 inches
Extension .... 7½ inches
Diameter of glass.............. 4½ inches
One to a Standard Package
$150.00 – 175.00

***Specify: Number, Finish of Fixture and Finish of Glassware required

Listed under Label Service of Underwriters' Laboratories, Inc.

Outdoor Weatherproof Lanterns
Made of Cast Aluminum

Wired complete and packed in individual cartons with illustrated labels affixed denoting the contents.

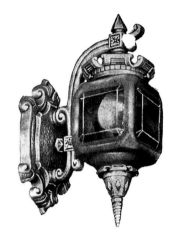

LN-119

Height overall .... 12 inches
Extension .... 7½ inches
Diameter of glass.............. 4½ inches
One to a Standard Package

$140.00 – 170.00

LN-120

Height overall .... 12 inches
Extension .... 7½ inches
Diameter of glass.............. 4½ inches
One to a Standard Package

$135.00 – 165.00

FINISHES

Swedish Iron with Frosted Crystal glass and Clear Crystal Highlights.

Antique Copper with Frosted Amber glass and Clear Amber Highlights.

LN-121

Height overall .... 12 inches
Extension .... 7½ inches
Diameter of glass.............. 4½ inches
One to a Standard Package

$150.00 – 175.00

LN-122

Height overall .... 12 inches
Extension .... 7½ inches
Diameter of glass.............. 4½ inches
One to a Standard Package

$150.00 – 175.00

***Specify: Number, Finish of Fixture and Finish of Glassware required

Listed under Label Service of Underwriters' Laboratories, Inc.

Outdoor Weatherproof Lanterns

Made of Cast Aluminum

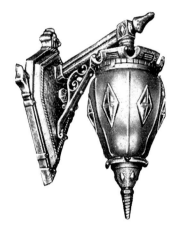

Wired complete
and packed in in-
dividual cartons
with illustrated
labels affixed de-
noting the con-
tents.

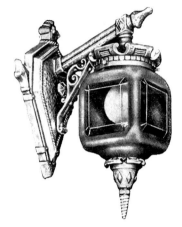

LN-124

Height overall .... 12 inches
Extension .... 7½ inches
Diameter of glass.............. 4½ inches
One to a Standard Package

$140.00 – 170.00

LN-125

Height overall .... 12 inches
Extension .... 7½ inches
Diameter of glass.............. 4½ inches
One to a Standard Package

$135.00 – 165.00

FINISHES

Verdi Antique
with Frosted
Crystal glass and
Clear Crystal
Highlights.

Antique Bronze
with Frosted
Amber glass and
Clear Amber
Highlights.

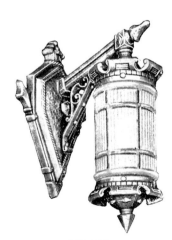

LN-126

Height overall .... 12 inches
Extension .... 7½ inches
Diameter of glass.............. 4½ inches
One to a Standard Package

$150.00 – 175.00

LN-127

Height overall .... 12 inches
Extension .... 7½ inches
Diameter of glass.............. 4½ inches
One to a Standard Package

$150.00 – 175.00

***Specify: Number, Finish of Fixture and Finish of Glassware required

Listed under Label Service of Underwriters' Laboratories, Inc.

ILLUMINATION CALCULATION PROCEDURE
FOR
GILL ILLUMINATING GLASSWARE

FIRST

Determine foot-candles required from Table I.

SECOND

Determine "Conditions Factor" for the interior, whether "Favorable," "Average" or "Unfavorable," from Table II, following page. The "Conditions Factor" will depend upon the room proportions, color of ceiling and upper walls, and the maintenance of equipment. Typical "Average Conditions Factor" consists of:

Room proportions . . . .
    Width approximately twice ceiling height

Color of ceiling and walls. . . . . .Medium

Maintenance of equipment. . . . . .Fair

The "Conditions Factor" becomes more "Favorable" as the width of the interior increases in proportion to its height; as the color of ceiling and upper walls becomes lighter; and as the maintenance of equipment improves.

THIRD

Decide which type of illuminating glassware ("Hyperion," Semi-Indirect, Creamtone).

FOURTH

Decide mounting height. Ordinarily, an overall fixture length (ceiling to underside of enclosing globe) of one-fourth ceiling height may be used for all Gill enclosing globes. Ceiling type fitters should be used on low ceilings.

FIFTH

Locate in first column, Table II, the contemplated "Area Per Outlet" or "Approximate Spacing" and further narrow this down to the "Conditions Factor" determined in second step. Then traverse Table II horizontally to the right until the desired foot-candle intensity (as determined in first step) is located in the correct glassware section. If not so found, then go to a closer spacing until desired foot-candle intensity is located. Directly above in the column heading is the required lamp size.

TABLE I. LIGHTING INTENSITIES FOR GENERAL ILLUMINATION
OF COMMERCIAL INTERIORS

Specific Commercial Interiors	Foot-Candles		Specific Commercial Interiors	Foot-Candles	
	Recommended	Minimum		Recommended	Minimum
Auditoriums	5	3	Lunch Rooms	12	8
Automobile Show Rooms.	15	10	Markets	12	8
Bank Lobbies	10	6	Office Buildings		
Barber Shops	15	10	Private and General	15	10
Churches			Same—no close work	10	8
Auditorium	3	2	File Room	6	4
Sunday School Room.	8	5	Corridors	5	3
Club Rooms			Restaurants	8	5
Lounge	5	3	Schools		
Reading Room	12	8	Auditorium	8	5
Court Rooms	10	6	Class Rooms, Library and Office.	12	8
Dance Halls	6	4	Corridors and Stairways.	5	3
Depot Waiting Rooms.	8	5	Drawing Rooms	25	15
Drafting Rooms	25	15	Manual Training	12	8
Gymnasiums			Laboratories	12	8
Main Exercising Floor	12	8	Sewing Rooms	25	15
Swimming Pool	8	5	Study	12	8
Shower and Locker Rooms.	6	4	Stores—Department and Large		
Halls, Passageways in Interiors.	3	2	Specialty		
Hospitals			Main Floors	15	10
Corridors	3	2	Basement Store	15	10
Private Rooms	8	5	Other Floors	12	8
Wards (with local illumination).	5	3	Stores—Medium Size		
Laboratories	15	10	Clothing	15	10
Hotels			Drug	15	10
Lobby	8	5	Dry Goods	15	10
Dining Room	6	4	Grocery	12	8
Bed Rooms	8	5	Furniture	15	10
Corridors	3	2	Shoe	15	10
Libraries			Confectionery	12	8
Reading Rooms	12	8	Meat	12	8
Lodge Rooms	6	4	Toilet and Wash Rooms.	6	4

TABLE II. DETERMINATION OF LAMP SIZE AND OUTLET SPACING

GILL GLASS & FIXTURE COMPANY

Using the proper section for glassware selected, the mounting height* and conditions factor decided upon, choose such spacing and lamp size as will give the desired foot-candle intensity

Area per outlet or †approximate spacing	Conditions factor	HYPERION Average foot-candles					CREAMTONE Average foot-candles					"EXCELITE" "SUPERBA" SEMI-INDIRECT LIGHTING Average foot-candles				
		100-watt	150-watt	200-watt	300-watt	500-watt	100-watt	150-watt	200-watt	300-watt	500-watt	100-watt	150-watt	200-watt	300-watt	500-watt
55 to 65 sq. ft. or 7¾x7¾-ft. spacing	Favorable	8-10	12-15	18-23			5-7	9-12	13-18			7-9	10-14	15-22		
	Average	6-7	9-12	12-16			3-5	6-9	8-13			5-6	7-10	11-15		
	Unfavorable	4-5	6-8	9-11			2.5-3.0	4-6	5-8			3-4	4-6	7-9		
65 to 75 sq. ft. or 8½x8½-ft. spacing	Favorable	7-8	11-15	15-20			4-6	8-11	11-15			6-7	9-13	13-19		
	Average	5.0-5.5	8-11	11-15			3-4	5-8	7-11			4.5-5.0	6-9	9-13		
	Unfavorable	3.0-3.5	5-7	7-9			2-3	3.5-5.0	5-7			2.5-3.0	4-6	6.5-8.0		
75 to 85 sq. ft. or 9x9-ft. spacing	Favorable	6-7	10-13	13-18			3.5-5.0	7-9	8-12			5-6	8-11	11-17		
	Average	4.5-5.0	7-10	10-13			2.5-3.5	4-7	6-8			5-8	5-8	8-11		
	Unfavorable	3.0-3.5	5-6	6-8			1.5-2.5	3-4	4-6			3.5-5.0	3.5-5.0	6-7		
85 to 95 sq. ft. or 9½x9½-ft. spacing	Favorable	4.5-6.0	8-11	11-16	18-25		3-4	6-8	8-11	14-19		4.0-5.5	7-10	10-14	17-24	
	Average	4.0-4.5	6-8	8-10	12-18		2-3	4-6	5-8	9-14		3.5-4.0	5-7	7-9	11-17	
	Unfavorable	2.5-3.0	4-5	6-7	8-12		1.5-2.0	2.5-4.0	4-5	6-9		2.0-2.5	3-4	5-6	7-11	
95 to 110 sq. ft. or 10x10-ft. spacing	Favorable	4.0-5.5	7-10	10-14	16-22		3.0-3.5	5-7	7-10	12-17		3.5-5.0	6-9	9-12	15-21	
	Average	3.5-4.0	5-7	7.5-9.0	11-16		2.0-2.5	3-5	5-7	8-12		3.0-3.5	4-6	6-8	9-15	
	Unfavorable	2.0-2.5	3-4	5-6	7-10		1.5-2.0	2.5-3.0	3.5-5.0	5-8		1.5-2.0	2.5-4.0	4.5-5.0	6-9	
110 to 125 sq. ft. or 11x11-ft. spacing	Favorable	4-5	6-9	9-12	14-20		2.5-3.5	4-6	6-9	11-15		3-4	5-7	8-11	13-19	
	Average	3.0-3.5	4.5-6.0	7.0-8.5	10-14		1.5-2.0	3-4	4-6	7-11		2.5-3.0	4.5-5.0	5.5-7.0	8-13	
	Unfavorable	2.0-2.5	3-4	4.5-5.5	7-9		1.0-1.5	2-3	3-4	5-7		1.5-2.0	2.5-3.0	4.0-4.5	6-8	
125 to 145 sq. ft. or 11½x11½-ft. spacing	Favorable	3.5-4.5	5.5-8.0	8-11	12-17	18-25	2-3	3.5-5.0	5-7	9-13	17-23	2.5-3.5	5-6	7-9	11-16	17-25
	Average	2.5-3.5	4-5	6.5-8.0	9-13	12-18	1.0-1.5	2.5-3.5	3.5-5.0	6-9	11-17	2.0-2.5	3.5-4.5	5-6	7-11	11-17
	Unfavorable	1.5-2.0	2.5-3.5	4-5	6-8	8-12		1.5-2.5	2.5-3.5	4-6	8-11	1.0-1.5	2-3	3.5-4.0	5-7	7-11
145 to 170 sq. ft. or 12½x12½-ft. spacing	Favorable	3-4	5-6	7-10	10-15	16-22		3.5-4.0	4-6	8-11	15-20		3.5-5.0	6-8	9-14	14-21
	Average	2.0-2.5	3.5-4.0	6-7	8-10	11-16		2.0-3.5	3-4	5-8	9-15	1.5-2.0	3.0-3.5	4.5-5.0	6-9	9-14
	Unfavorable	1.0-1.5	2-3	3.5-4.0	5-7	7-10		1.5-2.0	2-3	3.5-5.0	6-9	0.5-1.0	1.5-2.5	3.0-3.5	4-6	6-9
170 to 200 sq. ft. or 13½x13½-ft. spacing	Favorable	2-3	4.5-5.5	6-8	9-12	14-20		3-4	3.5-5.0	7-9	12-17		4-5	5-6	8-11	12-18
	Average	1.5-2.0	3.0-3.5	5-6	6-9	10-14		1.5-3.0	2.0-3.5	4-7	8-12	1.5-2.5	2.5-3.0	4.0-4.5	5-8	8-12
	Unfavorable	1.0-1.5	2.0-2.5	3.0-3.5	4-6	7-10		1.0-1.5	1.5-2.0	3-4	5-8	1.0-1.5	1.5-2.0	2.5-3.0	3.5-5.0	6-9
200 to 230 sq. ft. or 14¾x14¾-ft. spacing	Favorable		4-5	5-6	8-11	12-17		2.5-3.5	3.5-4.0	6-8	10-14		3-4	4-5	7-10	10-14
	Average		2.5-3.0	4.0-4.5	5-8	8-12		1.5-2.0	2-3	4-6	7-10		2.0-2.5	3.5-4.0	4-7	7-10
	Unfavorable		1.5-2.0	2.5-3.0	3.5-4.5	5-8			1.5-2.0	2.5-4.0	5-7		1.0-1.5	2.0-2.5	3-4	5-7
230 to 260 sq. ft. or 15½x15½-ft. spacing	Favorable		3.5-4.0	4.0-4.5	7-10	10-15		2-3	3-4	5-7	9-12		2.5-3.5	3.5-4.0	6-9	10-14
	Average		2.0-2.5	3.5-4.0	4.5-7.0	9-13		1.5-2.0	2.0-2.5	3-5	6-9		1.5-2.0	3.0-3.5	3.5-6.0	7-10
	Unfavorable		1.5-2.0	2.0-2.5	3-4	6-8			1.5-2.0	2.5-3.0	4-6		1.0-1.5	1.5-2.0	2.0-3.5	5-7
260 to 300 sq. ft. or 16¾x16¾-ft. spacing	Favorable	2-3	3-4	3.5-4.0	6-8	10-14		3-4	2.5-3.0	4-6	8-11		2-3	3-4	5-7	9-13
	Average	1.5-2.0	1.5-2.0	3.0-3.5	4-5	8-10		1.5-2.0	1.5-2.0	3-4	6-8		1.0-1.5	2.5-3.0	3-5	6-9
	Unfavorable	1.0-1.5	1.0-1.5	1.5-2.0	3-4	6-8		1.0-1.5	1-2	2-3	3-4			1.0-1.5	2.5-3.0	4-6
300 to 340 sq. ft. or 18x18-ft. spacing	Favorable			3.5-4.0	5-7	9-12			2-3	3.5-5.0	7-9			2.0-2.5	4-6	8-10
	Average			2.5-3.0	3.5-4.0	6-9			1.0-1.5	2.5-3.0	5-7				3-4	5-8
	Unfavorable			1.0-1.5	2.5-3.0	4-6				1.5-2.5	3-5				2.5-3.0	3.5-5.0
340 to 390 sq. ft. or 19x19-ft. spacing	Favorable		3.5-4.0	3.0-3.5	4-6	8-10			3-4	3-4	6-8		2.5-3.5	2.5-3.0	3.5-4.5	7-10
	Average		2.0-2.5	2.0-2.5	3.0-3.5	5-8			2-3	2-3	4-6		1.5-2.0	1.5-2.0	2.5-3.5	4-7
	Unfavorable		1.5-2.0	1.0-1.5	2.5-3.0	3.5-5.0			1.5-2.0	1.5-2.0	3-4		1.0-1.5		2.0-2.5	3-4
390 to 440 sq. ft. or 20½x20½-ft. spacing	Favorable		2.5-3.0	2.5-3.0	3.5-5.5	7-9				3-4	6-9			2.0-2.5	3-5	6-9
	Average		1.5-2.0	1.5-2.0	2.5-3.0	4.5-7.0				1.5-3.0	4-6			1.0-1.5	2.0-3.5	4-6
	Unfavorable		1.0-1.5	1.0-1.5	2.0-2.5	3-4				1.0-1.5	3-4				1.5-2.0	3-4
440 to 500 sq. ft. or 21¾x21¾-ft. spacing	Favorable		2.0-2.5	2.0-2.5	3-4	5-8			2.5-3.5	2.5-3.5	4-6			1.5-2.5	5-8	
	Average		1.0-1.5	1.0-1.5	2-3	3-5			1.5-2.0	1.5-2.5	3-4					
	Unfavorable					2.5-3.0					2-3					2.5-3.0

*Note—Ordinarily units may be mounted using an overall fixture length equal to one-fourth the ceiling height. For low ceilings, fitters of the ceiling type should be used.

†Note—Between walls and first rows of lights allow not more than ½ the spacing.

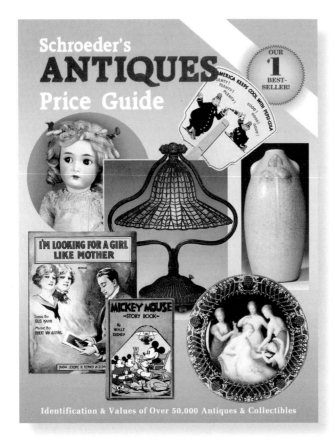